... or Worse

Jacques Lacan

... or Worse

The Seminar of Jacques Lacan
Book XIX

Edited by Jacques-Alain Miller

Translated by A. R. Price

polity

First published in French as *Le Séminaire, Livre XIX. . . . ou pire (1971–1972)*,
© Éditions du Seuil, 2011

This English edition © Polity Press, 2022

Polity Press
65 Bridge Street
Cambridge CB2 1UR, UK

Polity Press
101 Station Landing
Suite 300
Medford, MA 02155, USA

ISBN-13: 978-0-7456-8244-0
ISBN-13: 978-0-7456-8245-0 (pb)

A catalogue record for this book is available from the British Library.

Typeset in 10.5 on 12 pt Times NR MT by
Servis Filmsetting Ltd, Stockport, Cheshire
Printed and bound in the UK by CPI Group (UK) Ltd, Croydon

The publisher has used its best endeavours to ensure that the URLs for external websites referred to in this book are correct and active at the time of going to press. However, the publisher has no responsibility for the websites and can make no guarantee that a site will remain live or that the content is or will remain appropriate.

Every effort has been made to trace all copyright holders, but if any have been inadvertently overlooked the publisher will be pleased to include any necessary credits in any subsequent reprint or edition.

For further information on Polity, visit our website: politybooks.com

Contents

Contents

APPENDICES

Book XIX

. . . or Worse

1971–1972

OF ONE SEX AND THE OTHER

I

THE SMALL DIFFERENCE

The empty place
Prosdiorismoi
Nature and discourse
Let them muddle through!
Modality and negation

I could pass over my title, the meaning of which you're going to be able to see in a short while. Nevertheless, out of kindness, since it was devised to catch your attention, I shall introduce it with a commentary. Perhaps some of you have understood it, though. All in all, . . . *or worse* is what I'm always quite capable of doing. I just have to show you as much to take us to the heart of the matter, and this I do constantly.

However, to avoid remaining at the level of meaning, which like all meaning amounts to opacity, I'm going to give a textual commentary on the title. It so happened that some people read it wrongly. They thought it said . . . *ou le pire,* . . . or the worst, which really isn't the same thing. *Pire* is an adverb, like *well* or *better*.[1] You say, *I do it well*, or *I do it worse*.

It's an adverb, but it's disjoined. It's disjoined from something that is summoned to a place – precisely, the place of the verb – which here has been replaced by three dots. These three dots refer to the customary use in printed texts – and this is a curious thing – for denoting or creating an ellipsis.

My title underscores the importance of this empty place and also demonstrates that this is the only way to say something with the aid of language.

1

The remark that this empty place is the only way to catch hold of something by means of language allows us precisely to penetrate the nature of language.

You know that as soon as logic first succeeded in facing up to something that sustains a reference to truth, it produced the notion of the *variable*. I'm speaking of the *apparent variable*.[2] The apparent variable *x* is formed whenever an *x* marks an empty place in whatever is at issue. The precondition for this to work is that we put exactly the same signifier in each of the places set aside as empty. Only in this way can language get to something, and this is why I employed the formula – *There is no such thing as metalanguage*.

What does this mean? It would seem that in saying this all I would be doing is formulating a paradox, for where would I be saying it from? Since I am saying it in language, this would already be sufficient affirmation that there is one language from which I can say so. And yet this is clearly not the case. Whenever logic is at issue, it is necessary to create the fiction of metalanguage. That is, within a discourse, one forges what is known as an object-language, in view of which it is language that becomes *meta*. By *discourse* I mean common discourse, without which there are simply no means of establishing this division. *There is no such thing as metalanguage* denies that this division can be upheld. That there could be any discordance in language is foreclosed by this formula.

So, what occupies the ellipsis that I have produced to catch your attention? I said that it had to be a verb, because there is an adverb. However, eliding the verb by means of three dots is the one thing that may not be done in language once it is being examined in logic.

In this instance the verb is not hard to find. You just have to swivel the first letter of the word *pire* and you get *dire*. In logic, however, the verb is precisely the only term from which you cannot make an empty place. Indeed, when you try to turn a proposition into a function, the verb becomes a function, and you form an argument from what lies around it. So, by emptying out the verb, I'm turning it into an argument, that is to say, I'm turning it into substance. It's not *saying* per se, it's *one* fact of saying.

This fact of saying, which I'm taking up from last year's Seminar, is expressed, as is any fact of saying, in a complete proposition – *There is no such thing as sexual relation*. What this year's title proposes is that there's no ambiguity about this – move outside it and what you will say will only be worse.

There is no such thing as sexual relation is proposed, therefore, as a truth. I've already said, however, that truth can only come midsay. So, what I'm saying is that, all in all, what the other half says is worse. How much simpler things would be if there were no worse!

The question is whether this doesn't already simplify matters. Since I've started with what I *can* do, and this is exactly what I'm *not* doing, doesn't this suffice to simplify matters? Yet there you go, it is not possible for me not to do this worse, just like everyone else.

When I say that *there is no such thing as sexual relation*, I'm asserting precisely the truth that sex does not define any relation in speaking beings.

I'm not denying the difference that there is, from the earliest age, between what are known as a young girl and a young boy. This is even my starting point. You should twig right away that when I take this as my starting point, you don't know what I'm talking about.

I'm not talking about the notorious small difference for which, with respect to one of the two, when he becomes sexually mature, letting out a hurrah will appear altogether equivalent to a *bon mot*, a quip. *Hurrah for the small difference!* The mere fact that this is funny is enough to indicate to us, by denotation, by reference, the complexual relationship with this organ. This relationship is fully inscribed in the analytic experience and we were led to it by the experience of the unconscious, without which there wouldn't be any quips.

Even then at this early stage, the small difference is separated off as an organ, which already says it all – ὄργανον, instrument. Does an animal have any idea that it has organs? Has anyone ever seen such a thing? And whatever for? Will it be enough to state that *all animals* – I said this somewhere else, it's another way of taking up what I stated recently about supposing so-called sexual jouissance to be instrumental in animals, but here I shall put it differently – *all animals that have pincers do not masturbate*? That's the small difference between *homme* and *homard*, between man and lobster. There you go. That always has its little effect.

In view of which, the historical aspect of this sentence escapes your notice. On no account is it because of what it asserts – I'm saying no more than that, the sentence asserts – but on account of what it introduces at the level of logic. This is concealed within it, but the only thing you haven't noticed is that it contains the *pastout*, the *not-all*, which is very precisely and very curiously what Aristotelian logic eludes in so far as it produced and isolated the function of the προσδιορισμοί, the *prosdiorismoi*, which are exactly what you are familiar with, namely the use of *all*, πᾶν, of *not*, μή, of *some*, τί, around which Aristotle took the first steps in formal logic.[3]

These steps have far-reaching consequences. They allowed for the development of what is known as the function of quantifiers. It was with the *all* that the empty place I was speaking about earlier was established. When Frege comments on the function of the assertion in relation to a function $f(x)$ that is either true or false, in order for the x to have the existence of an argument – here placed in this little hollow, which is an image of the empty place – he makes sure to put something in front of it that is called *all x*, which is appropriate to the function.[4]

A *Höhlung* in the *Begriffsschrift*

Introducing the *not-all* is essential here. The *not-all* is not a denied universal. The *not-all* is not *none*. Namely, it is not *no animal that has pincers* masturbates. It is *not all animals that have pincers* are thereby necessitated to what follows. There are organs and then there are organs, just as we have *il y a fagots et fagots*,[5] the one who deals the blows and the one who receives them. And this brings us to the heart of our problem.

Indeed, you can see that simply by taking this first faint step we have thereby slid, without even the time to backtrack, into the midst of something where there is a machine that sweeps us along. It is this machine that I'm dismantling. However – this remark is intended for the use of certain people here – this is not to demonstrate that it is a machine, nor, even less, so that a discourse should be taken for a machine, as some have done in seeking to gear into my discourse. In so doing, what they have demonstrated is how they fail to gear into the very thing that forms a discourse, namely the real that passes through it. Dismantling the machine is on no account the same thing as what we have just done, namely to proceed without any further ado to the hole in the system, that is, to the site at which the real passes through you. And how it passes! Because it lays you flat!

Naturally, I would like, I really would like, I would very much like, I would like to preserve your natural knavery, which really is the nicest thing there is, but which, alas, alas forever starting over, as a certain someone says, is eventually reduced to foolishness by the very effect of this discourse that I'm demonstrating. Whereby you must surely have the immediate sense that there are at least two ways of demonstrating this discourse – it remaining open that my way of demonstrating it might be yet a third way.

You mustn't make me insist on this energetics of knavery and foolishness, to which I only ever make distant allusions.[6] Of course, from the standpoint of energetics it doesn't hold water. It's purely metaphorical. But it belongs to that brand of metaphor by which the speaking being subsists. I mean that for him it is his bread and leaven.

So, I have asked you to let me off insisting, in the hope that the theory should make up for it. You can hear the subjunctive accentuation. I've picked it out because it might have been covered up by the interrogative accentuation. Spare a thought for all this, as and when it happens, especially so that you can avoid overlooking what appears there, namely the relationship between the unconscious and truth.

The right theory is the one that clears the very path along which the unconscious had been reduced to insisting. There would be no further need to insist had the path actually been cleared, though this doesn't mean that everything would be resolved, quite the contrary. Since it would offer this facility, the right theory ought to be light to the point that it seems not to touch it. It ought to possess the naturalness that, until now, has only been possessed by errors. Once again, *not all* of them, of course. But does this make it any more certain that there might be some that can sustain this naturalness which so many others affect a semblance of?

For these others to be able to affect this semblance, it is my assertion that among these errors that sustain naturalness, there has to be at least one, *hommoinzune*. You ought to recognize what I wrote last year, albeit with a different ending, with regard to the hysteric and the *hommoinzun* she requires.[7] The role of this *hommoinzune* can be no better sustained than by naturalness itself.

This is why, at the start, I didn't deny the difference that exists, that is perfectly noticeable, and from a very early age, between a young girl and a young boy. This difference, which asserts itself as something innate, is indeed altogether natural. It corresponds to the real by the fact that, within the species that has itself given itself the name *Homo sapiens* – a self-made species, in this and in many other respects – the sexes appear to be shared out into two sets of individuals that are pretty much equal in number. Fairly early on, earlier than one might expect, these individuals are distinct. It is quite certain that they are distinguished.

However, I would point out to you in passing that this does not partake of logic. They recognize themselves as speaking beings only by rejecting this distinction by means of all sorts of identifications, and it is the common practice of psychoanalysis to notice how this forms the mainspring behind the phases of every childhood. This is just a parenthesis, however.

Logically speaking, the important thing, and this is what I didn't deny, is that they *se distinguent*. There is a slide here. What I did not deny is precisely not that. One distinguishes them. It is not *they* who distinguish *themselves*.

So it is that people say – *Oh, what a proper young lad he is. You can already see how different he is from a little girl. He's already restless, investigating, already in want of kudos.* The little girl, meanwhile, is far from resembling him. She's already thinking only of playing at hiding behind a fan, as it were, which consists in tucking her face into a niche and refusing to say hello. But there you go, people only marvel at this because this is exactly how it will be later on, in conformity with the *types* of man and woman such as they will be constituted from something quite different, namely from the consequence of the value that the small difference will have acquired in what comes next.

Needless to say, *hurrah for the small difference* had already been there for the parents for a long while. It had already had its effects on the way that the little lad and the little lass would be treated. It's not entirely sure. It's not always like that. But you don't need this for the judgement of recognition from adults in the child's ambit to be based on an error, the error that consists in recognizing them from what distinguishes them, no doubt, but recognizing them solely in accordance with criteria that have been shaped under language dependence. This assumes that it is the case, as I say it is, that the castration complex exists because these beings are speaking beings. I'm adding this in order to insist, so that you will understand properly what I mean.

It is in this respect that the *hommoinzune*, of error, lends consistency to the naturalness – which moreover is incontestable – of this premature calling, if I may put it like that, which each and every one of us experiences for our sex. Furthermore, it should be added that in cases where this calling is not apparent, it doesn't undermine the error, because it can be rounded out with ease by being attributed to nature as such, and no less naturally so. When things don't match, they say that she's a *garçon manqué*, a tomboy, don't they? In such cases, *manque*, lack, has great facility for being considered a success, to the extent that nothing stops one from imputing a little extra femininity to this lack. Woman, true woman, the proper young lass, hides behind this very lack. Moreover, this is a refinement that fully conforms to what the unconscious teaches us, never better succeeding than in failing.

In these conditions, to get to the other sex one really has to pay the price, the price of the small difference, which deceptively passes over to the real through the intermediary of the organ. This happens precisely when it stops being taken for an organ. By the same stroke, it reveals what it means to be an organ. An organ is an instrument only through the intervention of the fact that it is a signifier, which is what founds any instrument.

It is qua signifier that the transsexual wants rid of it, and not qua organ. Thus, he suffers because of an error, the common error. The transsexual's passion is the madness of wanting to free himself from this error, the common error that doesn't see that the signifier is jouissance, and that the phallus is only its signified. The transsexual wants to be no longer signified phallus by sexual discourse, which, I say, is impossible. He is wrong in just one respect, in wanting to force, by means of surgery, sexual discourse which, qua impossible, is the point of passage to the real.

This is the same thing I once stated in a programme for a congress on female sexuality. I said, for those who know how to read of course, that only the homosexual, to be written in the feminine, *homosexuelle*, sustains sexual discourse in total safety.

This was why I called upon the testimony of Les Précieuses who, as you know, remain a model for me, Les Précieuses who, if I may say so, define so admirably the *excès au mot*, the excess in the word – allow me if you will to stop the word right there – the *Ecce homo* of love, because there's no way they will take the phallus for a signifier. *O fie, fie, fie!* O fie, phi, signi-Φ! It is only by breaking up the signifier at the level of its letter that one gets to the bottom of it with its final term.

It is unfortunate, though, that for her, the female homosexual, this amputates the psychoanalytic discourse, because it's a fact that this discourse completely blinds these very dear women to what is involved in feminine jouissance.

Contrary to what can be read in a famous play by Apollinaire, the same play that introduced the word *surréaliste*, Theresa becomes Tiresias – don't forget that I've just been speaking about blindness – not by letting go, but by retrieving the two *birds of her weakness* – I'm quoting Apollinaire, for those who haven't read it – namely, the large and small balloons that represent them on the theatre stage, and which are perhaps – I'm saying *perhaps* because I don't want to divert your attention, so I'll make do with a *perhaps* – the very thing owing to which a woman can find jouissance only in an absence.

The female homosexual is on no account absent in the jouissance that remains to her. I repeat, this puts her at ease with the discourse of love, but it's quite clear that it excludes her from the psychoanalytic discourse, which she can barely stammer through.

2

Let's try to move forward.

Given how late it is, I can only provide a quick indication of the following – that concerning what is involved in everything that is posited as sexual relation, instituting it through a sort of fiction that is called *marriage*, it would be a good rule for the psychoanalyst to tell himself on this score, *let them muddle through as best they can.*

This is the rule that the psychoanalyst follows in practice. He doesn't say so, nor does he even tell himself as much, through some kind of false shame because he believes himself duty-bound to overcome every tragedy. This is a legacy of sheer superstition. He plays the doctor, but never have doctors got caught up in ensuring conjugal happiness. Since psychoanalysts haven't yet noticed that there is no such thing as sexual relation, they are haunted by playing the role of Providence in couples.

All of the above – the false shame, the superstition, the inability to formulate a precise rule on this point, the same rule that I've just set out by saying *let them muddle through* – stems from a failure to recognize what their experience repeats to them, namely that there is no such thing as sexual relation.

I could even use the verb *seriner*.[8] It has to be said that the etymology of *seriner* leads us straight to *siren*. It's textual. It's in the *Dictionnaire étymologique de la langue française*. I'm not the one who's giving myself over to some such song here all of a sudden.

This is doubtless why the psychoanalyst, like Ulysses in similar conditions, stays lashed to a mast. Naturally, for as long it lasts – the Sirens' song that enchants him, that is to say, that makes him hear everything the wrong way round – he has to stay lashed to the mast, in which you cannot fail to recognize the phallus, that is to say, the major, all-embracing signified. This is only convenient for everyone in so far as it has no untoward consequences, because it's made for that, for the good ship psychoanalysis herself, that is, for all those who are in the same boat.

It is still the case that he hears the Sirens' song of experience the wrong way round, and this is why it has thus far remained a private domain – I mean, for those who are in the same boat. What happens on this boat, where there are also beings of both sexes, is none the less remarkable. It so happens that I hear from the lips of people who sometimes come to visit me from these boats – I who am, my goodness, on another one – that the same rules don't apply there. This would be rather exemplary, were the way I got wind of it not so peculiar.

In studying what emerges from a certain pattern to the misrecognition of what forms the psychoanalytic discourse, namely the consequences it has on what I shall call the style of what is related to *liaison* – because in the end the absence of sexual relation clearly doesn't prevent liaisons, far from it, but rather provides them with their conditions – this would perhaps afford a glimpse of what might result from the fact that the psychoanalytic discourse is still being accommodated on these boats, where currently it does its wandering. Something of this gives us to fear this might remain its privilege.

It could ensue that something of this style should come to dominate the realm of liaisons in what is improperly called *the vast field of the world* and, truth be told, this is not reassuring. It would surely be yet more untoward than the present state, which is such that it is from the misrecognition I have just pointed out that there arises what can often be seen at the start of a psychoanalysis, and which after all is not unwarranted, namely the fears that are sometimes expressed by subjects as to everything that might constrict or affect the engaging relationships, the enthralling acts, and even the creative upheavals, that are necessitated by the absence of relation.

They do not know that, all told, these fears are stirred up by giving credence to the institutionalized silence of psychoanalysis on this matter of there being no such thing as sexual relation.

3

Before taking leave of you I should like to make some headway into something, to explore what I called a new logic.

This new logic is to be constructed from what occurs on account of the following having been posited at the outset. Nothing of what occurs due to the instance of language can in any case whatsoever give rise to any formulation of relation that would be satisfactory.

This logical exploration is not only the questioning of what imposes a limit on language in its apprehension of the real. In the very structure of this effort at broaching it, in its specific handling, it demonstrates the aspect of the real that lies in the fact of having determined language. Can't we take something from this?

If it is at the site of a certain rift in the real – which is strictly speaking inexpressible because this rift is what would determine all discourse – that the lines of these fields lie, lines that we find in the psychoanalytic experience, is it not appropriate, probable, and fit to infer that what logic has traced out by referring language to what is posited as real can enable us to ascertain, along certain lines that stand to be invented, an orientation? Here lies the theoretical effort I am designating as the *facility* that would find an insistence.

Before leaving you today, I shall do no more than point out that there are three registers that, strictly speaking, have already emerged from the expansion of logic, three registers that my efforts shall revolve around this year, in order to develop what is involved by way of consequence in the following, which was posited at the outset – *there is no such thing as sexual relation*.

First, we have what you've already seen cropping up in my disquisition, the prosdiorismoi.

Today, in the course of this first approach, I have only touched on the statement of the *pas-tous*, the *not-all*. Already, last year, I thought I should isolate this statement for you by writing $\overline{\forall(x)}$ beside the function Φx, which I'm leaving in its entirely cryptic state. This is not the function of sexual relation, but rather the function that makes access to it impossible. It stands to be defined this year. Think of it as a function of jouissance. Why would it not be possible to set down a function of jouissance in writing? It is in putting it to the test that we shall see its tenability, as it were, or otherwise.

I was already led to put forward the function of the *not-all* last year, and certainly from a point that is far closer with respect to what is at issue. Today I am doing no more than landing on our terrain. Last year, I put forward this function using a negative bar placed above the term $\forall(x)$ that in the theory of quantifiers denotes the equivalent of *all*. It is only its equivalent. I shall go still further and say that it's a paring down in relation to Aristotle's naïve use of the prosdiorismos *all*.

The important thing for today is to have put before you the function of the *pas-tout*, the *not-all*.

Everyone knows that what arises, as it were naïvely, from the proposition that Aristotle calls the *particular proposition* is that there exists something that is reckoned to correspond to it. Whenever you use the word *some*, this does indeed seem to go without saying. Yet it does not go without saying, because it is not enough to negate the *not-all* for existence to be affirmed for each of the two bits, if I can put it like that. Of course, should existence be affirmed, the *not-all* is produced. Our way forward has to take in this *There exists*.

On this score, ambiguities have been sustained for such a long time that people have come to mix up essence and existence, and even more astonishingly, to believe that it means more *to exist* than *to be*. The whole problem is perhaps precisely that *There exist*, certainly, men and women, who do nothing more than exist, all told. Because after all, in the correct use that stands to be made of it once logic has allowed itself to peel apart a little from the real, which in truth is the only way for it to be identified in relation to the real, that is to say, once it has been guaranteed only by the portion of the real in which a truth is possible, that is to say, a mathematics, one can clearly see that any *There exists* whatsoever is but a number that fulfils the terms of an equation, for example.

I'm not settling the question as to whether number is to be considered real or not. So as not to leave you in any ambiguity, I can tell you that I do settle the question – number is part of the real. It is, however, a privileged real, in regard to which the handling of truth allows logic to progress. Be that as it may, the mode of existence of a number is not, strictly speaking, something that can guarantee for us what is involved in existence each time the prosdiorismos *some* is asserted.

There is a second plane that I shall do no more than pick out here as a reference point of the field we are going to have to move into, a logic that will be advantageous for us – the field of modality.

As everyone knows, by looking into Aristotle, modality is what is involved in the *possible*. It is what *may* occur. I shall do no more here than indicate the frontispiece to it.

Aristotle plays four categories against one other. There is the *possible*, which he pits against the *impossible*, and the *necessary*, which he pits against the *contingent*. We shall see that nothing in these oppositions holds water. For today, I'm simply pointing out to you what is involved in the formulation of the necessary, which is strictly speaking *not to be able not to*. This is what specifically defines necessity for us. Where does that lead? From the impossible, *not to be able*, to an *able not to*. Is the latter possible or contingent? Either way, what is quite certain is that should you care to take the opposite route, what you find is *able not to be able*, that is, it joins up with the unlikeliness, the obsolescence, of what may occur, namely, not the impossible to which one would return by looping the loop, but quite simply powerlessness. This is just to indicate the second field of questions to be opened, as a frontispiece.

The third term is *negation*.

Considering what I have written, and what completes it in the formulae from last year written up on the blackboard, $\exists x.\overline{\Phi x}$, does it not strike you that there are two utterly distinct possible forms of negation?

The grammarians have already tackled these forms, but, in truth, they did so in a grammar that claimed to go *from words to thought*, which says it all. You embark in semantics and shipwreck is guaranteed! The distinction they draw between foreclosure and discordance is worth recalling, however, as we enter what we shall be dealing with this year. I still need to specify – and the purpose of the following sessions will be to afford each of these chapters suitable development – that foreclosure cannot in itself be bound, contrary to what Damourette and Pichon have said, to *pas*, to *point*, to *goutte*, to *mie*, or even to some of the other accessory terms that seem to support it in French.[9] Nevertheless, it should be noted that what runs counter to this is precisely our *not-all*. Our *not-all* is discordance.

But what is foreclosure? It is certainly to be placed in a register that is very different from that of discordance. It is to be placed at the point where we have written the term known as *function*. It is here that the importance of the fact of saying is formulated. There is no foreclosure but from the fact of saying so, but from this something that exists, since existence is already reserved for what we must surely furnish with its status – *that something may or may not be said.* This is what is at issue in foreclosure. Moreover, from the fact that something may not be said thereof, the only conclusion is a question that bears on the real.

For the time being, the function Φx, in the way I have written it, means solely that for everything that concerns the speaking being, sexual relation constitutes a question. All our experience lies here, I mean, the minimum that we may derive from it. As with any question, there would be no question were there not a response. The patterns this question follows when posed, that is, the responses, are precisely what it is a matter of setting down in writing in this function.

Without any doubt, this is going to enable us to form a juncture between what has been developed by way of logic and what can be grounded on the principle, considered as an effect of the real, that it is not possible to set sexual relation down in writing, namely the function that regulates everything that is involved in our experience.

By constituting a question, sexual relation, *which is no such thing*, in the sense that one cannot write it, determines everything that is developed in terms of a discourse the nature of which is to be a ruptured discourse.

8 December 1971

II

THE FUNCTION Φx

The written: the return of the repressed
A matheme verging on doltishness
Aristotle, Being, and the One
Castration and existence
The *not-all*

This morning I was given a little pen as a present. If you knew just how hard it is for me to find a pen that I like, you would be able to sense how much pleasure this has given me. I thank the person who brought it to me, who is perhaps here. This person admires me, as they say. I don't give a damn about being admired. What I like is to be treated well. Yet even from those who admire me, this seldom happens.

Be that as it may, I made use of this pen straightaway to do some writing, and this is where my reflections began. It's when I am writing that I find something. This is a fact. At least, it is for me. It doesn't mean that if I were not to write, I wouldn't find anything. But then, perhaps I wouldn't even notice.

1

With respect to this function of the *écrit*, of the written, which is on the agenda thanks to a few smart Alecs, perhaps I didn't really care to take sides, but my hand is being forced, so why not?

I'm going to spell out my idea of it – and this is perhaps what has led to some confusion in certain cases – emphatically, with no frills. Indeed, I said to myself, today in fact, that something written could be very helpful for me to find something, but writing something down just for the sake of sparing myself strain or risk, shall we say, or a good many other things besides, does not in the end make for particularly good results. Better to have nothing to read for you. Furthermore, the written work in which now and then I do produce a few findings is not the same as that whereby I might prepare what I have to say here.

Then, there is also what is written for print, which is something more different still. More accurately, it would be untoward to believe that whatever I might once have written down in order to speak to you should constitute written work that would be fully admissible, or which I would anthologize.

I will venture, therefore, to say something that takes the plunge. My idea of the written – to situate it, to start from there, which may be debated afterwards – well, let's say it, colon, is the return of the repressed.

It's in this form that it might have led to confusion in some of my *Écrits*. If I have sometimes appeared to lend credence to the belief that I identify signifiers with letters, this is precisely because the signifier touches me most, as an analyst, in the form of the letter. It's as a letter that I most frequently see the signifier coming back, the repressed signifier. So, in *L'instance de la lettre*, it's all the more legitimate for me to have imaged this signifier with a letter given that everyone else does as much.

The first time that logic, strictly speaking, was opened up with Aristotle and the *Analytics*, there too, letters were used. This is not altogether in the same way as the letter comes back to the place of the signifier that makes a return. The letter comes there to mark out a place, the place of the signifier, which is a signifier that is lying around, that may at the very least be lying around all over the place. In the end, however, we can see that the letter is in some sense designed just for this, and all the more so given that this is how the letter first manifests itself.

I don't know whether you are fully aware of this, but in the end I do hope you will think about it, because even so, it does presuppose something that has not been said in what I have been putting forward. There has to be a kind of transmutation that occurs, from signifier to letter, when the signifier isn't there, when it's gone off course, when it's scarpered. One would have to ask oneself how this transmutation might come about. But this is not what I mean to go into today. I might turn to it some other day.

Even so, on the subject of this letter, one cannot feign that one is not dealing, in a field that is called mathematics, with a site at which one cannot write just any old thing. I'm not about to go into this either. I will simply point out that it's in this respect that this domain sets itself apart, and that probably this is even what constitutes what I have not yet alluded to here, at this Seminar I mean, but which I reported in a few remarks at Sainte-Anne, which doubtless some of you here attended, namely what may be called a *matheme*. I posited that this *matheme* is the pivotal point of all teaching. In other words, mathematical teaching is the only teaching. The rest is banter.

Of course, this hinges on a different status of the written from the one I gave at the outset. I shall be trying to form a juncture between them during the course of the year.

In the meantime, my difficulty, the one that I hold to in spite of it all – I don't know whether this comes from me or whether it's not rather through your participation – is that, in view of the field of discourse that I have to establish, my own *matheme* invariably verges on doltishness.

This is self-evident, given what I've told you, since all in all what is at issue is that when it comes to sexual relation, *y en a pas*. There's no such thing. It ought to be written *hi-han* and *appât*, with a double *p*, a circumflex accent on the second *a*, and a *t* at the end.[1] Naturally, sexual relation shouldn't be confused with sexual intercourse, which is all there is.

However, these sexual encounters are always bungled, even, and above all, when they are acts. Well, let's move on.

2

While there is still time, I should like you to read a very fine introduction, something essential – Aristotle's *Metaphysics*.

By the time I come back to it, perhaps at the beginning of March, you will need to have read it attentively, so that you can see its relationship with this business of ours. Naturally, I won't be speaking to you about the *Metaphysics*. Not that I don't admire doltishness. I daresay I bow low before it.

You lot, you don't bow low. You're an organized and mindful electorate. You don't vote for dolts. That's your undoing. A favourable political system should allow doltishness to have its place. Moreover, things go well only when doltishness dominates. That said, this is no reason to bow low.

Therefore, the text I'm going to take up is an exploit, and one of many such exploits that are, as it were, unexploited. This text is Plato's *Parmenides*, which is going to be of service to us. However, properly to comprehend the depth this text possesses, a text that is not doltish, one needs to have read Aristotle's *Metaphysics*.

When I recommend reading the *Critique of Practical Reason* as a novel – it's brimming with humour – I don't know whether anyone has ever followed this advice and managed to read it as I do. At least, no one has confided as much. This invitation is somewhere in *Kant avec Sade*, which I never know if anyone has read. So, I'll do the same again. I'm going to tell you to read Aristotle's *Metaphysics*. And I hope that, like me, you will sense that it's truly doltish. I don't want to dwell too long on this. These are brief sidelong remarks that have occurred to me. You cannot help but be struck by this character of doltishness, when you read the text, of course.

This is not about Aristotle's *Metaphysics* in its essence, in the signified, in everything that has been explained to you on the basis of this magnificent text, that is, everything that has gone to make up metaphysics in this part of the world in which we find ourselves. Because everything came out of this. It's quite fabulous. People speak about the end of metaphysics, but in the name of what? So long as this book exists, one can still do metaphysics.

This book, because it is a book, is very different from metaphysics. It's a *written* book, which I was speaking about earlier. It has been given a meaning that is called metaphysics, but even so, meaning has to be differentiated from the book. Naturally, once it has been given all this meaning, it's not easy to get back to the book. If truly you do get back to it, you will nevertheless see what has been read into it by people who have a discipline, which is a method that is called historical, critical, exegetical, what you will. Evidently they are capable of reading the text with a certain way of barring themselves off from the meaning, and when you look at the text, well, you are beset by doubts.

This obstacle, arising from everything that has been understood therein, can exist only at the academic level, and universities haven't always been in existence. Well, in Antiquity, three or four centuries after Aristotle, they started to air the most serious doubts about this text, because they still knew how to read. They voiced doubts, saying that it was a series of notes, or else that a pupil had put it together, amassing stuff. I must say I am not convinced in the slightest. It might be because I've just read a book by a certain Michelet, not our Michelet, not our poet – when I say our *poet*, by that I mean that I place him very highly – but instead a fellow who was a professor at the University of Berlin, also named Michelet, Karl Ludwig. He wrote a book on Aristotle's *Metaphysics*, published in 1836, because the historical method that was then flourishing had mildly annoyed him with the doubts it was airing, which were not unfounded since they reach back to Late Antiquity. I must say that Michelet is not of this opinion, and nor am I.

Indeed, truly – how shall I put it? – doltishness is a mark of proof when it comes to authenticity. The dominant factor is the authenticity, as it were, of doltishness. Perhaps the term *authentic* is still a little bit complicated for us, with its etymological resonances of Greek. There are languages in which it is better represented. It is *echt*. I don't know how you turn it into a noun. It must be *Echtheit*, or something of the like. No matter. There is nevertheless nothing more authentic than doltishness. So, this authenticity is perhaps not Aristotle's authenticity, but the *Metaphysics* – I'm speaking about the text – is authentic. It cannot be composed of pieces or fragments. It is constant in its doltishness.

What is the justification for calling it doltishness? One slides into doltishness when one pitches the questions at a particular level that is determined precisely by the fact of language, namely when one nears its essential function, which is to fill in everything that has been left gaping wide by the fact that there can be no such thing as sexual relation, meaning that nothing written, as a product of language, can account for it in a satisfactory way.

Of course, since the moment we first caught a view of gametes we have been able to write on the blackboard *man = bearer of spermatozoa*. This would be a rather odd definition because he's not the only one who bears spermatozoa, there's a host of other animals. Let's start talking about biology, then. Why are the spermatozoa of man the same that men carry? Because, since it's the spermatozoa of man that makes man, we are in a circle that turns around. So what? It can be written down.

Yet this bears no relation whatsoever to anything that may be, so to speak, sensibly written, that is, which would bear a relation to the real. Just because it's biological, this doesn't make it more real. It is the product of science that is called biological. The real is something else.

The real is what commands the entire function of *signifiance*. The real is what you encounter precisely on account of not being able, in mathematics, to write just any old thing. The real is what is entailed in the fact that, in the most commonplace function, you are immersed in *signifiance*, yet you cannot grasp all the signifiers at the same time. This is forbidden by their very structure. When you have some, a mass of them, you no longer have the others. They are repressed. This does not mean that you don't utter them none the less. Precisely, they are said *inter*. There is an *inter-diction*. It doesn't stop you from uttering them. But they are said censured. Either everything that psychoanalysis is possesses no meaning and can be slung in the bin, or else what I'm telling you here has to be your home truth.

This is what will be at issue this year. When one poises oneself at a certain level, Aristotle or not – either way the text is there and it's authentic – there's no plain sailing. It's engaging to see someone so sharp, so learnèd, so alert, and so lucid, starting to flounder in this way. Why does he flounder? Because he wonders about the principle. Naturally, he hasn't the faintest idea that the principle is that there is no such thing as sexual relation. And yet one can see that it is solely at this level that he poses himself all the questions.

So, what is it that comes out of him like a bird on the wing, from the top hat into which he had simply placed a question the nature of which he was unacquainted with? It's like the conjurer who thinks he has put a rabbit in the top hat to emerge from it later, and out pops a rhinoceros instead. That's exactly how it is for Aristotle. Where is the principle? If it's the genus, he gets angry – because is it the broad genus or the more specified genus? It's clear that the broader is the most essential, but that even so, the more specified is what readily supplies what is most unique to each entity.

So, he doesn't even realize, but thank goodness he doesn't, for owing to this he doesn't mix them up. Because this business of essentiality and this business of oneness are the same thing, or more accurately, it is homonymous with what he examines. Thank goodness, he doesn't mix them up. He doesn't make them emerge from there. He asks himself – *is the One the principle, or is Being the principle?* This is when things start to become a damned awful muddle. The One must, at any cost, be. And Being must be One. This is where we lose our pedalling because, precisely, the way not to mess up is strictly to separate them. This is what we shall be trying to do later.

That's enough of Aristotle.

3

Last year, I took the step of announcing to you that this non-relation, if I can put it like that, needs to be written. It needs to be written at any cost. I mean that the other relation needs to be written, the one that blocks the possibility of writing the first one.

I put some items on the blackboard last year which I think it would not be a bad idea to posit here at the outset.

Naturally, there is some arbitrariness here. I'm not about to excuse myself by using the mathematicians as a shield to hide behind. They do as they please, and so do I. Even so, just for those who feel the need to make excuses for me, I can say that in Bourbaki's *Elements* they start by chucking letters around without saying a single word about what they might be used for. Let's call them written symbols, because they don't even look like letters. These symbols represent something that one can call *operations*. Not a word is said about which operations are at issue. Only twenty pages in is one able to deduce this retroactively, based on the way they have been used.

I won't be going that far. I shall attempt to examine right now what is meant by the letters I wrote. However, since I reckon that for you it would be far more complicated were I to set them out one by one, as they become animated and assume a functional value, I would rather posit these letters as the items around which I will have to navigate afterwards.

Since you can't hear me when I turn to the blackboard, there are two ways of going about this – either I write and keep my mouth shut, then speak afterwards, or I carry on speaking a bit if you manage to keep within earshot. So, can you hear me?

Already, last year, and for reasons that are tentative, I thought I would write Φ*x* as they do in mathematics, as a function. This is the function constituted by the fact that the jouissance called *sexual jouissance* exists, which is specifically what forms a barrier to sexual relation.

For the speaking being, sexual jouissance opens the door to jouissance. Train your ears and you will perceive that jouissance, when we refer to it like that *tout court*, might be what jouissance is for some – I don't exclude this – but it's really not sexual jouissance.

This is the merit that can be bestowed on Sade's text, for calling a spade a spade. Jouissance is the jouissance of a body. Jouissance is the embracing, the clutching, the fragmenting of the body. In legal parlance, *avoir la jouissance* of something is precisely that, to be able to treat some thing as a body, that is, to wreck it. This is the most regular mode of jouissance, and this is why these statements invariably have a Sadean resonance. *Sadean* is not to be confused with *sadistic*. So much rubbish has been spoken about sadism that the term has been devalued. I won't go any further on that point.

What is produced by the relationship between signifier and jouissance is what I am expressing with this notation Φ*x*. This means that *x* merely designates a signifier. Each of you here can be a signifier, precisely at the slender level at which you exist as sexuated. It is, if I may say so, very slender in width, but it has a far larger surface than it does in animals. When they are not on heat, you can't differentiate in animals between what in the last lesson I was calling the young boy and the young girl. Lion cubs, for example, look utterly alike in their behaviour. But not you, precisely for as much as you sexuate yourselves *comme signifiant*, as signifying.

It is not about underscoring the signifier *man* as distinct from the signifier *woman*, calling one *x* and the other *y*, because this is precisely the question – how are they distinguished? It is for this reason that I'm putting the *x* in the place of the hole that I'm making in the signifier, that is to say, I'm setting down this x as an apparent variable. This means that each time I have to deal with this sexual signifier, with this something that has to do with jouissance, I will be dealing with Φx. Among these $x$es, there are some that are specified in such a way that one can write *for all x* – whatever or whoever it may be – Φx. This means that what functions here is what is known in mathematics as a Φ function, that is, it can be written $\forall x.\Phi x$.

I'm going to enlighten you straightaway. Well, enlighten … You're the only ones who will be enlightened. You will be enlightened for a short while. As the Stoics used to say, *if it is day, it is light*. As for me, as I wrote on the back cover of my *Écrits*, I take the side of the Enlightenment thinkers. I shine a light, in the hope that the day will come, of course. However, it's precisely this day that is in question. The day won't come tomorrow. The first step to be taken in Enlightenment philosophy is to know that the day hasn't dawned, that the daylight at issue is one of a faint shaft of light in a perfectly dark field. In view of which, you're going to think that it's clear when I tell you that Φx means the function that is called castration.

Since you think you know what castration is, well, I presume you're glad, at least for the time being. Yet can you imagine that if I'm writing all this on the board, which I'm going to continue to do, it's because I have no idea what castration is. It's because I'm hoping, with the help of what is played out in these letters, finally to see day dawning, namely to know that one really does have to pass through this, through castration. So long as one is unaware of this, no discourse can be sound, sound in the sense that it leaves half of its status and conditioning in the shadows. And one can become aware of this only by enabling a particular changing of the letters to be played out across different levels of topological relationship, and by seeing how this is shared out.

Until then, you are reduced to little stories – namely, *Dad said we're going to snip it off* – as though this were not the epitome of doltishness. So, somewhere there is a site at which it may be said that everything that is articulated by way of signifiers falls under the sway of Φx, under the sway of this function of castration.

There is one small advantage to formulating it in this way. You might get the idea that, if earlier I made the remark, not unintentionally – I'm more cunning than I might seem – about the subject of inter-diction, namely that never can all the signifiers be there, all together, it's because this perhaps bears a relation to castration. I'm not saying – *the unconscious = castration*. I'm saying that it bears a strong relation. Obviously, writing this as Φx amounts to writing a function that carries, as Aristotle would say, an incredibly broad scope.

I haven't said anything yet about the relation between this function and a certain signifier, but let's say it. This signifier is, for instance, *a man*. All this is exhausting because there is a lot to wade through, and then, since no one has ever done this before me, it runs the risk of toppling down on our heads at any moment.

Un homme, a man. I didn't say *l'homme*. It's rather funny, though, how the signifier gets used. People say to the lad, *Be a man*. They don't say, *Be man*. Why is that? What is curious is that you don't hear *Be a woman* very often. On the other hand, people speak of *la femme*, with a definite article, *the woman*. There has been much speculation about this definite article. Well, we'll be coming across this when the moment is right. What I simply want to say is that what is written in terms of Φ*x* produces the effect that one no longer has the entirety of signifiers at one's disposal. I'm not even saying these two signifiers here, precisely, but these and a certain number of others that link up with them. Perhaps, right here, this is a first inroad to what is involved in castration from the point of view of this mathematical function, which is imitated in what I have written.

In a first phase, I ask no more of you than to acknowledge that my way of writing it is an imitation. This doesn't mean that for me, having already reflected on it, it doesn't go a great deal further. Anyway, there is a means of writing it such that, given any *x*, this functions.

This is specific to a way of writing that stems from the first skeleton of logic, for which Aristotle is responsible, which earned him prestige due to the fact that logic harbours a formidable jouissance, because it touches on the field of castration.

How otherwise could you explain how so broad a period, of such searing intelligence and such abundant output as our Middle Ages, was able to get excited to this extent about these affairs of logic, of Aristotelian logic? For it moved hordes of people, given that through the intermediary of logicians it had consequences in theology, where the *logic* dominated the *theo* a great deal. This is not the case in our time, where only the *theo* remains, still as solid as can be in its doltishness, and from which the logic has fairly evaporated. For it to have put people in that state in the Middle Ages, the matter must procure jouissance.

It was from here that was derived all the prestige that, in Aristotle's construction, reflected onto the famous *Metaphysics*, in which he writes such copious drivel.

I'm not going to give you a lesson today on the history of logic. I will tell you simply to hunt out the *First Analytics*, which is called more accurately the *Prior Analytics*. Even for those, who of course are the majority, who will never muster the courage to read it, fascinating though it is, I recommend nevertheless that you read in what is known as Book I, chapter 46, what Aristotle produced on negation. He writes about whether saying *the man is not white* is indeed the contrary of *the man is white*, or whether, as many believed, and already believed in his time – which didn't hold him back, however – the contrary is to say *the man is non-white*.

It's absolutely not the same thing. I think that just in stating it like this, the difference is palpable. It is most important to read this chapter, however, because you have been told so many things about the logic of predicates, at least those who have already tried to tackle some of the places where people speak about this stuff, that you could imagine that syllogisms fall squarely within the logic of predicates. This is a brief indication that I'm giving on the side. Since I didn't want to dwell on it, I might have the time to take it up some other day.

I simply want to say that, for me to be able to write Φx, there was an essential mutation at the start of the nineteenth century, namely the attempt to apply this logic to the mathematical signifier, the special status of which I indicated earlier. This furnished the mode of writing, the depth and originality of which I think I will have the time to make tangible for you in what comes next. In short, it no longer says in any respect whatsoever the same thing as the propositions – because that's what's at issue – that function in syllogisms. As I wrote last year, $\overline{\forall x}.\Phi x$, the sign of negation placed at the level of the $\forall$, is a possibility that was opened for us precisely by the introduction of quantifiers. They are generally termed [in French] *quantificateurs*, but I prefer to call them *quanteurs* – I'm not alone in this, nor am I the first – because the important thing is that you should know that this has absolutely nothing to do with quantity, which is obvious. They have been so termed because no better has been found, which in itself is a sign.

This articulation of the quantifiers allows us to posit the function of the *pas-tous*, the *not-all*, which has never been done in this logic of quantifiers, and which I'm doing because I consider that it may be very profitable for us. There is a set of these signifiers that supplements the function of what is sexuated, which supplements it with respect to jouissance, at a site where this *not-all* is functioning within the castration function.

I make further use of the quantifiers. There is a way of articulating them, which is to write $\exists x$, meaning *There exists*. What exists? There exists a signifier.

When you are dealing with mathematical signifiers, which have a different status from our little sexuated signifiers, and which bite into the real in a different way, you ought perhaps to try to bring to the forefront of your minds how there is at least one thing that is real, the only thing we can be sure about, and this is number. What people manage to do with number! They've done rather a lot. To manage to build the real numbers – that is, precisely the ones that are not real – number has to be something real. I'm addressing this in passing to the mathematicians, who might lob a few rotten tomatoes at me. But what matter. They will do so in private because they find me intimidating here.

Let's come back to what we have to say. *There exists.* The reference I've just made is not merely a digression. It tells you that this is where *There exists* carries a meaning. It's a precarious meaning.

It is indeed qua signifiers that you exist, all of you. You surely do exist, but this doesn't go far. You exist qua signifiers. Try imagining yourselves cleansed of this business, and let me know how you get on. After the war we were being incited to exist in a strongly contemporary fashion. Well, look what's left of that. I daresay people nevertheless had a few more ideas in their heads when they were proving the existence of God. It's clear that God exists, but no more so than you. This doesn't get us very far. Well, that is for the sake of developing what is involved in existence.

What is it that might interest us about this *There exists* in respect of the signifier? It would be that there exists *at-least-one* for whom this business of castration does not function. This is precisely why the *at least one* was invented. This is what is called the Father, and this is why the Father exists at least as much as God does, that is to say, not much.

So, naturally, there are a few smart Alecs – I'm surrounded by smart Alecs, who transform what I put forward into intellectual pollution, as a patient of mine put it, and I thank her for supplying me with that, she found it all on her own because she's a sensitive woman, and moreover, by and large only women understand what I'm saying – there are a few smart Alecs who discovered that I was saying that the Father was a myth because it's blindingly obvious that, indeed, Φx doesn't work at the level of *Totem and Taboo*.[2] The Father is not castrated. Otherwise, how could he possess all the women? Do you realize? It is even here alone that they exist as *toutes*, as all, because the *not-all* is suited to women. I'll be commenting on this at greater length in the near future.

So, it's on the basis of this *There exists one*, in reference to this exception, that all the rest can function. Yet there you go, having fully understood that the rejection of the function Φx can be written down, it is not true that this one gets castrated. This is the myth. But what the smart Alecs didn't notice is that this is correlative to existence, and that this posits the *There exists* of the *it is not true* of castration.

It's two o'clock. So, I will simply mark out for you the fourth way of making use of what is involved in the negation grounded on the quantifiers, which is to write $\overline{\exists}x$, *There exists not.*

Who, or what, doesn't exist? Why shouldn't it be true that it is the function Φx that dominates what is involved in the usage of the signifier? Is that what this means? Just now, I differentiated existence from exception. If the negation here were to mean $\overline{\exists}x.\overline{\Phi x}$, that is, *without the exception of this signifier position,* it could be inscribed into the negation of castration, into the rejection, into the *it is not true* that castration dominates everything.

It is on this little enigma that I shall take leave of you today, because, in truth, this is very enlightening for the subject. One can make use of negation in a way that is not so straightforwardly univocal as the use that is made of it in the logic of propositions, where everything that is not true is false, and where – this is confoundedly big – all that is not false becomes true.

I'll leave things now as the hour hand is cutting me off, which is only right. I'll pick them up next time at the precise point at which I've left them today.

15 December 1971

III

FROM ANECDOTE TO LOGIC

Favouring the real of logic
A disturbed relation to the body
Function and argument
The *not-all* and the *at least one*
The possible and the contingent

$$\exists x.\overline{\Phi x} \qquad \overline{\exists x.\Phi x}$$

$$\forall x.\Phi x \qquad \overline{\forall x.\Phi x}$$

		0			
nad	0	1			
monad	0	1	1		monad
	0	1	2	1	dyad
	0	1	3	3	1 triad
0	1				tetrad

On the blackboard

Were we to find in logic a means of articulating what the unconscious demonstrates by way of sexual values, this would come as no
surprise to us.

I mean this would come as no surprise, right here, at my Seminar,
that is, right down at the level of this experience, analysis, which was
put in place by Freud and whereby a structure of discourse that I
have defined was established.

1

Let's take up what I have just said in the density of my opening sentence.

I have spoken of sexual values. I will note that these values are accepted values – accepted in each and every language. *Man, woman*, these are what are called sexual values. That man and woman should be there at the outset is first and foremost a matter of language. This is the thesis I will start from today.

Language is such that any speaking subject is either *he* or else *she*. This exists in all the languages of the world. It is the principle behind the functioning of gender, feminine or masculine. Whenever there is a hermaphrodite, this is just an occasion to play, with more or less mindfulness, at bringing the *him* and the *her* into the same sentence. On no account does one call a hermaphrodite *it*, unless thereby to evince a horror of the sacred type. One does not refer to a hermaphrodite in the neutral.

That said, we don't know what man and woman are. For a while, this bipolarity of values was taken to be sufficient to support, to suture, what is involved in sex. It was from this very fact that resulted the muted metaphor that for centuries underpinned the theory of cognizance. As I have noted elsewhere, the world used to be what was perceived, even apperceived, as though it stood at the place of the other sexual value. The involvement of νοῦς, of the power of cognizance, was placed on the positive side, the active side, of what I will be examining today by asking what relation it bears to the One.

On any tight inroad to the sexual approach, the step that analysis has led us to take shows us, reveals to us, the detour, the barrier, the course, the chicane, the narrow pass, of castration. This step can be properly taken only on the basis of the articulation that I have provided of the analytic discourse. This is what leads us to think that on no account can castration be reduced to anecdote, to mishap, to the clumsy intervention of a word of threat or even of censure. The structure is logical.

What is the object of logic?

You know from experience, just by opening a book with the title *Traité de logique*,[1] how fragile, uncertain, and eluded, the first stage can be in any tract that goes under the heading of something along the lines of *the art of good conduct in one's thinking* – but where is this thinking to be conducted, and from which end is it to be taken? – or otherwise, some such recourse to a normality whereby what is rational would be defined independently of the real. It's clear that after this kind of attempt to define the object of logic, what presents itself belongs to a different order and is consistent in a different way. I could simply leave a blank here, but I won't do that. I propose to define the object of logic as what is produced by the necessity of a discourse.

No doubt this is ambiguous, but it's not idiotic because it entails the implication that logic can change meaning completely, depending on where any given discourse draws its meaning from. Any given discourse can take its meaning from another discourse.

For a long time now I've been asserting fairly clearly, for it to be enough just to recall it here, that the real – a category from the triad with which my teaching got under way, *the symbolic, the imaginary, and the real* – is affirmed in the impasses of logic.

Let me explain. At the start, in its conquering ambition, what logic proposed was nothing less than the network of discourse qua articulated. In being articulated, this network was supposed to close into a universe that was reckoned to surround what is offered to cognizance, and to cover it like a net. The experience of logicians showed that things were different.

I needn't go into details here, because this audience is sufficiently well informed of where in our time the effort of logic has been able to start afresh to know the following. It's a matter of broaching something that in principle has been fined down to a real, namely arithmetic. It has been demonstrated that, in arithmetic, something can always be stated – whether or not it is put to logical deduction – which is articulated as though it stood in advance of the very thing which premises, axioms, and grounding terms, whereby the said arithmetic can find a base, enable us to presume to be provable or refutable. Here, in a domain that in appearance is the surest, we put our finger on what stands in opposition to the entire grasp of discourse, of logical exhaustion, which introduces a wide, irreducible gap here. This is where we designate the real.

Before arriving at the proving ground that might be looming on the horizon, which is indeed uncertain for those who have not formed a firm grasp of its latest proofs, it will be enough to call to mind what naïve discourse is.

Naïve discourse proposes itself at the outset, inscribes itself as such, as truth. Apparently it has never been hard to demonstrate to this naïve discourse that it doesn't know what it is saying. I'm not speaking of the subject. I'm speaking of discourse. This was the dawning – why not say so? – of the Sophist's critique. When somebody states what is invariably posited as truth, the Sophist demonstrates to him that he doesn't know what he is saying. This is even the origin of dialectic as a whole. And then, it's always ready to get a new lease of life. Whenever someone is put in the witness box, the ABC of the barrister is to show him that he doesn't know what he's saying. But here we fall to the level of the subject, of the witness, whom it's a matter of throwing into a muddle. At the level of Sophistic action, it is always the discourse itself that the Sophist lays into. Since I announced that I would have to give an account of the *Parmenides*, we might this year have to show what is involved in Sophistic action.

In the development of what logicians have enunciated, to which I made reference just now, some of you perhaps noticed that what was at issue was nothing less than Gödel's theorem concerning arithmetic. Gödel proceeds to his demonstration that, in the field of arithmetic, there will always be something that can be stated in the specific terms it comprehends which does not lie within the scope of what it posits to itself as a mode to be taken as accepted in the proof. The remarkable thing is that Gödel does not proceed on the basis of truth values. He doesn't proceed to his demonstration on the basis of truth, but rather on the basis of the notion of derivation. It's by leaving the value of *true* or *false* as such in abeyance that the theorem is provable.

What I'm saying about the logical gap with regard to this point – a vital point in that it illustrates what I intend to push forward – is accentuated by the following. If the real, which is certainly of easy access, may be defined as the impossible – the impossible inasmuch as it is borne out by the very holding power of discourse, of the logician's discourse – this impossible, this real, is the one that ought to be favoured by us. When I say *by us*, I mean *by analysts*. Because it obtains in an exemplary way that this is the paradigm of what calls into question what can arise from language. From language, certain types of discourse arise which I defined as establishing a very definite type of social bond. But language questions itself about what it grounds as a discourse. It is striking that it can only do so by fostering the shadow of a language that would surpass itself, which would be metalanguage. I have often remarked that it can do so only by scaling back in its function, that is, by begetting, for a start, a particularized discourse. In turning our attention to this real inasmuch as it is affirmed by the logicians' interrogation of language, I propose that here lies the model of what is important for us, namely the model of what is offered up by the exploration of the unconscious.

What is offered up by the exploration of the unconscious is far from being a universal sexual symbolism, which is what the likes of Jung thought they would be able to revive by sliding back into the most ancient rut. Far from it being a universal sexual symbolism, it is very precisely what I called to mind earlier by way of castration, underscoring, however, the requirement that it should not be reduced to the anecdote of a heard remark. Without this, why would one isolate it and accord it the privilege of goodness knows what trauma, or even the efficacy of a gap? It is only too obvious that it has nothing anecdotic about it. It is rigorously fundamental, not in what establishes, but in what renders impossible the statement of sexual bipolarity as such.

The curious thing is that we go on imagining sexual bipolarity at the animal level, as though every illustration of what constitutes in each species the tropism of one sex for the other were not just as variable for that species as their corporeal constitution is. Moreover, haven't we known already for some time now that, regarding sex, not at the level of what I have just defined as the real but at the level of what is articulated within each science, where its object is defined once and for all, there are at least two or three stages in what constitutes the sex, from the genotype to the phenotype? Following the most recent steps in biology – need I mention which? – it's quite sure that sex merely takes up its place as a particular modality of what allows for the reproduction of what is known as a living body. Far from sex being its typical instrument, it is merely one of its forms. Even though Freud indicated this, albeit approximately, people still far too often confuse the function of sex with the function of reproduction.

Things are far from being such that there is the lineage of the gonad on one side, what Weismann called the *germen*, and on the other the branch of the body, the *soma*.[2] It's clear that the genotype of the body does pass on something that determines the sex, but that this is not sufficient. From its bodily production, from its corporeal stasis, hormones are released that can interfere in this determination.

So, it's not that, on one side, there is sex inextricably associated with life because it is in the body, sex imagined as the image of what, in the reproduction of life, would supposedly amount to love, and then, on the other side, the body as having to fend off death. The reproduction of life, such as we have managed to examine it at the level of the appearance of its initial forms, emerges from something that is neither life nor death. Quite independently of sex, and even on occasion of something that is already living, something intervenes which we will call the *sequence*, or even the *codon*, as is said regarding one or another unit that has been ascertained in chromosomes.

The life-and-death dialogue occurs at the level of what is reproduced. From what we know, it only assumes a dramatic character from the moment that jouissance intervenes in the balance between life and death. The vital point, the point of emergence of something that all of us here more or less believe we form part of, namely speaking being, is this disturbed relation to our bodies that is called jouissance.

The analytic discourse demonstrates that the centre of this, its point of departure, is a privileged relation to sexual jouissance. The value of the other partner, which I began by designating respectively as man and as woman, is unapproachable through language very precisely because language functions, from the start, by standing in for sexual jouissance. It thereby gives order, in bodily repetition, to this intrusion of jouissance.

Today I am going to start to show you how, by making use of logical functions, it is possible to provide what is involved in castration with an articulation that is different from the anecdotal one.

2

In the lineage of the logical exploration of the real, the logicians started with propositions. Logic only got under way when it was known how to isolate in language the function of what are called prosdiorismoi, which are *one*, *some*, *all*, and the negation of these propositions.

Aristotle defined, in order to set them in opposition, the universals and the particulars, and, in each of them, the affirmative and the negative. I want to stress the difference there is between this use of prosdiorismoi and something else that came about which – for requirements of logic, namely for an approach that was none other than the real that is called number – was completely different.

The logical analysis of what is called the propositional function is articulated by isolating something in the proposition, or more exactly through the lack, the void, the hole, the hollow that is made, in what has to function as an argument. To wit, it will be said that any argument in a domain that we can label as you wish, with an x or a gothic a, placed in the empty place in the proposition,[3] shall suffice, that is, shall supply its truth value. This is an inscription of what is here on the bottom left, the $\forall x.\Phi x$. It matters little what is here in the proposition. The function takes on a true value for any x in the domain.

What is this x? I have said that it is defined as though by a domain. Even so, does this mean we know what this is? Do we know what a man is when we say *all men are mortal*? We learn something about him from the fact of saying that he is mortal, and precisely from the knowledge that this is true for all men. However, before introducing this *all men*, we only know the most approximate features, which can be defined in the most variable fashion. This is the story, which I suppose you've known for a long time, of the plucked chicken that Plato recounts. This means that we need to examine the phases of the logical articulation.

Indeed, whatever the prosdiorismos holds does not carry any meaning until it functions as an argument. It only takes on a meaning through entering the function. It takes on the meaning of true or false. It seems to me that this is just what it takes to make us touch on the wide gap that lies between the signifier and its denotation, because meaning, if it lies somewhere, lies in the function, yet denotation only begins when the argument comes to be inscribed within it.

By the same token, this calls into question the following, which is different, namely the use of the letter E, likewise inverted, ∃, meaning *There exists*. There exists something that can serve in the function as an argument and thereby assume, or not, a truth value. I would like to give you a sense of the difference that lies in this introduction of *There exists* as a problematic. It calls into question the very function of existence in relation to what was implied by the use of particulars in Aristotle, namely that the use of *some* would seem to bring existence along with it, such that, since the *all* was supposed to comprehend this *some*, the *all* assumed the value of what it is not. It assumed the value of an affirmation of existence.

The status of the *all*, namely the universal, lies only at the level of the *possible*. Given how late it is, we will only be able to see this next time. It is *possible* to say, among other things, that *all humans are mortal*. However, the curious thing is that, far from settling the question of the existence of the human being, one has first of all to be sure that the human being exists.

3

I want now to indicate the path that we will start on next time.

The domain from which each x assumes a value can be defined solely by the articulations of the four argument-function conjunctions, under the sign of quantifiers. It is possible to propose the following truth function, namely that all men are defined by the phallic function, the phallic function being specifically what obturates sexual relation.

The universal quantifier will be defined in a different way when the upside-down A is furnished, which is what I have been doing, with a bar that negates it, $\overline{\forall}$. I have put forward the essential trait of the *pas-tous*, the *not-all*, $\overline{\forall}x.\Phi x$, as that by which a fundamental statement can be articulated regarding the possibility of denotation that a variable assumes in functioning as an argument.

Woman is situated through it being *pas toutes*, *not all* of them, who may be truthfully said to be functioning as an argument within what is stated of the phallic function. What is this *pas toutes*? It is very precisely what deserves to be examined as a structure. Indeed, contrary to the function of the particular negative, namely that there are *some that are not*, it is impossible to extract such an affirmation from the *pas toutes*. To this *pas toutes* is restricted the indication that somewhere, and nothing more, woman has a relation to the phallic function.

It is from here that the values to be given to my other symbols find their point of departure. Nothing can adapt this *all* to this *not all*. Between what symbolically grounds the argumental function of the terms *man* and *woman*, there remains the wide gap of an indeterminacy in their common relation to jouissance. They are not defined in relation to this jouissance by the same order.

The denotation of man hinges on the *all* of the phallic function. However, in spite of this *all*, *There exists* . . . – and here, *There exists* means that it exists exactly as it does in the solution of a mathematical equation – . . . *at-least-one* for whom the truth of its denotation does not hold in the phallic function.

Is there any need to spell it right out for you? *Totem and Taboo* is what was fashioned to give some idea of this logical condition that is the condition of indirect approach that woman can make to man.[4] Already, it is in itself extraordinary that it doesn't seem farcical to state the myth in terms of an originary man who is purported to enjoy precisely what does not exist, namely all the women. This is not possible, not simply because clearly one has one's limits, but because there is no such thing as *all the women*.

So, what is at issue is of course something else, namely that at the level of *at-least-one* it is possible for the prevalence of the phallic function to be subverted. It is possible for it no longer to be true.

Just because I said that sexual jouissance is the pivotal point of all jouissance, this doesn't mean that I have sufficiently defined what is involved in the phallic function. For the time being, let's say that they are the same thing.

Something is introduced at the level of the *at least one* of the Father. This *at least one* means that it is one that can work by itself. As the myth demonstrates – for it is designed especially for this – this means that sexual jouissance will be possible but it will be limited. It presupposes, for each man, at the very least some mastery of this jouissance in his relation with woman. For the woman, at least this much is required – that castration should be possible. This

is her approach to man. When it comes to enacting the said castration, she takes care of it.

I would not like to leave you before articulating what is involved
in the fourth term. I will have to come back to this, because we've
been set back a little today.[5] I had intended, as I intend each time,
to cover a much wider field, but since you are patient, you will come
back the next time.

We have said that the *There exists* is problematic. This year will
be the occasion to examine what is involved in existence. After all,
what exists? Has anyone ever even realized that alongside the fragility, the futility, and the inessentiality constituted by the *There exists*,
the *There does not exist* does actually mean something? What does it
mean to assert that *There does not exist* an *x* that would be such that
it could fulfil the function Φx endowed with the bar that establishes
it as being untrue? That is, $\overline{\exists x.\Phi x}$.

This is precisely what I called into question earlier. If *not all
women* have dealings with the phallic function, does this mean that
there are women who do have dealings with castration? Well, this is
very precisely the point at which man has access to woman.

I'm saying this for the analysts as a whole, those who dawdle,
those who spin around, mired in Oedipal relations on the side of
the Father. When they can't get out of this, when they can't move
beyond what happens on the side of the Father, it has a very precise
cause. It's that the subject would have to admit that the essence of
woman is not castration.

To spell it right out, on the basis of the real, aside from a mere
insignificant nothing – I'm not saying this by chance – women
cannot be castrated because they don't have the phallus. I stress
that I have still on no account said what this phallus is. From the
moment it is impossible as a cause, woman is not linked to castration essentially and access to woman is possible in its indeterminacy.

Doesn't this suggest to you – I'm sowing this seed so that it might
resonate here next time – that what is up here on the top left, $\exists x.\Phi x$,
the *at-least-one* in question, results from a necessity, and it's in this
precise respect that it's a matter of discourse? There is only any
necessity qua spoken, and this necessity is what makes the existence of man possible as a sexual value. Contrary to what Aristotle
put forward, the possible is the opposite of the necessary. The
mainspring of the possible lies in $\exists x$ being opposed to $\forall x$.

I told you that the *There does not exist* is asserted in a fact of
saying, by the fact of being said by man. The impossible is that it is
from the real that woman assumes her relation to castration. This
is what delivers us the meaning of the $\overline{\forall x}$, that is, of the *pas-toute*.
Just like what was involved in the left-hand column a moment ago,

the *pas-toute* means *not impossible*. It is *not impossible* that woman should know the phallic function.

What is this *not impossible*? It bears a name that is suggested by the Aristotelian tetrad, but which here is arranged differently. In the same way that the possible stood in opposition to the necessary, the contingent stands in opposition to the impossible. It is in so far as woman presents herself to the phallic function by way of an argument in contingency that what is involved in the sexual value *woman* can be articulated.

It is sixteen minutes past two. I'm not going to push any further today. The cut-off point is falling at a place that is really not especially desirable. I think I have advanced enough with this introduction to the functioning of these terms to have given you a sense of how the use of logic is not unrelated to the content of the unconscious.

Just because Freud said that the unconscious knows no contradiction, this doesn't mean that it is not a land of promise for logical conquest. Have we got to this century without knowing that logic can readily bypass the principle of contradiction?

To say that in everything Freud wrote on the unconscious, logic does not exist, or that the unconscious cannot be explored by the paths of logic, would imply never having read the use he makes of certain terms, for instance, *I love her, I don't love him*, and all the ways there are of negating *I love him* by taking grammatical paths.

12 January 1972

IV

FROM NECESSITY TO INEXISTENCE

The symptom, between truth and jouissance
Phallic jouissance
The emergence of the number 1
Leibniz, Frege, Pascal
The two Ones

The art of producing a necessity of discourse

$\exists x.\overline{\Phi x}$	$\overline{\exists x}.\overline{\Phi x}$		the signification of the phallus
$\forall x.\Phi x$	$\overline{\forall x}.\Phi x$		*die Bedeutung des Phallus*

Objective genitive: a desire → of a child

Subjective genitive: a desire ← of a child

The Law of Talion

```
0   1   0   0   0   0   0   0   0   0
    0   1   1   1   1   1   1   1   1
        0   1   2   3   4   5   6   7
            0   1   3   6  10  15  21
                0   1   4  10  20  35
                    0   1   5  15  35
                        0   1   6  21
                            0   1   7
```

On the blackboard

The art of producing a necessity of discourse is the formula that last time I slipped in, rather than proposed, for what logic is.

Amid the hubbub made by everyone getting to their feet, I left you with the remark that the fact that Freud noted, as a characteristic of the unconscious, that it neglects the principle of contradiction, isn't enough to mean that logic has nothing to do with the elucidation of the unconscious, as some psychoanalysts imagine.

If there is a discourse that deserves to be pinpointed by the recent establishing of analysis, it is more than probable that its logic can be extracted, as for any other discourse.

The least one can say about discourse is that its meaning remains veiled. In truth, what constitutes discourse is very precisely formed through the absence of this meaning. There is no discourse that must not receive its meaning from another discourse. Moreover, concerning the appearance of a new structure of discourse – which is what the analytic discourse is, as I situated it for you last year – if it does take on meaning it is not just by receiving it in this way, but also because it becomes palpable that something original has been produced in the circle that closes through this final shift in what is articulated in the name of *signifiance*. Indeed, this discourse represents the final shift in a tetradic structure, a *quadripode*, as I have reminded you in a published text.

1

The art of producing a necessity of discourse is something other than this necessity itself.

Reflect on this. Logical necessity – there can be no other – is the upshot of this production. Necessity, ἀνάγκη, only begins with the speaking being, and by like token, everything that might appear to have been produced by it is invariably the doing of a discourse. If this really is what is at issue in tragedy, it's precisely in so far as tragedy is made concrete as the upshot of a necessity that is logical. This is obvious, for here it's a matter only of speaking beings.

It seems to me that nothing of what is properly speaking ἀνάγκη appears anywhere else but among speaking beings. This is also why Descartes saw animals as mere automatons. That was certainly an illusion, the impact of which we shall show in passing, in connection with what I am about to attempt to open up regarding this art of producing a necessity of discourse.

Produce has a double meaning here. First, it means to demonstrate what was there beforehand. Already, it is by no means sure that something is not reflected in, or does not contain the beginnings of, the necessity that is at issue in the precondition of animal existence. However, for want of any demonstration, what is to be produced must indeed be held to have been inexistent beforehand.

Second, the other sense of *produce* is the one that a whole research project issuing from the elaboration of a discourse that has already been constituted, known as the discourse of the master, has already put forth under the heading *achieving through labour*.

It is precisely inasmuch as I myself am the logician in question, the product of the emergence of this new discourse, that production in the sense of demonstration can be declared here in front of you. It has to be supposed that it was already there, through the necessity of the demonstration, as a product of the supposition of the necessity of always, but also vouching precisely for the necessity – which is not a lesser necessity – of the labour of actualizing it. At this point of emergence, however, this necessity by the same token furnishes the proof that initially it can be supposed only as *inexistent*.

So, what is it then, necessity? No, I shouldn't say *it then*, which already entails too much Being, but rather, directly, *what is necessity?* such that from the very fact of producing it, it can only, before being produced, be presupposed as inexistent, which means *posed* as such in discourse. There is a response to this question, as there is to any question, due to the reason that it is posed, as is any question, only when one already has the response. You have the response, therefore, even if you don't know it. In response to the question *what is necessity?* you logically cobble together your *bricolage*. Even if you don't know it, you respond in your day-to-day *bricolage*. A certain number of you here – not all of you, of course – by virtue of being in analysis with me, come along to confide in me, without moreover being able to assume the sense that in coming to see me, prior to taking a particular step, you presume that I am myself this *bricolage*. Indeed, by cobbling together this *bricolage*, all of you, even those who do not confide in me, are already responding to the question. How so? Quite simply by repeating it, by tirelessly repeating this *bricolage*. This is what is called, at a certain level, the symptom. At another level, it is automatism, which is a somewhat improper term but which can be accounted for by its history.

From one instant to the next, inasmuch as the unconscious exists, you are carrying out the demonstration by which inexistence is grounded as what is preliminary to what is necessary. This is the inexistence of what lies behind the principle of the symptom. It has been so ever since the term assumed its value in emerging with Marx. It is the very consistence of the said symptom. What lies behind the principle of the symptom is the inexistence of the truth that it presupposes, even though it marks out its place. There you have it for the symptom inasmuch as it attaches itself to truth that no longer has currency. In this respect, it can be said that like anyone who scrapes by in the modern age, not a single one of you is unacquainted with this modality of response.

In the second case, it is the inexistence of jouissance that the so-called automatism of repetition brings to the light of insistence, of this stamping at the door that is designated as the exit towards existence. Beyond the door, however, what lies in wait for you is not altogether what is called existence. It is rather jouissance, such as it is operative as the necessity of discourse.[1] And, you see, it operates only as inexistent.

Of course, I'm reminding you of these old refrains, these old chestnuts, with the intention of reassuring you, of giving you the sense that I'm merely delivering you speeches that answer for the fact that there is a particular substance, jouissance, truth in this case, the truth that is lauded in Freud. It still remains, however, that you cannot get down to the bone of structure when you stay at this level.

I asked, *what is the necessity that is established on the basis of a supposition of inexistence?* In this question, what counts is not that which is inexistent, but rather the *supposition* of inexistence, which is merely a consequence of producing necessity.

Inexistence only becomes a question on account of already having a response – the twofold response, certainly, of jouissance and of truth – but it already *inexists*. It is neither through jouissance nor through truth that inexistence assumes a status, that it may inexist, in other words that it may come to the symbol that designates it as inexistence, not in the sense of not having existence, but rather of only being in existence through the symbol that would make it inexistent and which, for its part, does indeed exist. As you know, this is a number that is generally designated as nought. This shows very well that inexistence is not what you might think it is, namely nothingness, for what could come out of nothingness?

The answer to that is nothing, of course, except belief. Belief in itself. There are not umpteen beliefs. *God made the world from nothingness.* It's no surprise that this should be a dogma. It is belief in itself, it is the rejection of logic, which is here expressed in accordance with the formula – it was one of my pupils who came up with this, all on his own, and I thank him for it – *Surely not, but all the same.* On no account will this be sufficient for us.

Inexistence is not nothingness. It is, as I've just told you, a number that is part of the series of integers. There can be no theory of integers if you don't take into account what is involved in nought. It is not by chance that this was noticed in an endeavour that was coeval – slightly earlier, actually – with Freud's research. This is the path that was opened by a certain Frege – who was born eight years before Freud and died fourteen years before him – through examining logically what is involved in the status of number.

This has a weighty destiny in our examination of what is involved in the logical necessity of the discourse of analysis. It's what I was pointing out as what could escape your notice in the reference that I was illustrating it with just now as an application, in other words as a functional use, of inexistence. Inexistence is only produced in the retroaction from which there first arises necessity, namely from a discourse in which it manifests itself prior to the logician reaching it himself as a second consequence, that is, at the same time as inexistence itself. Its end is to be reduced right where this necessity manifests itself, prior to him.

I repeat – demonstrating it this time at the same time as I state it – this necessity is repetition itself, in itself, by itself, for itself, that is to say, the very thing through which life demonstrates that it is merely a necessity of discourse, because it finds nothing by which to hold out against death, that is, against its lot of jouissance, apart from recourse to this same thing, which is produced by an opaque sequencing. I stressed that this sequencing is very different from vital power, from love, or from some other poppycock. It's a radical sequencing, which has only started to emerge from the shadows a little with what the biologists have been doing at the level of bacteria, and the consequence of which is precisely the reproduction of life.

What discourse does – in demonstrating this level at which nothing of a logical necessity manifests itself except through repetition – here appears to join up, as a semblance, with what comes about at the level of a message. But this is a message that is in no way easily reduced to what we know of this term. It belongs to the realm of what is located at the level of short combinations, the modulations of which are those that pass from deoxyribonucleic acid to what of this is transmitted at the level of proteins, by the good will of a few intermediaries that are qualified as enzymatic or catalytic.

That here lies what allows us to refer to what is involved in repetition can only come about precisely by elaborating what is involved in the fiction whereby all of a sudden something appears to us to reverberate from the very foundation of what, one fine day, made a living being capable of speaking.

Indeed, among them all there is one living being who does not elude a particularly senseless jouissance, and which I would describe as local, in the sense of accidental. This is the organic form that sexual jouissance assumed for this living being. He colours all his basic needs with jouissance, needs which in other living beings are merely ways of sealing off jouissance. If animals feed on a steady basis, it's quite clear that this is so as to avoid knowing the jouissance of hunger. With jouissance, he who speaks – and this is Freud's discovery – colours all his needs, that is to say, that by which he fends off death.

Just because of this, it shouldn't be thought, however, that sexual jouissance is life. As I told you earlier, it is a local, accidental, and organic production, which is very exactly centred on what is involved in the male organ. Clearly, this is particularly grotesque.[2] Detumescence in the male has generated the special type of appeal that articulated language is, by virtue of which the necessity of speaking is introduced into its dimensions. From this arises logical necessity as a grammar of discourse.

You can see that this is meagre. To notice it, it required nothing less than the emergence of the analytic discourse.

I was careful to put in my *Écrits* the pronouncement I made a while ago, in 1958, *The signification of the phallus*. Beneath it, I wrote *Die Bedeutung des Phallus*. I didn't do that just to take pleasure in making you think that I know some German, though it was indeed in German because it was in Munich that I thought I ought to give voice to what I provided in a retranslated text. It struck me as a timely opportunity to introduce under the term *Bedeutung* what in French, in view of the degree of culture we had reached back then, I could only decently translate as *signification*.

The Germans themselves, given that they were analysts – I indicate the shortcoming in a brief note added at the head of the text – didn't cotton on in the slightest to *Die Bedeutung des Phallus*. It wasn't long after the war, and it can't be said that analysis had made a great deal of progress during that time. As I underscore in the final term of the note, all of that struck them as, strictly speaking, *unheard of*. Moreover, it's curious that things have moved on to the extent that what I am saying today might already have become common currency for some of you, and rightly so.

Die Bedeutung was, nevertheless, in precise reference to the use that Frege makes of the word, to contrast it with the term *Sinn*, which corresponds most exactly to what I thought I should remind you of in what I have stated today, namely the meaning of a proposition. What is involved in the necessity that leads to this art of producing it as the necessity of discourse could be expressed differently, and you'll see that this is not incompatible. It could be expressed as, *what does it take for a word to denote something?* This is the sense that Frege gives to *Bedeutung* – pay attention, there will be some small changes now – to wit, *denotation*.

If you would care to open the book called *The Foundations of*

Arithmetic – it has been translated [into French], which makes it wholly accessible for you, within arm's reach, by a certain Claude Imbert, who if I remember rightly used to come to my Seminar – it will strike you as clear, as might have been anticipated, that for there to be reliable denotation it would not be a bad idea to turn first of all, gingerly, to the field of arithmetic as defined by the integers.

There was someone by the name of Kronecker who couldn't help himself, so great is the need for belief, from saying *the integers were created by God*. In view of which, he adds, *everything else is the work of man*. Since he was a mathematician, for him this *everything else* was everything else that has to do with number.

Nothing in this realm is certain. But a logical endeavour can at least attempt to account for the integers, and this is why I'm bringing Frege's work into the field of consideration.

2

Nevertheless, I would like to pause for a moment, if only to encourage you to reread it, on the pronouncement that I produced from the angle of *the signification of the phallus*, from which you will see that, at the point I've reached – I pride myself on this minor merit – none of it needs revising, even though at the time truly no one understood any of it. I was able to observe as much, then and there.

What does *the signification of the phallus* mean? In a determinative construction, you always have to ask whether it's an objective or subjective genitive. I'm illustrating this difference through the comparison of two *thrusts*, indicated here by the two little arrows. *A desire of a child* with an objective genitive is a child that one desires. *A desire of a child* with a subjective genitive is a child who desires.[3]

You can try it out. It's always very useful. The thrust of *The Law of Talion*, which I've written underneath without adding any commentary, can be either that the law is talion – I establish it as law – or what the talion articulates as law, that is, *eye for an eye, tooth for a tooth*. It's not the same thing. What I would like to get you to notice is that the signification of the phallus – and what I am going to develop will be designed to make you discover this – with the meaning that I have just specified for the word *thrust*, that is, the little arrow, is neutral. What is ingenious in the signification of the phallus is that what the phallus denotes is the power of signification.

This Φx is not, therefore, a function of the ordinary type. Provided you articulate it with a prosdiorismos, which is something that initially needn't carry any meaning whatsoever and which is itself a product of the research of logical necessity, and nothing else, the argument of the function thus pinpointed will take on the signification of man or of woman depending on the prosdiorismos that is chosen, that is to say, either *There exists*, or *There does not exist* – either *all* or *not all*.

It is clear none the less that we cannot avoid taking into account what has been produced by a logical necessity, by confronting it with the integers, for the reason that this retroactive necessity implies the supposition of what *inexists* as such. Now, it is remarkable that it was in examining the integer, in having broached its logical generation, that Frege was led to found the number 1 upon the concept of inexistence.

For him to have been led to this, it has to be thought that what had hitherto been circulating on the foundation of the 1 did not give him satisfaction, a logician's satisfaction. For a long while, people had been content with very little. They thought that it wasn't very difficult. There are several of them, there are many of them, so, they count them. Of course, this poses unsolvable problems for the advent of the integer because it's merely a matter of doing what has been settled on, of coming up with a sign with which to count them.

Such signs exist. I've just been handed a little book with an Arabic poem at the start that indicates in verse what you have to do with your little finger, and then your index finger, and with your ring finger and some of the others, to convey the sign of the number. But precisely because it's a matter of making a sign, number must have another kind of existence besides simply designating, for example, each of the people present here, even letting out a bark for each one. For them to have the value of 1, they have to be divested of all qualities, without exception. People have always been aware of this. So, what remains? Of course, there were a few philosophers, called empiricists, to articulate this by making use of little objects, like small beads. A rosary, of course, is the best thing for it. But this doesn't resolve in the slightest the question of the emergence of the 1.

This was spotted very well by Leibniz, who thought he should start off from identity, which is what he compelled himself to do, specifically positing first of all –

> *Two* is one and one
> *Three* is two and one
> *Four* is three and one[4]

He believed he had solved the problem by showing that, by reducing each of these definitions to the preceding one, it could be demonstrated that 2 and 2 is 4.

Unfortunately there is a small obstacle that the logicians of the nineteenth century noticed fairly quickly, which is that his demonstration is only valid on the condition that one neglect the utterly necessary parentheses that have to be inserted in $2 = 1 + 1$, namely the parentheses around $1 + 1$. What he neglects is that it is necessary to posit the axiom –

$$(a + b) + c = a + (b + c)$$

This negligence on the part of a logician who was as true a logician as Leibniz surely deserves to be explained, and, in one respect, something does justify it. Be that as it may, that this condition should have been omitted is enough, from the logician's point of view, for Leibnizian generation to be rejected, besides the fact that it also neglects any foundation of what is involved in 0.

Here, I'm merely indicating to you which notion of concept has to be chosen as a base – a concept that is supposed to denote something – so that everything will hold together. But after all, it cannot be said that the concepts they chose, the moons of Mars or of Jupiter, do not have sufficient scope of denotation for it to be said that a number is matched to each of them. Nevertheless, the self-subsistence of number can only be assured on the basis of the equinumerosity of the objects that a concept subsumes.[5]

Thereafter, the order of numbers can be furnished by the trick that consists in moving in exactly the opposite direction from Leibniz's procedure, so to take 1 away from each number. The predecessor number is the concept that – aside from any object that might have served as a support in the concept of any particular number – is identical with a number that is very precisely characterized by not being identical with the number before, let's say, with the exception of 1.

This is how Frege works his way backwards to the conception of the concept as an emptiness, under which no object falls. It is the concept, not of nothingness – because it's a concept – but of inexistence. He does this precisely by considering what he believes nothingness to be, namely the concept for which the number would be equal to the 0 that he believes he can define by formulating the argument *x different from x*, $x \neq x$, that is to say, *x* different from itself.

This is certainly an extremely problematic denotation, because what do we get? If it is true that the symbolic is what I have said about it, namely that it is entirely within speech, that there is no such thing as metalanguage, then where in language can an object be designated about which one can be certain that it is not different from itself? Nevertheless, it is upon this hypothesis that Frege constitutes the notion that the concept *equal to nought* – in accordance with the formula that he provided at the start, of the predecessor number – yields a number that is different from what is involved in the 0 that is well and truly held to be nothingness. In other words, it yields a number that is different from the one for which what is suitable is not *equality with 0*, but the number 0.

Thereafter, it is in reference to this that the concept to which the number 0 is suited is – *identical with 0 but not identical with 0.*[6] The one that is quite simply *identical with 0* is held to be its successor, and as such is equal to 1. The whole thing is founded on a point of departure known as equinumerosity. Clearly, the equinumerosity of the concept under which no object falls, in the capacity of inexistence, is always equal to itself. There is no difference between 0 and 0. It was from the angle of this *no difference* that Frege sought to establish the foundation of 1.

Either way, for us this conquest remains a precious one to the extent that it furnishes us with 1 on account of it essentially being – listen carefully to what I'm saying – the signifier of inexistence.

Nevertheless, is it so certain that this is able to establish the foundation of 1?

3

This discussion could certainly be pursued along purely Fregean paths. Nevertheless, I thought I should reproduce for clarity's sake what could be said to bear no relation to the integer, namely the arithmetical triangle.

The arithmetical triangle is organized as follows. It starts off, as a given, from the sequence of integers. Each term to be inscribed is constituted without further commentary by the addition – you will note that so far I have not spoken of addition, any more than Frege does – of two figures, the one that stands immediately to its left and the one that stands to its left on the level above it.

0	1	0	0	0	0	0	0	0	...
	0	1	1	1	1	1	1	1	...
		0	1	2	3	4	5	6	...

When we have a whole number of points that we shall call *monads*, you can easily confirm that this automatically gives us, for example, what is involved in the number of subsets that can, within the set that subsumes all these points, be formed of any number, chosen as lying underneath the integer at issue.

Thus, for example, if you take the line of the dyad, having encountered one dyad, what immediately obtains is that there will be two monads in the dyad.

1

2

1

It's not hard to imagine a dyad. It's a line with two terms, a beginning and an end.

Now let's take something more amusing. If you examine what is involved in the tetrad, you will obtain something that amounts to four possibilities of triads, in other words, to turn this into an image for you, the four faces of the tetrahedron. You next obtain six dyads, that is, the six edges of the tetrahedron. You also obtain the four vertex corners of a monad.

1

4

6

4

1

This is to lend support to what is to be expressed only in terms of subsets.[7] It's clear that you can see that, as the integer increases, the number of subsets that can be produced within it very quickly surpasses by far the integer itself.[8]

This is not what is of interest to us. It was simply that, in order for me to account for the series of integers by means of the same procedure, I had to start off from what lies at the origin of what Frege came up with.

Frege designated that the number of objects that fall under a concept qua concept of the number n, shall by itself be what constitutes the successor number. In other words, if you start counting from 0 –

0 1 2 3 4 5 6

this will invariably make what is here, namely 7 – 7 what? – 7 of this something that I have termed inexistent, on account of it being the foundation of repetition.

For the rules of the triangle to be met, the 1 that is repeating here still needs to arise from somewhere. And, since we have flanked the triangle at each level with 0 –

$$0 \quad 1 \quad 1 \quad 1 \quad 1 \quad 1 \quad 1 \quad 1 \ldots$$

there is, therefore, a point here, a point to be situated at the level of the row of zeros. This point is 1.

$$0 \quad 1 \quad 0 \quad 0 \quad 0 \quad 0 \quad 0 \quad 0 \quad 0 \ldots$$

What does it articulate? It articulates the important thing to distinguish in the generation of 1, namely the distinction of *no difference* between each of these zeros, on the basis of the generation of what repeats, but which repeats as inexistent.

Frege does not, therefore, account for the sequence of integers, but rather for the possibility of repetition. Repetition is posited first and foremost as repetition of the 1, qua 1 of inexistence.

In the fact that there is not just a single 1, but rather 1 that repeats, and 1 that is posited in the sequence of integers, is there not – I can only ask the question, here – something that suggests that we have to uncover in this gap something that belongs to the realm of what we have examined by positing, as the necessary correlate to the question of logical necessity, the foundation of inexistence?

19 January 1972

THE OTHER:
FROM SPEECH TO
SEXUALITY

V

TOPOLOGY OF SPEECH

A TALK AT SAINTE-ANNE

Where does meaning come from?
Speech between semblance and jouissance
Analysis started with the norm
Science behind the wall . . .
. . . and discourse in front of it

During the same academic year that Lacan was delivering his Seminar in the Law Faculty on the Place du Panthéon, he was also delivering 'talks' in the chapel at Sainte-Anne Hospital. From the fourth talk on, they were devoted to clarifying and extending his elaborations in the Seminar. In the present book can be found, in their chronological position, the talks that pick up the thread of . . . or Worse *– JAM*

Two years ago I explained something that, once it got on the right highway, the *poubellic* highway, took the name *quadripode*. I was the one who chose the name, and you can only wonder why I gave it such a strange one. Why not *quadruped* or *tetrapod*? These would have had the advantage of not being crossbreeds. In truth, as I was writing it I asked myself the same question. I don't know why I kept it. Then I asked myself what we used to call these crossbreed terms when I was young, these half-Latin–half-Greek terms. I was sure I used to know what the purists called them but I've since forgotten.[1] Is there anyone here who knows how terms are designated when they are composed, for example, of a Latin element and a Greek element, like the word *sociology*, or *quadripode*? If anyone knows, I implore you, out with it!

Well, this is not encouraging. I started searching the day before yesterday and as I still couldn't find it I telephoned a dozen different people whom I thought most likely to be able to give me the answer. Well, too bad.

I called them *quadripodes* to give you the idea that one can sit on them. It was just to reassure people a little, because I was speaking through the mass media. In reality, however, when I'm on the inside, I explain that what I have isolated by way of four discourses results from the emergence of the last one to arrive, the discourse of the analyst. Indeed, the discourse of the analyst brings some order to a particular current state of thought, an order that clarifies the other discourses that emerged earlier. I have arranged them in accordance with a topology. It's one of the simplest, but it is no less a topology, in the sense that it's mathematizable. It's a topology in the most rudimentary fashion, namely in that it hinges on the grouping of no more than four points that we shall call monads.

It doesn't seem so, but it is so forcefully inscribed in the structure of our world that there is no other foundation to the fact of the space we live in. Note if you will the following, that putting four points at an equal distance from one another is the highest number with which you can do this in our space. You will never be able to put five points at an equal distance from one another.

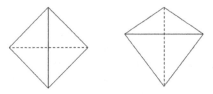

This little shape is here to help you to sense what is at issue. The quadripodes are not tetrahedral, but tetradic. The number of vertex corners is equal to the number of surfaces, and this is linked to the same arithmetical triangle that I drew in the last lesson of my Seminar.

As you can see, to sit on it, whether the one on the left or the one on the right, affords no rest. You've got used to the one on the left-hand side of the board, to the point that you don't even feel it any more. The one on the right, however, isn't any the more comfortable. Imagine yourself sitting on a tetrahedron that is poised on its tip. Yet this is where we have to begin for everything that is involved in what constitutes a type of social base that is supported by what is called a discourse. This is what I specifically put forward in my antepenultimate Seminar.

The tetrahedral, to refer to it in its present appearance, possesses some curious properties. If it is not like this one, which is regular in shape – the equal distance is just to remind you of the properties of the number four with regard to space – if it is just any old how, then it will be strictly impossible for a symmetry to be defined in it.

Nevertheless, it does have the following particularity. If you take these edges – namely these short dashes that join what are known in geometry as *vertices* – and vectorize them, that is, give them a direction, you just have to posit as a principle that none of the vertices shall be privileged, that nowhere shall there be a convergence of three vectors at the same vertex, nor shall there be three vectors that depart from the same vertex – otherwise there would be at least two vertices that would not benefit from vectors – and you will necessarily obtain the following distribution.

2 incoming   1 outgoing
2 incoming   1 outgoing
1 incoming   2 outgoing
1 incoming   2 outgoing

This means that each of the said tetrahedrons will be strictly equivalent. In each case, by removing one of the edges you will obtain the formula with which I schematized my four discourses.

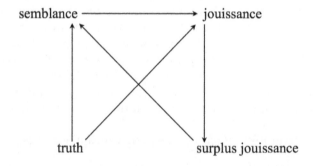

You can observe that one of the vertices has the property of divergence, but without any incoming vector to feed it. On the other hand, you've got this triangular trajectory. The number and the orientation of the vectors suffice to distinguish these four poles through a character that is altogether special. I state their terms as truth, semblance, jouissance, and surplus jouissance.

This is the fundamental topology from which any function of speech results, and it deserves to be commented on. What is the function of speech? The discourse of the analyst is formed in such a way as to make this question emerge. *The function and field of speech and language* – that's how I introduced what would lead us to the present point of defining a new discourse. Not that this discourse is mine, because at the time of speaking, this discourse has in fact been in place for three-quarters of a century.

That the analyst is capable, in some quarters, of rejecting what I say about this discourse is not a reason for him not to be its support. In truth, in this instance, *to be the support* means only *to be supposed*. However, that this discourse should assume meaning from the very voice of someone who is – this is my case – just as much of a subject as anyone else, is precisely what deserves to be paused over, so as to know where this meaning is drawn from.

In hearing what I've just put forward, the question of meaning might not seem to you to pose any problems. It seems that the analyst's discourse makes enough of an appeal to interpretation for the question not to arise. Effectively, going by a certain analytic scribbling, it seems that one can read – and this comes as no surprise, you're going to see why – all the meaning one wants, going right back to the most archaic. One can purportedly find an echo, the sempiternal repetition, of what has come down to us from the depths of ages under the term *meaning* in all the forms that, it has to be said, only become meaningful in their superposition.

Indeed, to what do we owe our comprehension of anything whatsoever in the symbolism in common use, for example in Holy Scripture? Everyone knows that comparing it with a mythology, whatever mythology it may be, is one of the most misleading types of slippage. For a while now, no one has stopped there. When one studies in a serious way what is involved in mythologies, one doesn't go to their meaning, but rather to the combinatory of mythemes. On this score, look up the works by an author whom I needn't, I think, name yet again.

The question is, therefore, as to where meaning comes from.

To introduce what is involved in the analytic discourse, I had no qualms about helping myself, because it was quite necessary, to the facilitation provided by what is called *linguistics*. To quell the ardour that might have been too quickly aroused in my vicinity, and which might have sent you back to the usual mire, I reminded you that this something that is worthy of the title *linguistics* as a science, which seems to have language and even speech as its object, was supported only on the condition that the linguists swear amongst themselves never – or never again, because this is what people had been doing for centuries – even remotely, to allude to the origin of language. This was one, among others, of the watchwords I gave to the form of introduction that was articulated in my formula *the unconscious is structured like a language*.

When I say that it was to avoid my audience returning to a particular miry equivocation – I'm not the one who helped myself to the term, it was Freud himself, and specifically with respect to so-called Jungian archetypes – this is certainly not in order now to lift this prohibition. On no account is it a matter of speculating about any origin of language. I said that it's a question of formulating the function of speech.

A very long time ago I asserted that the function of speech is to be the only form of action that posits itself as truth. It is an otiose question to ask oneself what speech is. Not only do I speak, do you speak, and even *ça parle, it speaks,* as I said, but this carries on all by itself. It's a fact, and I would even say that it lies at the origin of all facts, because whatever might be at issue only assumes the rank of a fact *when it has been said.*

Note that I didn't say *when it has been spoken.* There is something distinct between speaking and saying. A word that founds a fact is a fact of saying, but speech functions even when it doesn't found any fact. When it gives a command, when it prays, when it insults, or when it voices a wish, it doesn't found any fact.

Today, we can indulge in some fun. These are not things I would come out with at the other place, at my Seminar, where fortunately I say more serious things, as I did in the last lesson. Here, because it is implied in the seriousness that I'm always sharpening to a finer edge, we can have a bit of a laugh while still holding ourselves on this edge. I do hope there will be fewer people there the next time, because that was no laughing matter.

In an amusing register, it's not for nothing that in cartoons, speech is spelt out on banderoles. Speech is where *ça bande,* where hard-ons occur, *role* or not. It is not for nothing that this establishes the dimension of truth, because truth, the actual truth, the truth that we have only started to glimpse with the analytic discourse, is what this discourse reveals to each and every person who simply commits himself to it in an agentive manner, as an analysand. It's that *bander,* getting a hard-on – excuse me for using the term again, but since I've started I'm not going to abandon it – which up there, on the Place du Panthéon, I've been calling Φx, bears no relation to sex, no relation to the other in any case.

Here we're surrounded by these walls, so I will say that to get a hard-on for a woman means – because one really ought to call a spade a spade – giving her the function of Φx, which means taking her as a phallus.

The phallus is no small matter. I've already explained to you – up there, where's it's serious – that the signification of the phallus is the sole case of a fully balanced genitive. This means that the phallus is signification. This is what Jakobson was explaining to you this morning. I'm saying this for those who are a little switched-on.

The phallus is that by which language signifies. There is only one *Bedeutung*, and it's the phallus.

Let's begin with this hypothesis. It will explain for us to a very large extent the entirety of the function of speech. Indeed, speech is not always being applied to denoting facts. Denoting *facts* is all it can do – one doesn't denote *things* – but it does so completely by chance, once in a while. Most of the time it makes up for the fact that the phallic function is precisely what means that in mankind there are only the relations you know between the sexes – poor relations – whereas everywhere else things seem to coast along, at least to our eyes.

This is why in my little quadripode you can see, at the level of truth, two diverging vectors.

Jouissance, which is at the end of the right-hand branch, is certainly a phallic jouissance, but one which cannot be called sexual jouissance. On the left, so that any one of these odd animals who have fallen prey to speech can maintain themselves, there has to be this pole, which is correlative to the pole of jouissance inasmuch as it is an obstacle to sexual relation. It is this pole that I designate as semblance. If we dare, as is done on a daily basis, to pinpoint our partners by their sex, it is striking that man and woman alike affect a semblance, each of them in this role. The important thing, however, at least when the function of speech is at issue, is that the poles should be defined as that of semblance and that of jouissance.

Were there in mankind what we quite needlessly imagine there to be, namely a specified jouissance of sexual polarity, we would know it. Perhaps it was once known, because whole ages have boasted as much and, after all, we have numerous testimonies – though sadly they are purely esoteric – that there were times when people really believed they knew how to hold that together. A certain van Gulik, whose book struck me as excellent, prods around here and there. Of course, he does as everyone does. He goes prodding around near what is involved in the Chinese written tradition. His subject is sexual knowledge, which is not very extensive, I assure you. Nor is it very enlightened. Well, have a look at his book should this amuse you, *Sexual Life in Ancient China*. I defy you to get anything out of it that could serve you in what earlier I called the current state of thought.

What is of interest in what I'm pointing out does not lie in saying that things have always been the same as here at the point we've now reached. There might once have been, and perhaps there still are, places where there is a harmonious conjunction between man and woman, which would purportedly take them to seventh heaven. But, at any rate, it's curious that this is always in places where one has seriously to prove one's credentials before being allowed in. You only hear about it from the outside.

On the other hand, it's quite clear that each of us has a relation with capital Φ rather than with the other. This is plainly confirmed when one takes a look at those who are called, using a term that fits nicely thanks to the ambiguity of the Latin, or the Greek, *homos*. *Ecce homo*, as I was saying. It's quite certain that among homos there are better, firmer, and more frequent hard-ons. It's curious, but no one who has spent a certain amount of time hearing about such things can be in doubt about this fact. Still, don't be deceived. There are homos and homos. I'm not talking about André Gide. You oughtn't to believe that André Gide was a homo.

Let's not lose the thread. It's about meaning. For something to have meaning in the current state of thought, it's sad to say so, but it has to be pitched as normal. This was why André Gide wanted homosexuality to be normal. And, since you perhaps have the lowdown on this, within this meaning there are a host of different meanings. In two shakes of a lamb's tail it will fall under the cover of the normal, to such an extent that we will have new clients in psychoanalysis coming to tell us, *I've come to see you because I'm not a normal pederast.*[2] It's going to produce a traffic jam.

Analysis got off to a start with this. Had the notion of *normal* not taken on such an extension following certain vagaries of history, analysis would never have seen the light of day. It's very clear when you read Freud that a precondition to enter analysis, the minimum, to begin with was to have a good university education. This is the case for all patients, not only those whom Freud took on, but Freud says so in clear language. I have to underscore this, because the university discourse, which I have spoken badly of, and for the best reasons, is nevertheless what irrigates the analytic discourse.

You understand that you can no longer imagine, and I'm saying this to make you imagine something – if you are capable, who knows? – in being pulled along by my voice, a stretch of time that is called, because of this, *Antiquity*, when there was δοχα that was not academic. You know the famous δοχα that is spoken about in the *Meno. Mais non, mais non!* Nowadays, there is no δοχα, however futile, shaky, bumbling, or even daft it may be, that does not feature somewhere in university teaching. There is no example of an opinion, however stupid it may be, that has not been detected and, indeed, on the occasion of being detected, taught.

This falsifies everything, because when Plato speaks of δοχα as something that he literally doesn't know what to make of – even though he is a philosopher who is striving to found a science – he notices that there are true forms of this δοχα that he meets on every street corner. Naturally, he didn't bother saying why, no more than any other philosopher, but no one doubts that they are true, because truth is something that imposes itself. The fact that δοχα had not been normalized provided a completely different context from what is called *philosophy*. There is no trace of the word *norm* anywhere in antique discourse. We invented that, and naturally we did so by hunting out a Greek noun that was hardly ever used.

One nevertheless has to start from there in order to see that the discourse of the analyst did not appear by chance. Things needed to have reached the highest state of extreme urgency for it to emerge.

Of course, because it's a *discourse of the analyst*, as with each of the four discourses that I have named, this takes on the sense of the objective genitive. The discourse of the master is discourse *about* the master. This was clearly seen at the peak of the philosophical epic in Hegel. It's the same thing with the discourse of the analyst. One is speaking about the analyst. He is the object *a*, as I have often stressed. Naturally, this doesn't make it easy for him to grasp what his position is, but from another angle it's a restful position because it's the position of semblance.

So, our Gide, to continue weaving – I take up this Gide, then let go again, then we take up this Gide together, and so on – our Gide is nevertheless exemplary here. He doesn't get us out of our little concern, far from it. His concern is to be desired, which is something we commonly find in our analytic probing. There are people who, in their early childhood, missed out on being desired. It drives them to do things so that it will come about late in life. This is even very widespread.

However, we need to divide things up carefully. It's not at all unrelated to discourse. These are not the kind of words that pop up left, right and centre at carnival time. Here, discourse and desire bear the closest relation. This is even why I have managed to isolate – at least, I think so – the function of the object *a*. This is a key point that, I must say, hasn't been taken advantage of to any great extent. It will happen, slowly and surely.

The object *a* is that by which the speaking being is determined when he is taken up in a discourse. He doesn't know at all what determines him. It's the object *a*. How is he determined? He is determined as a subject, that is, he is divided as a subject. He falls prey to desire. This sounds like it occurs at the same site as those words that subvert, but it's not at all the same. It's quite regular. It has to be said that it's a product. It produces, mathematically, the object *a* as cause of desire.

The object *a* is also the one that I called, as you know, the meto-nymic object, which courses throughout what unfurls as discourse, discourse that is more or less coherent, until it stumbles and peters out. It is still the case that we get our idea of the cause from this. We believe that everything in nature has to have a cause, on the pretext that we have been caused by our own blather.[3]

In André Gide, all the features are there to indicate that things are as I've told you. First of all, there is his relationship with the supreme Other. On no account should one believe, despite what he said, that the big Other had no impact. Where the *a* takes shape, Gide even had an exceedingly specific notion, namely that the big Other's pleasure was to disturb the pleasure of all the little ones. In view of which, he twigged very well that there was a point of bother there, which clearly saved him from his childhood neglect. All his teasing with God was something deeply compensatory for someone who had got off to such a poor start. This is not a special privilege of Gide's.

Some time ago I started a Seminar on the Name-of-the-Father. I gave just one lesson. Naturally, I began with the Father. I spoke for an hour and a half about God's jouissance. If I said that it was mys-tical banter, it was so as never to speak about it again. It is certain that, since the time that there has only been a single God, the one and only, the God that ushered in a certain historical era, He has been precisely the one who disrupts the pleasure of others. It is even this alone that counts.

There were the Epicureans, who did all they could to teach the method whereby each individual can avoid being disrupted in his pleasure, but it failed. There were others, called Stoics, who said, *But on the contrary, one should dive head first into divine pleasure.* This, however, also falls flat. You know it can only be played out between the two of them. What counts is the bother. With that, you are each in your natural environment. You don't get any jouissance, of course. It would be an exaggeration to say this, all the more so given that, either way, it's too dangerous. But still, it can't be said that you don't take any pleasure. It is even upon this that the primary process is grounded.

All of this puts us in a tight spot. What exactly is meaning? Well, we would be better off starting again at the level of desire.

The pleasure that the other gives you – this is commonplace – is even called, in a nobler region, *art*. This is where the wall should be attentively considered, because there is a region of meaning here that is thoroughly enlightened. It was thoroughly enlightened, for example, by the man known as Leonardo da Vinci, who as you know left behind a few manuscripts and some little knickknacks – not a great deal, he didn't fill up the museums – but he uttered some profound truths that everyone ought to remember. He said, as have I, *Look at the wall*. Since then, he has become the Leonardo of families. They make gifts of his manuscripts. There is a luxury edition and, can you imagine, I've even been given a couple of these myself. This doesn't mean, however, that it's illegible. So, he explains to you – *Look carefully at the wall*.

This wall here is rather unclean. Were it better kempt, there might be damp stains and perhaps even mould. Well, going by Leonardo, when there is a mildew stain, it's invariably a fine opportunity to transform it into a Madonna or some muscular athlete. It lends itself to it far better because in mildew there are always shadows and hollows. It's very important to note that there is a class of things on walls that lends itself to the figure, to the creation of art, as they say. The stain in question is figuration itself.

All the same, we need to find out about the relation between this and something else that can occur on a wall, namely gullies. These are not only gullies of speech – though this can happen, indeed this is always how things get going – but gullies of discourse. In other words, we need to find out whether it belongs to this same order of mould on the wall, or to writing. This should be of interest to a few people here who, I think, not so long ago – it's getting on a bit now – used to be very taken with writing love letters on walls. It was a damned good time. Some of them never got over this time when one used to be able to write on walls and when, from this stuff in *Publicis*, one could surmise that the walls had the power of speech, as though such a thing could happen.

I would simply like to remark that it would be better were nothing ever to be written on walls. What has already been written on them should even be removed. *Liberté, égalité, fraternité*, for instance, it's indecent. *No smoking*, it's not possible, especially given how everybody smokes. There's a tactical error here. I've already said this concerning the *lettre d'amur*.[4] Everything that is written reinforces the wall. This is not necessarily an objection, but what is certain is that it oughtn't to be believed that this is absolutely necessary. It's useful none the less because, had no one ever written on a wall, whichever wall it might be, this one or another, it's a fact that no one would have taken a step into the meaning of what might be there to be beheld beyond the wall.

You see, there is something here of what I will be led to speak to you about a little this year, namely the relationships between logic and mathematics. To tell you straightaway, beyond the wall there is only, to the best of our knowledge, the real that is signalled precisely by the impossible, the impossibility of reaching it beyond the wall. It no less remains that this is the real.

How did we manage to form some idea of it? Language certainly served in part. This is even why I'm trying to build this little bridge that you have been able to see taking shape in the latest lessons of my Seminar. How does the One make an entrance? This is what I have already been expressing for three years now with symbols, with S_1 and S_2. So that you might understand something from them, I designated the first as the master-signifier and the second as knowledge.

Would there be S_1, however, were there no S_2? This is a problem, because they need first of all to be twain in order for there to be S_1. I broached this in the latest lesson of my Seminar by showing you that, either way, they are at least twain, so that one alone may emerge. Nought and one, as they say, makes two. But this is in the sense that is said to be insurmountable. Nevertheless, you can surmount it when you are a logician, as I have already indicated for you in reference to Frege. I hope, however, that it appeared to you none the less that it was surmounted with a jaunty step. There and then – I will be coming back to this – I indicated that there was perhaps more than a short stride. This is not the important thing.

Someone whose name a few of you doubtless heard for the first time this morning, René Thom, who is a mathematician, doesn't think that logic – that is, the discourse that stays on the wall – is something that suffices even to account for number, the first step of mathematics. On the other hand, it does seem to him that he is able to account not only for what is traced out on the wall – this is nothing less than life itself, which as you know begins with mould – but also, through number, algebra, functions and topology, for what occurs in the field of life. I *will* be coming back to this. I'm going to explain to you that the fact that he finds in a mathematical function the very line of these curves formed by primal mould, before moving on up to mankind, pushes him to the extrapolation of thinking that topology can furnish a typology of natural languages. I don't know whether it's possible to settle the question at present. I'm going to try to give you an idea of where its current repercussion lies, no more than that.

In any case, what I can speak about is the cleaving performed by the wall. There is something in place in front of it, which I have called speech and language, and then there is another side that this works upon, perhaps mathematically. It's quite certain that we cannot form any other idea of it. There can be no doubting that science hinges not on quantity, as some have been saying, but on number, function, and topology. A discourse that is called science has found the means to construct itself behind the wall.

Only, what I do believe I can formulate clearly, and in this respect I believe I am in agreement with everything that is most serious in scientific construction, is that it is strictly impossible to endue with the faintest shadow of meaning anything whatsoever that is articulated in algebraic or topological terms. There is meaning for those who, standing before the wall, take pleasure in mildew stains that are so readily transformed into Madonnas or athletes' backs. It is evident, however, that we cannot content ourselves with these confusional meanings. At the end of the day, this serves only to reverberate on the lyre of desire, on eroticism, to call a spade a spade.

In front of the wall, however, other things happen, and this is what I call discourses. There have been others besides the four of mine that I have listed, and which, moreover, are specified only by making you note straightaway that they are no more than four. It is quite sure that there have been others, nothing of which we are still familiar with nowadays, besides what converges in the four that remain. These four that remain are articulated in the ring of a, S_1, S_2, and indeed the subject – who is left to pick up the pieces. These four terms, in moving around in this ring to each of the four vertex corners, as follows, have allowed us to isolate something by which to take our bearings. This is something that gives us the current state of what is grounded, by way of a social bond, as discourse. In discourse, whichever place one occupies – the place of the master, of the slave, of the product, or of what sustains the whole affair – one doesn't get it in the slightest.

Where does meaning arise? It is in this respect that it's very important to have made the division, which is doubtless a heavy-handed division, that Saussure made between signifier and signified, as Jakobson was reminding us this morning. Moreover, this was something Saussure inherited from the Stoics, whose very peculiar position in these sorts of manipulations I told you about earlier. What is important, of course, is not that signifier and signified unite, or that the signified would allow us to distinguish what is specific in the signifier. On the contrary, what is important is that the signified of a signifier – which I articulate in the little letters I told you about earlier – to which one attaches something that may resemble meaning, always comes from the place that the same signifier occupies in another discourse.

This was precisely what went to their heads, all of them, when the analytic discourse was introduced. It seemed to them that they understood everything, the poor souls. Fortunately, through the care I've taken, this is not your case. Were you to understand what

I say elsewhere, the place where I'm serious, you wouldn't believe your ears. This is even why, in general, you don't believe your ears. It's because, in reality, you do understand it, but in the end you keep your distance. And this is understandable because, for most of you, the analytic discourse hasn't caught hold of you yet. This will happen, unfortunately, because it's becoming increasingly important.

I would nevertheless like to say something about the analyst's knowledge, on the condition that you don't stay at this level.

My friend René Thom manages with great ease to find, by means of cuts in complicated mathematical surfaces, something like a drawing, a crest line, ultimately something that he also calls a spike, a flake, a cusp, a fold, and to turn it to truly captivating use. In other terms, a slice is made through a thing that only exists because one can write *There exists an x that would satisfy the function f(x)*. However, while Thom performs this with such ease, it is still the case that so long as this has not accounted exhaustively for the very thing with which, in spite of it all, he is forced to explain this, namely common language and the grammar around it, there will remain a zone here, which I call the zone of discourse. It is upon this zone that the analytic discourse sheds a clear light of day.

What of this can be transmitted by way of knowledge? Well, you have to choose! It is the numbers that know. They know because they have managed to stir this organized matter at a point, an immemorial point, of course. They still know what they do. There is something quite certain here, which is that meaning is only put into this most improperly. The same goes for any idea of evolution or perfection process. In the supposed animal chain we can see absolutely nothing that attests to this so-called continual adaptation, to the point that at the end of the day they had to give up on it and say that, after all, those that made it through are those that were able to make it through. They call it natural selection. Strictly speaking, this doesn't mean anything. It has a little meaning that has been borrowed from the talk of a crook. Why not this one or some other?

The clearest thing that appears to us is that a living being does not always know very well what to do with one of its organs. After all, this is perhaps a particular case of the analytic discourse evincing the cumbrous aspect of the phallus. We are unable to say any more than the following – there is a correlation between this and what is stirred up by way of speech.

At the point we've reached in the current state of thought . . . This is the sixth time I've employed this wording and it doesn't look like it's bothering anyone. Yet this really is something worth returning to, because I'm turning this current state of thought into a permanent fixture. It's true, though. Saying that thoughts are just as strictly determined as the latest gimmick is no idealism.

In any case, in the current state of thought, we have the analytic discourse which, when one cares to hear it for what it is, shows that it is linked to a curious adaptation, because in the end, if this business of castration is true, it means that, in man, castration is the means of adapting to survive. It's unthinkable, but it's true. All this is perhaps merely an artifice, an artefact, of discourse. That this discourse, which rounds out the others so knowingly, should be sustaining itself is perhaps just a historical phase. The sexual life of ancient China may perhaps flourish again. It will have a certain number of scruffy ruins to dispatch before that happens.

For the time being, however, what does the meaning we bring tell us? When all is said and done, this meaning is an enigmatic riddle, and it's an enigmatic riddle precisely because it is meaning.

Somewhere, in the second edition of a book that I allowed to come out, and which is called *Écrits*, there is a short addendum called *The metaphor of the subject*. I played at length on the expression that my dear friend Perelman repeated with relish, *an ocean of false learning*. You can never be sure what's in the back of my mind when I'm amusing myself, and I recommend you start off from there. *An ocean of false learning* could well be the analyst's knowledge. Why not? Why not, because it's only from the analyst's perspective that the following is clarified – that learning has no meaning, and that any meaning of discourse is merely partial, sustained as it is by another discourse.

If truth can only ever come midsay – this is the kernel, the essential part, of the analyst's knowledge – then, in what I have called a tetrapod or a quadruped, S_2 stands in the place of truth. This knowledge is a knowledge that is, therefore, always to be called into question.

On the other hand, there is one thing that is to be claimed of analysis, which is that there is a knowledge that is drawn out of the subject himself. At the place of the pole of jouissance, the analytic discourse positions the barred S. This knowledge is the result of the stumbling, the bungled action, the dreams, and the work of the analysand. As far as this knowledge is concerned, it is not supposed, it is a deciduous knowledge – scrap of knowledge upon scrap of knowledge.

This is what the unconscious is. I take this knowledge on board and I define it as only being able to be posited – a newly emerging term – on the basis of the subject's jouissance.

3 February 1972

VI

I ASK YOU TO REFUSE ME MY OFFERING

... because: this isn't it
Linguistic analysis
Schematizing speech
Grammar and signification
The Borromean rings

蓋　請
非　拒
也　收
　　我
　　贈

On the blackboard[1]

You're fond of *conférences*.[2] This is why, by means of a short note that I delivered to him at about a quarter past ten, I asked my friend Roman Jakobson to give you the *conférence* he didn't give yesterday. I was hoping he would be present today. After announcing it – I mean, after writing on the blackboard something equivalent to what I've just written here – he thought he should stick to what he called *generalities*, doubtless reckoning that this is what you would rather hear, that is to say, a *conférence*. Unfortunately – he telephoned me early this morning – he is tied up in a lunch appointment with some linguists, so you won't get the *conférence*.

I don't give *conférences*. As I have already said elsewhere in all seriousness, I amuse myself, whether in serious amusements or pleasant amusements. Elsewhere, specifically at Sainte-Anne, I tried my hand at some pleasant amusements. This speaks for itself. And while I said, over at Sainte-Anne, that this was also perhaps an amusement, here I say that I stick to the serious. But, even so, this is still an amusement.

Instead of relating it, at Sainte-Anne, to pleasant amusement, I related it to what I called *la lettre d'amur*.

1

La lettre d'amur? Well, here's a typical one – *I ask you to refuse me my offering*. There's a stop here, because I hope that for it to be understood there's no need to add anything. It's very precisely this, *la lettre d'amur*, the true one – *to refuse my offering*.

It can be finished off, for those who by chance might never have understood what *la lettre d'amur* is – to refuse my offering *because this isn't it*.

You see, I've slipped in – because my goodness, I'm speaking to you, to you who are fond of *conférences* – *ça n'est pas ça*. I've added the *n'*. When the *ne* is added, it doesn't need to be expletive to mean something, namely the true and rightful presence of the enunciator. The enunciation would be full precisely because the enunciator wouldn't be there. It should be written – *parce que*, colon, *c'est pas ça*.

I said that here the amusement is serious. What might that mean? I looked up the ways of saying *serious* in different languages. For my conception of it, I couldn't find any better than our way, which lends itself to a play on words. I don't speak the others well enough to work out what their equivalent would be, but in ours, *sérieux*, as I understand it, is *sériel*.

As a certain number of you already know, I hope, without me having to tell you, the principle behind the *serial* is the sequence of integers that no one has found any other way of defining but to say that a property is transferable from n to $n + 1$, which can only be the same property that transfers from 0 to 1. They also refer to this as reasoning by recurrence or mathematical induction.

Only, there you go, this is precisely the problem I tried to broach in my latest amusements – what exactly is it that could transfer from 0 to 1? It's a tall order. Yet this is the goal I set myself, for this year, to secure . . . *or worse*.

I won't be moving into the interval of what transfers from 0 to 1 today, which at first blush is bottomless. What is quite sure, however, is that, taking them one by one, you have to be clear in your mind about what you're doing, because whatever effort people might have made to logicize the sequence of integers, they didn't find any better than to designate the property that is common to all of them – and it's the only such property – as the property of what transfers from 0 to 1.

In the meantime, you were advised – well, those from my School were advised – not to miss the clarification that Roman Jakobson could bring you regarding what is involved in language analysis. This will be extremely useful for where I'm going to steer the question now. However, just because I took this as my starting point to get to my present amusements, it doesn't mean I should be bound to it.

What struck me, among other items, in what Roman Jakobson put before you was something that concerns the historical point that finding language on the agenda is not a recent occurrence. Indeed, he spoke to you about a certain Boetius de Dacia, who was very important, as Jakobson stressed, because he articulated *suppositiones*. I think that at least for some of you this will echo what I have long been saying about the subject, the subject that is radically *supposed* by the signifier. Then he told you that this Boetius, Dacia as he was called, which means Dane – he's not the same Boëthius whom you are familiar with, the one who is in the Bouillet dictionary, the one who extracted images of the past[3] – Boetius de Dacia took off, just like that, over a little question of deviation. In fact, he was accused of Averroism, and though it can't be said that it was unpardonable in those days, it might not be pardoned when the person concerned had caught people's attention with something that sounded a bit solid, like speaking about *suppositiones*, for example. It would not be altogether accurate to say that the two things are unrelated, and this is what I find striking.

What I find striking is that, for centuries, one had to be careful when one was dealing with language. There is a letter that only appears on the absolute margins in phonetic composition, the letter aitch, pronounced *hache* in French. Don't touch the *hache*![4] For centuries, this was wise when dealing with language, because it turns out that when one dealt with language in public, it used to produce an effect that was different from amusement.

One of the questions that it wouldn't be a bad idea for us to have a quick look at, right at the end – although I've indicated where it is that I amuse myself in a pleasant way, in the shape of this famous wall – is the question as to why nowadays linguistic analysis is part of scientific research. What might that mean, exactly? You don't have to look far. The definition of scientific research – here, I'm letting myself get swept along a bit – is very precisely the following. *Research* is the right word in that it's not a matter of *finding*, in any case, it's not about finding anything that would upset the public I was speaking about just now.

I recently received from a distant shore – I don't want to cause anyone any bother, so I won't say where – a question to do with scientific research. It came from a *committee for scientific research on weapons*. Word for word. Someone who is no stranger to me – this was why I was being consulted about him – intended to carry out a research project on fear. For this he was to receive financing that, converted into French francs, would amount to slightly more than a cool million in old francs, which would allow him – it was written in the text, which I can't give you, but I have a copy – to spend three days in Paris, twenty-eight days in Antibes, nineteen days in Douarnenez, and a fortnight in San Montano. Antonella, are you in the audience? San Montano must have a rather nice beach, I suppose? You don't know. Well, maybe it's close to Florence. Anyway, we don't know. He would then spend another three days in Paris.

Thanks to one of my pupils, I was able to sum up my appraisal [in English] in the following terms – *I am bowled over with admiration*. Then, I put a big cross over all the details of the appraisal I was being asked for, regarding the scientific quality of the programme, its social and practical impact, the competence of the person concerned, and all the rest. This story is only of limited interest, but it does offer some comment on what I was indicating. It doesn't get to the bottom of scientific research, but none the less it does denote something, and this is perhaps the sole interest of the affair.

Naturally, you don't know what [the English word] *bowl* means. Nor did I. It refers to the bowling ball. Therefore, I'm like a full set of skittles when a well-bowled ball has knocked them all over. Well, you'll believe me if you will, not knowing the expression *bowled over*, what I said on the phone when they called was *I'm blowed over*. I was trying to say *Je suis soufflé*. Naturally, it was completely wrong. *Blow*, which does indeed mean *souffler*, would become *blown*, not *blowed*. So, if I said *blowed*, was it because, without knowing, I did indeed know that it was *bowled over*?

Here, we're moving into the slip of the tongue, that is, into serious matters. At the same time, however, this is all it takes to indicate that, as Plato glimpsed in the *Cratylus*, it's not altogether sure that the signifier is arbitrary. After all, it's not for nothing that *bowl* and *blow* are so close, because this is precisely how I only missed *bowl* by a hair's breadth. I don't know how you would qualify this amusement, but I find it serious.

In view of which, we come back to linguistic analysis, which, certainly, in the name of research, you're going to be hearing about more and more.

It's hard to wend one's way through this where the division is worthwhile. You learn things, for instance that there are parts of discourse. I've kept away from this like the plague. I mean, I've avoided dwelling on it, so as not to bog you down.

In the end, however, since research will certainly make itself heard here just as it does elsewhere, I'm going to start with verbs.

2

You are told that verbs express all sorts of things, and that it's hard to disentangle an action from its opposite. Intransitive verbs obviously create an obstacle here, and they become very hard to classify.

To stick to what has been most accentuated in this definition, you are told, as far as typical verbs are concerned, about a binary relationship, where it has to be said that the same sense of the verb cannot be classified in the same way in every language.

There are languages in which one says *the man beats the dog*. There are languages in which one says *there is beating of the dog by the man*. This is not the essential thing, because the relationship is still binary.

There are languages in which one says *the man loves the dog*. Is it still binary when one expresses oneself as follows in a language – *the man loves to the dog* – not to say that he *likes*, in the same way that he likes some trinket, but that he has love for his dog? There are differences here.

To love to someone, has always delighted me. I mean that I regret that we speak a language in which we say *I love a woman*, in the same way as saying, *I beat her*. *To love to a woman* seems more appropriate to me. This is so even to the extent that one day I noticed – since we're in the parapraxis, let's continue – that I was writing *tu ne sauras jamais combien je t'ai aimé*. I didn't put an *e* on the end, which is a slip, a spelling mistake if you like, incontestably.[5] On reflection, I told myself I'd written it like that because I must have felt *I love to you*. Well, this is a personal matter.

Be that as it may, one distinguishes with care between these first verbs and those that are defined by a ternary relationship. *I give you something.* This can range from a punch on the nose to a trinket, but in the end there are three terms. You've been able to note that I have always used *I . . . you* as an element of the relationship. This already pulls you in the direction that is precisely the one in which I'm steering you, because, as you can see, it is a piece of *I ask you to refuse me my offering.* This doesn't go without saying, because one can say *the man gives the dog a little pat on the brow.*

This distinction between the ternary relation and the binary relation is utterly essential. When the function of speech is schematized, you are told that there is S and R for Sender and Receiver.[6] To this is added the relationship that, in the commonly used scheme, is identified with the message, and it is stressed that for it to work out the Receiver has to be in possession of the code. If he doesn't have it, he will have to get it, and he will have to decode it.

Is this a satisfactory way of writing it out? The relationship that passes through speech, if indeed there is such a relationship – you know that such a thing may be called into question – implies that the ternary function should be inscribed, namely that the message should be distinguished, here –

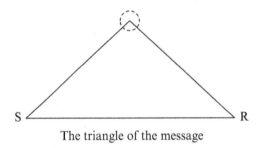

The triangle of the message

Therefore, there is a sender, a receiver, and a message. I claim, however, that it is no less the case that what is stated in a verb is distinct from this. The fact that what is at issue is a Demand deserves to be singled out, in order to group the three elements together.[7] It is precisely in this respect that this is evident only when I employ *I* and *you*, or *you* and *me.* This *I* and this *you,* this *you* and this *me,* are precisely specified by the utterance of speech. There can be no ambiguity whatsoever here.

In other words, there is not only what is called, vaguely, *code,* as though it were only present at one point. Grammar forms part of the code, namely this tetradic structure that I have just marked out as essential to what is said. When you trace out your objective scheme of communication – sender, message and, at the other end, the receiver – it is less complete than grammar, which forms part of the code. It is in this respect that it was important for Jakobson to voice this generality for you – that grammar also forms part of signification, and that it is not for nothing that it is employed in poetry.

This is essential when it comes to specifying the status of the verb, because soon enough the substantives will be sifted out for you in accordance with their respective weights. There are, so to speak, heavy substantives that are called *concrete*, as though there could be some other kind of substantive besides substitutes. But in the end, there has to be substance. I, meanwhile, think it is more pressing to indicate first of all that we are dealing only with subjects. Let's set these items aside for the time being.

You will recognize the scope of what I have been putting forward when you consider a criticism that curiously has only reached us after reflection, from the attempt to logicize mathematics. The criticism is that, in taking a proposition as a propositional function, we will have to note down the function of the verb, and not the function of what is done with it, namely the predicative function.

For the function of the verb, let's take the verb *to ask*. *I ask you*, F, and, opening the parentheses, *I* and *you* are x and y. Thus we have –

$$F(x, y$$

What do I ask you? *To refuse.* Another verb. This means that, in the stead of what here could be the little pat on the dog's head, that is, z, you have for example f and, again, x, y –

$$F(x, y, f(x, y$$

Are you compelled to end here, that is, to put z? On no account is this necessary, because you can perfectly well have a ϕ. Let's not put Φ because it will only lead to confusion later. So, I'm putting a lower-case ϕ, and again x, y, for *my offering to you*. In view of which, we have to close three parentheses –

$$F(x, y, f(x, y, \phi(x, y)))$$

What I'm steering you towards is this – it's a matter of seeing, not how meaning arises, but how the object arises from a knot of meaning. I named this object, as best I could, the object *a*.

3

I know that reading Wittgenstein is very captivating.

Throughout his whole life, with admirable asceticism, Wittgenstein stated the following, which I'm condensing – *whereof one cannot speak, thereof one must be silent.* In view of which he would hardly say anything at all. From one instant to the next, he would come off the footpath and into the stream, that is, he would then get back up on the footpath, the footpath defined by this exigency.

My friend Kojève expressly formulated the same rule. Goodness knows he didn't follow it. However, just because he formulated it, this doesn't mean that I should think myself obliged to stay at the level of the living demonstration that Wittgenstein gave thereof.

It seems to me that *whereof one cannot speak* is very precisely what is at issue when I designate as *this isn't it* that which alone prompts a request such as *to refuse my offering.* And yet, if there is one thing that should be palpable for everyone, then it's the *this isn't it.* This is where we are, at each instant of our existence. So, let's try to see what it means.

We could leave the *this isn't it* in its place, in its dominant place, in view of which we would clearly never see the end of it. Instead of cutting it off, however, let's try to insert it into the statement itself. *This isn't it* – isn't what, exactly? Let's put, in the simplest way possible, the *I* here, the *you* here, and *I ask you,* capital D for *Demand,* here, *to refuse me,* capital R, *my offering,* capital S for *Supply,* and then there is this that is lost – lower-case *i.*

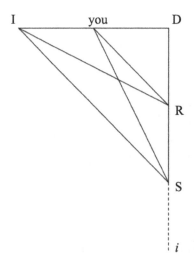

This isn't it inserted in the statement

However, if my offering isn't this, if I'm asking you to refuse it because *this isn't it*, then what you refuse is not my offering, so I needn't ask this of you. So, this is truncated at R. In view of which, if I needn't ask you to refuse it, why do I even ask you? Thus, this truncates at D.

To take this up in a more accurate diagram, the *I* and the *you* are here, the *Demand* here, the *Refusing* here, and the *Supply* here. This is, namely, a first tetrad, here – *I ask you to refuse.*

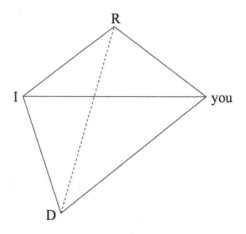

This is a second, here – *refuse my offering to you.*

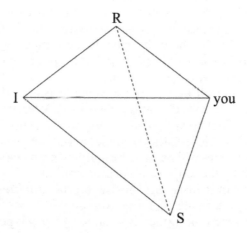

Perhaps we can see, which will not astonish us, in the distance that lies between the distinct poles of *Demand* and *Supply*, between the poles of asking and offering, that maybe here lies the *this isn't it*.

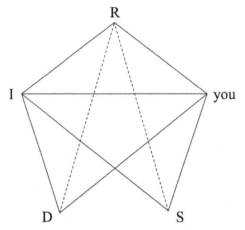

Diagram of the double tetrad

However, as I've just explained, if we are to say that this is the space that lies – that can lie – between what I have to ask you and my offering to you, it is equally impossible to sustain the relation between asking and refusing, and between refusing and offering.

Do I need to give a detailed commentary? This might be useful, after all.

First, you might be wondering why I'm giving you a spatial diagram of all this. It's not about space. Space is at issue to the extent that we project our objective schemes into it. But this already indicates enough about it, namely that our objective schemes perhaps govern something of our notion of space even prior to it being governed by our perceptions.

I know full well that we are inclined to believe that our perceptions provide us with the three dimensions. A certain Poincaré, who is not unfamiliar to you, made a very nice attempt to demonstrate as much. Nevertheless, this reminder about the precondition of our objective schemes will perhaps be useful when it comes to appreciating more fully the scope of his demonstration.

What I want to insist on is not merely the turn from *this isn't what I'm offering you* to *this isn't what you can refuse*, nor even to *this isn't what I'm asking you*. Rather, it's that *my offering* is perhaps not at all *what I'm offering you*, but rather *the fact of my offering*. It is on this basis that we get things wrong.

Indeed, what does *my offering* mean? It's enough to reflect on it to realize that it doesn't mean at all that I'm *giving*. Nor does it mean that you're taking, which would endow the *refusing* with a meaning. When I offer something, it's in the hope that you will reciprocate. This is precisely why the potlatch exists.

The potlatch is what drowns out, what outstrips, the impossible aspect of offering, the impossibility of it being a gift. And this is precisely why the potlatch has become completely foreign to us in our discourse. This is what makes it unsurprising that, in our nostalgia, we turn it into something that supports the impossible, namely the real – but the real as impossible.

If the *this isn't it* doesn't lie in the whereof of *my offering* either, let's observe what results from examining the fact of offering as such. It's not *what I'm offering*, but rather *the fact of offering*, as a gerund.[8] Remove supply and we see that demand and refusal lose all meaning, because what can it mean to ask to refuse?

A little exercise will be sufficient for you to notice that it is strictly the same if you withdraw any of the other verbs from the knot of *I ask you to refuse me my offering*. If you withdraw the refusal, what could the supply of a demand mean? As I told you, the nature of supply is that, if you withdraw demand, then refusing no longer has any signification. This is precisely why the question that arises for us is not about what is involved in the *this isn't it* – which plays out across each of these verbal levels – but to realize that it is by untying each of these verbs from its knot with the two others that we can uncover what is involved in this meaning-effect, in so far as I have called it the object *a*.

Now here's a strange thing. While I was wondering yesterday evening how I might present this to you today with my geometry of the tetrad, it so happened that, dining with a charming person who attends the courses of Monsieur Guilbaud, I was given, like a ring slid on my finger, something that I should like to show you now. It would seem to be nothing less – this I learnt yesterday evening – than the family crest of the House of Borromeo.

You need to take a bit of care over this, and this is why I'm doing just that. There you go. I haven't made any mistakes.

The Borromean rings

You can remake it with pieces of string. If you copy it down carefully, you will realize that – pay close attention – by removing this one, the third one, the other two are separated. This one passes over at this point here on the left, and again over the same ring here. They only hold together because of the third one. If you're lacking in imagination, you have to try it with three short lengths of string. You will see that they hold together.

You only have to cut one for the two others to come free, even though they might seem to be knotted together in the same way as those with which you are well acquainted, namely the rings of the Olympic Games, but the latter still hold together when one of them clears off. Well, there's no more of that with these Borromean rings! This is something that is nevertheless of great interest, because it shouldn't be forgotten that when I spoke about the signifying chain, I always implied this concatenation.

People don't seem to have realized that binary verbs have a special status that is very closely related to the object *a*. If, instead of taking the man and the dog as an example – these two poor animals – we had taken *I* and *you*, we would have noticed that what is most typical of a binary verb is, for example, *I bore you shitless*, or *I look at you*, or *I speak to you*, or *I gobble you up*.[9] These are the four guises, which only hold interest in their grammatical analogy, namely, on account of being grammatically equivalent.

Is it not the case that we now have, here in reduced form, in miniature, this something that enables us to illustrate the fundamental truth that any discourse only gets its meaning from another discourse? Assuredly, demand is not enough to constitute a discourse, but it possesses its fundamental structure, which is to be, as I put it, a quadripode. I stressed that a tetrad is essential for representing this demand, just as a quaternion of letters, F, x, y, z, is indispensable.

It's clear that, in the knot that I have put forward today, *demand*, *refusal*, and *supply* only take on their meaning each from the other. However, what results from this knot, in the way that I have tried to unravel it for you, or rather, in taking on the test of its unravelling, from telling, from showing you, that this never holds together with just two on their own, is that this is the fundament, the root, of what is involved in the object *a*.

I've given you the minimal knot, but you could add others to it. *Because this isn't it.* Isn't what? It isn't of my desiring. And who doesn't know that what is specific to demand is very precisely the fact of not being able to locate what is involved in the object of desire? With this desire, my offering, which is not of your desiring, we would easily be able to tie this thing up with your desiring of my asking.[10] And thus, the *lettre d'amur* will extend indefinitely.

Who can fail to see the fundamental character of a concatenation such as this for the analytic discourse?

I once said, long ago, and there are some who still find it soothing, that an analysis ends only when someone can say, not *I speak to you*, nor *I speak of me*, but *it's from me that I speak to you*. That was a first sketch. Is it not clear that the discourse of the analysand is grounded precisely on this – *I ask you to refuse me my offering, because this isn't it*? This is the fundamental request, and it's the same request that the analyst renders that much heavier when he neglects it.

I once quipped ironically – *with supply, the analyst creates demand*. But the demand that he satisfies is the recognition of the fundamental fact that what is being asked for, *this isn't it*.

9 February 1972

VII

THE VANISHED PARTNER

A TALK AT SAINTE-ANNE

The illusion of sexual relation
The *Hun* and the *Hautre*
All and *not-all*
The duality of woman's jouissance
The exorbitant emergence of the One

Please excuse me. This is the first time I've arrived late. I warn you
that I'm unwell. You're here, and so am I. This is all well and good.
It's all well and good for you. What I mean by this is that I feel
abnormally well under the influence of a slightly high temperature
and some medicine, and so, were this situation to change all of a
sudden, I hope that those who have been listening to me for some
time would explain to the newcomers that it's the first time this has
happened to me.

So, this evening I'm going to try to live up to your expectations,
here where I said I amuse myself. It is by no means certain that the
tone will stay the same throughout. So, please excuse me, it certainly
won't be due to my abnormal state. It will be in line with what I
intend to say to you this evening.

Elsewhere, at my Seminar, obviously I don't make it easy on my
audience. I see that a few of them are here, and they might remember that last time I spoke about this thing I encapsulated with the
Borromean knot – I mean, a link of three rings made in such a way
that by detaching one of them from the link, the two others will hold
together not an instant more. What does this hinge on? I really do
have to explain this for you because, after all, in its raw state I'm not
sure this will be sufficient for everyone.

It has to do with a question concerning the condition of the
unconscious, a question directed at what language is. Indeed, this is
a question that has not been settled. Should language be broached in

its grammar? – in which case, this is certain, it hinges on a topology
. . .

WOMAN IN THE AUDIENCE: *What is a topology?*

How nice this person is! Topology has a mathematical definition. It is approached through non-metric relationships that can
be pulled out of shape. This was the case for those sorts of flexible
circles that constituted *I ask you to refuse me my offering*. Each of
them was a closed and flexible circle that only holds fast when linked
to the others. None of them can sustain itself on its own. By virtue
of its mathematical insertion, this topology is linked to relationships
of pure *signifiance*, as the latest lesson of my Seminar demonstrated.
It is in so far as these three terms are threefold that we can see the
presence of the third term establishing a relationship between the
two others. That's what the Borromean knot means.

There is another way of broaching language, and of course this
is of current pertinence. It is of current pertinence given the fact
that someone whom I mentioned by name – it so happens that I
mentioned him after Jakobson had, but actually I knew him from
before – a certain René Thom, attempts to broach the question of
language, certainly not without having already cleared a number of
paths, from the angle of semantics. That is to say, he doesn't broach
language on the basis of signifying combinatorics, in the way that
pure mathematics can help us to form a conception of it. The semantic angle doesn't prevent him from also drawing on mathematics,
from finding in certain curves, and in certain forms that are deduced
from these curves, something that would enable us to conceive of
language as something like an echo of these physical phenomena.

For example, these curves are elaborated on the basis of what is
purely and simply the communication of phenomena of resonance.
Holding validity in a certain number of fundamental relations, these
curves would purportedly, in a second phase, gather together and
homogenize, as it were, to be taken up in a single parenthesis from
which the various grammatical functions are purported to result. It
seems to me that there is already an obstacle to conceiving of things
in this way, which is that one is compelled to place very different
types of action under the same heading of *verbs*. Why would language have gathered in some way, into a single category, functions
that can only be conceived of originally in very different modalities of emergence? None the less, the question remains in suspense.
It is certain that there would be something extremely satisfying
about considering language to be modelled in some way on functions that are supposed to be functions of physical reality, even if
this reality can be broached only from the angle of a mathematical
functionalization.

For my part, what I'm putting forward for you is something that is necessarily attached to the purely topological origin of language. I believe I am able to account for this topological origin on the basis of its being linked essentially to something that occurs in the speaking being through the intermediary of sexuality. Does the speaking being speak because of this something that happened to sexuality, or did this something happen to sexuality because he is a speaking being? I abstain from settling this matter. I let you take care of that.

This evening, I'm going to try to push the fundamental scheme at issue a little further.

The function called sexuality is defined, to the extent that we know anything about it – we do know a bit about it, if only from experience – by the fact that the sexes are twain. This is so, regardless of what is thought by one famous author who, in her time, oriented by goodness knows what because in truth I hadn't started teaching anything yet, thought she should confer with me before delivering *The Second Sex*. She called me by phone to tell me that she would certainly need my advice in order to enlighten her as to what the psychoanalytic contribution to her book would be. As I remarked to her that it would take at least a good five or six months for me to unravel the question for her – which is a minimum because I've been speaking about it now for twenty years, and this is not by chance – she announced that of course it was out of the question for a book that was already being finalized to have to wait so long, the laws of literary production being such that it seemed to her that having more than three or four consultations with me was impossible. Following which, I declined the honour.

The fundament of what I've been coming out with for a while now, since last year, is very precisely that *there is no second sex*. From the moment language starts functioning, there is no second sex. Or, to put it differently, concerning what is called heterosexuality, the word ἕτερος, which is the term that in Greek is used to say *other*, is in the position – for the relation that in the speaking being is called sexual – of emptying itself of its Being. This emptiness which it offers to speech is precisely what I call the locus of the Other, namely the locus in which the effects of the said speech are inscribed.

I'm not going to fill what I have to say to you with etymological references because that would set us back. I'll spare you how ἕτερος, in one Greek dialect that I won't name, is called ἅτερος, and how this ἕτερος joins up to δεύτερος and marks out how this δεύτερος is, in this instance, elided, so to speak.

Clearly this might appear surprising, just as it is evident that, for many an age now, such a formula is precisely what has been

overlooked. Truth be told, I don't know whether there exists any reference for a time when it might have been formulated. Nevertheless,
I claim that this is what the psychoanalytic experience brings, and I
support this with what you can see on the blackboard.

$$\exists x.\overline{\Phi x} \qquad \overline{\exists x}.\overline{\Phi x}$$

$$\forall x.\Phi x \qquad \overline{\forall x}.\Phi x$$

For this, recall the basis of the conception we may have, not
of heterosexuality – because all in all, if you have followed what
I just put forward, heterosexuality bears the right name – but of
bisexuality.

At the point we've reached in statements about the said sexuality,
what have we got? What we refer to – and don't imagine that this
goes without saying – is the model that is supposed to be animal.
Therefore, there is a relation between the animal image of copulation and the sexes, which seems to furnish a sufficient model for
what is involved in relation. By the same token, what is sexual is
considered in terms of need.

This is far from having always been the case. Believe it. I don't
need to remind you what *know* means in the biblical sense of the
word. The relation between νοῦς and something that is purported
to receive its passive imprint – which is termed in various ways,
but which is most usually denominated in Greek as ὕλη – this
mode of relationship that is generated by the mind has always been
considered to model not merely the animal relationship, but the
fundamental mode of Being of what was held to be the world. The
Chinese have long called upon two fundamental essences that are
respectively the feminine essence, which they call *Yīn*, in opposition to the *Yáng* that I have written, doubtless not by accident,
underneath.

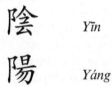

陰   *Yīn*

陽   *Yáng*

Were there such a thing as relation that could be articulated on
the sexual plane, were there such a thing as relation that could be
articulated in the speaking being, the question is whether it would
have to be stated of all those of one same sex with respect to all

those of the other. This is obviously the idea that is suggested to us, at the point we've reached, in reference to what I've called the animal model, which is the aptitude, if I may say so, of each of those on one side to be valid for all the others on the other side. You can see, therefore, that the statement is announced in keeping with the significant semantic form of the universal. If you replace in what I have just said *each of those* with *anyone* or *anybody* – anybody from one of these two sides – you would be wholly in the realm of the indeterminacy of what is being chosen in each *all* to correspond to *all the others*. Recognize if you will in this conditional mood something that echoes my discourse that would not be a discourse of semblance.

The *each of those* that I used at first has the effect of calling to your minds how, dare I say, the effective relation is not without an evocation of the horizon of *one to one*, of *every Jack has his Jill*. This one-to-one correspondence echoes what we know to be essential when it comes to presentifying number. Note that from the outset we can eliminate the existence of both of these dimensions, and it may even be said that the animal model is precisely what is suggestive of the animistic fantasy. Even if the choice happens through encounter, one-to-one coupling is what of this is apparent to us, namely that there are only two animals that are copulating together. If we didn't have this animal model, we would not have this essential dimension which is very precisely that the encounter is unique. When I say that it is here, and only here, that the animistic model is hatched, this is not by chance. Let's call it the soul-to-soul encounter.

In any case, it will come as no surprise to anyone who knows about the condition of the speaking being that, on the basis of this fundament, the encounter is to be repeated qua unique. There is no need to bring any dimension of virtue into play here. The very necessity of what is produced as unique in the speaking being is that it repeats. It is precisely in this respect that the fantasy I have called animistic is only hatched and sustained on the basis of the animal model. This fantasy is there to say *language does not exist*. Clearly this is not what interests us in the analytic field.

What gives us the illusion of sexual relation in the speaking being is everything that materializes the universal in what effectively amounts to herd behaviour in the relations between the sexes. I have already underscored that, in the sexual quest, or hunt if you prefer, the lads egg each other on in groups and the lasses like to pair up, so long as it is advantageous for them, of course. This was an ethological remark that I made, but which doesn't settle anything because a moment's reflection suffices to see in this a mirage that is equivocal enough for it not to last long.

To be more insistent here, and to hold myself at the most basal level of experience, I mean at the ground level of analytic experience, I will remind you about the imaginary. We reconstitute the imaginary in the animal model, and we do so in keeping with our own ideas, of course, because it's clear that we can only reconstruct it from observation. However, we do have an experience of the imaginary, an experience that is not effortless but which psychoanalysis has allowed us to extend. To put things crudely – it's not so *crude*, I ought rather to say *cruel* – I think it will not be difficult to make myself heard if I assert that in any sexual encounter, well, good Lord, if there is something that psychoanalysis enables us to assert, it's I know not what profile of other presence for which the vulgar term *partouze* is not to be altogether ruled out.[1]

In itself, this reference has nothing decisive about it, because, after all, one could assume an air of seriousness by saying that this is precisely the mark of the abnormal, as though the normal could be located somewhere. In putting forward this term – the vulgar name I have just uttered – I was certainly not striving to pluck the string of the erotic lyre for you, but simply to make a remark that may have something of the value of an awakening. At least this offers you, not the dimension that might echo Eros – I am certainly not here to amuse you in that key – but simply the pure dimension of a wake-up.

Let's try now to open up what is involved in the kinship between the universal proposition and our business, namely the statement that objects ought to be shared out into two *alls* of opposite equivalence. I've just told you that there is no cause to demand the equinumerosity of individuals, and I stuck, as best I could, to maintaining what I had to assert concerning simply the bi-uniqueness of coupling. If this were possible, it would amount to two universals defined solely as establishing the possibility of a relation of one to the other or of the other to one.

The said relation has absolutely nothing to do with what are commonly called *sexual relations*. We have stacks of relations to these relations. And, on these *rapports*, these relations, we also have a few little *rapports*, a few little reports. They keep us busy in our terrestrial life. However, on the level at which I position it, it's a question of grounding this relation in universals. How does the *man* universal relate to the *woman* universal? This is the question that forces itself upon us due to the fact that language demands very precisely that it should be grounded through this. Were there no such thing as language, well, there wouldn't be any question either. We wouldn't have to bring the universal into play.

To be more precise, and to render the Other absolutely alien to
what otherwise might be mere seconding, pure and simple, this relation is perhaps what will force me this evening to accentuate the A
– whereby I mark out the *Autre* as an emptiness – by means of something extra. With an extra aitch, the *Hautre* might not be such a bad
way of making audible the dimension of the *Hun* that can come into
play here.[2] It would enable us to perceive, for example, that all that
we possess by way of philosophical lucubration has come, perhaps
not by chance, from a certain Socrates. He was clearly a hysteric,
clinically speaking I mean. Well, there are reports of his cataleptic
manifestations.

The said Socrates was able to sustain a discourse that, not without
reason, stands at the origin of the discourse of science. He was able
to do so very precisely on account of having brought the subject to
the place of semblance, as I have defined it. He was able to do so precisely because of the dimension that presentified for him the *Hautre*
as such, namely his wife's hatefulness, to call a spade a spade. She
was *sa femme* to the point that she *s'affemait*,[3] to such an extent that
at the time of his death he had to adjure her kindly to withdraw so
as to allow his death to take on its full political signification. This is
simply a dimension indicative of the point at which the question we
are raising lies.

I mentioned that if we can say that there is no such thing as
sexual relation, this is surely not innocently. It's because of experience, namely a mode of discourse that is absolutely not that of the
hysteric but rather the one that I have inscribed with a quadripodic
distribution as the analytic discourse. From this discourse emerges
the dimension of the phallic function, which hitherto had never been
mentioned. The phallic function is what entails that at least one of
two terms is not typified by sexual relation. This term is the one to
which the word *Hun* is here being attached. It's not that its *Hun*
position is reducible to this something that is called either *male* or, in
the Chinese terminology, the essence of *Yáng*. On the contrary, it's
very precisely by virtue of what deserves to be recalled in order to
accentuate the meaning of the term *organ*. It is an organ only as an
implement. This meaning is veiled because it comes to us from afar.
The analytic experience prompts us to see everything that is stated
by way of sexual relation as revolving around the implement. This
is something new. I mean that it corresponds to the emergence of a
discourse that certainly had never come to light of day before, and
which would never have been conceived of without the precondition
of the discourse of science in so far as the latter is an insertion of
language on the mathematical real.

I have said that what stigmatizes this relation, on account of being profoundly undermined in language, is very precisely that no longer can it be written down in terms of male and female essences. This gets done nevertheless, but in a dimension that strikes me as being a mirage. What does this mean, that it *cannot be written down*, since, after all, it has already been written down? If I reject this ancient writing in the name of the analytic discourse, you could raise a far more valid objection, which is that I too am writing it down. What I have put once again on the blackboard is something that claims to support the channelling of this sexual business by means of a form of writing.

Nevertheless, this writing is only authorized, it only takes shape, through a highly specified form of writing, which allowed the sudden entrance of a mathematical topology to be introduced into logic. It is only on the basis of the existence of the formulation of this topology that we have been able to imagine turning any proposition into a propositional function, that is, into something that is specified by the empty place that is left in it, and which functions to determine the argument.

What on this occasion I am borrowing from mathematical inscription, in so far as it supersedes the first forms – I'm not saying *formalizations* – sketched out by Aristotle in his syllogistic, might, so it would seem, offer us under the term *argument-function* a comfortable term with which to specify sexual opposition. What would it require? It would be enough for the respective functions of male and female to be distinct in the same way as *Yīn* and *Yáng*. It's precisely because the function is unique, because it's always Φx that is at issue, that difficulty and complication are generated. The simple fact that you are here means that it's not possible for you not to have at least a little idea of this.

Here, Φx affirms that it is true – this is the meaning that the term *function* carries – that what is related to the practice, to the register, of the sexual act falls within the remit of the phallic function. It is very precisely inasmuch as the phallic function is at issue, from whichever angle we look at it – I mean, from one side or the other – that something urges us to ask in what respect the two partners differ. This is what is inscribed in the formulae that I have put on the blackboard.

If it turns out that, due to the fact of dominating both partners equally, the phallic function does not make them different, it is no less the case that first of all we must seek out the difference elsewhere. It is in this respect that the formulae inscribed on the blackboard deserve to be examined from both sides. The left side stands in opposition to the right side, while the upper level stands in opposition to the lower level. The meaning of this deserves to be

auscultated, if I may say so, namely to be examined first of all in
how they can show evidence of a certain misuse.

Just because I have made use of a formulation produced by the
sudden emergence of mathematics in logic, this doesn't mean that I
have employed it in quite the same way. Moreover, my first remarks
are going to consist in showing that, indeed, I make use of it in such
a way that on no account can it be translated into the terms of propositional logic. The mode of the variable – namely that which makes
a place for the argument – is specified here by the quadruple form
in which the relationship between argument and function is posited.

To introduce what is at stake, I'm going to remind you that in propositional logic we have on the foremost plane the four fundamental
relationships that are in some sense the grounding of this logic,
namely *negation, conjunction, disjunction* and *implication*. There are
others, but they are seldom the first, and all the others are reducible
to these.

I claim that the way our positions of argument and function have
been written here means that the relation called *negation*, whereby
all that is posited as truth can only be negated by passing over to
falsehood, is unsustainable here. Indeed, you can see that at either
level, both the upper and the lower, where the statement of the
function – namely that the function is phallic – is posited either as
a truth or as dismissible, the actual truth would be precisely what is
not written, which here can only be written in the form that contests
the phallic function, namely *It is not true that the phallic function is
what grounds sexual relation.* In both cases, at each of the two levels
that are as such independent, it is not at all a matter of making one
the negation of the other, but on the contrary of one standing as the
obstacle to the other.

What you can see distributed across the upper level is *There exists*
and *There does not exist.* Likewise, on the lower level, on one side
there is *all x,* namely the domain of what is here defined by the
phallic function, while the difference in the position of the argument
in the phallic function is that it is *not all woman* that is inscribed on
the other side.

You can see very well that, far from one standing in opposition to
the other as its negation, they subsist, quite to the contrary, by both
being negated. On one side there is an *x* that can be sustained here
beyond the phallic function, and on the other side there is not one,
simply because a woman cannot be castrated, and for the best of
reasons. This is the level of what is closed off for us as regards sexual
relation, while at the level of the phallic function it is inasmuch as
the *all* stands in opposition to the *pas-toute,* the *not-all,* that there is

a chance of a distribution, to the left and to the right, of what will be founded as male and as female. Therefore, far from the relationship of negation forcing us to choose, it is in so far as we have to *distribute* that the two sides stand in legitimate opposition to one another.

After negation, I spoke of *conjunction*. To put paid to this matter, I need only on this occasion remark – I hope there are enough people who have flipped through a book on logic for me not to have to insist – that conjunction is grounded in that it only takes on a value from the fact that two propositions can both be true. This is precisely what is in no way permitted by what is here on the blackboard, because you can see that from right to left there is no identity, and that at the level of what is posited as true, namely Φx, the universal propositions cannot conjoin. The universal proposition on the left-hand side stands in opposition to the right-hand side only by virtue of the fact that there is no articulable universal proposition, namely that woman, in regard to the phallic function, only situates herself as being *pas toute*, not all, subject to it.

The strange thing is that, in spite of this, *disjunction* doesn't apply either, if you recall that disjunction only takes on a value from the fact of it being impossible for two propositions to be false at the same time. Shall we say that this is the stronger or the weaker relationship? It is certainly the stronger in that it is the one that is the hardest nut to crack because, for there to be disjunction, the minimum requirement allows that one proposition is true and the other false, or else that both are true. Additionally, what I have called *one true, the other false*, may also be *one false, the other true*, so there are at least three combinatorial cases in which disjunction is sustained. The only thing that it cannot allow is for both to be false at the same time. Now, here on the board we've got two functions, the two at the top, which are posited as not being the truthful truth, as I said earlier. Seemingly, we've got something that gives hope that, at the very least, we might have articulated a veritable disjunction.

However, note what is written on one of the sides that has Φx with the sign of negation over it, the left side – and this is something that of course I will have occasion to articulate in a way that will bring it to life – namely that it's inasmuch as the phallic function is not functioning that sexual relation stands a chance. We have posited that there has to exist an x for this. Now, what do we have on the other side? Well, that there doesn't exist any other such x. This means that it may be said that the fate of a mode by which the differentiation of male and female, of man and woman, would be sustained in speaking beings, any chance of us having such a thing, is that while there is discord – and presently we shall see what I mean by this – at the level of the universals, these universals are not sustained by the fact of the inconsistency of either one of them.

What happens here, where we have dismissed the function itself? While on one side it is supposed that there exists an x that satisfies the negated Φx, on the other side we have the express formulation that there is *no x*. I illustrated the latter by saying that woman, for the best of reasons, can on no account be castrated. Precisely, there is only the statement, *no x*. This means that at the level on which the disjunction would have some chance of being produced, we have, to one side, just one – or at the very least what I have put forward as the *at-least-one* – and to the other, non-existence, that is to say, the relation of 1 to 0.

At the level on which sexual relation would stand a chance, not of coming about, but simply of being hoped for beyond the abolition, the dismissing, of the phallic function, we only ever find the presence, dare I say, of one of the two sexes. This is very specifically what must be related to the experience that I have accustomed you to see being stated in the form that woman educes, in that for her the universal cannot arise from the phallic function. As you know – and this is the experience, one that is, alas, far too everyday not to veil its structure – she only participates in the phallic function by wanting it, either by stealing it from the man or, good heavens, by ordering him to serve it to her, so that in the . . . *or worse* of cases – mark my word – she may serve it back to him. This does not, however, universalize her, apart from the fact – which is the root of the *pas-toute*, the *not-all* – that she harbours another jouissance besides phallic jouissance. This other jouissance is strictly termed *feminine*, and on no account does it depend on phallic jouissance.

If woman is *not all*, it is because of the duality of her jouissance. This is what Tiresias disclosed when he came back after having been, for a while – by the grace of Zeus – Theresa. Naturally this had the consequence we know about, and which was ultimately laid out, if I may say so, visibly – this being the operative word – for Oedipus, to show him what was in store for him, in return for having existed as a man of the supreme possession that resulted from the deception his partner exercised over him regarding the true nature of what she was offering to his jouissance. Or, let's put it differently, it was for want of his partner asking him to refuse her offering. This clearly shows, but at the level of myth, that for having existed as a man at a level that eludes the phallic function, Oedipus had no other woman but the very one who, for him, should not have existed.

Why *should not have*? Why the theory of incest? This would make it necessary for me to go down the path of the Names-of-the-Father, precisely where I said I would never venture again. Because it so happens that I've just reread, at someone's behest, this first lecture from the academic year of 1963/64, delivered here at Sainte-Anne. This was why I went back to it, because I enjoyed remembering it. I read it again, and it reads well. It even has a certain dignity, such that I would publish it, if I ever publish again. This doesn't depend on me. Others would have to publish with me. That would encourage me. If I do publish it, you will be able to see the care I took to pick out – though I'd already been saying it for five years – a certain number of registers, the paternal metaphor in particular, the proper noun, and so on. There was everything you need to give meaning, with the Bible, to the mythical lucubration of what I had said. But I won't ever do that again. I will never do it again because, after all, I can make do with formulating things at the level of logical structure which, after all, has every right here.

What I want to tell you is that at a certain level, the one where sexual relation stands a chance, this $\overline{\exists x}$, namely *There does not exist*, there is nothing else, this absent ἕτερος, is on no account necessarily a special privilege of the feminine sex. This is simply indicative of what, on my graph – I'm saying this because it's had its own small fate – I wrote as the Signifier of the barred Other. This means that, however you take it, from the moment sexual relation is at issue, the Other is absent.

Naturally, at the level of what is functioning – that is, the phallic function – there is simply the discord that I mentioned just a moment ago. It so happens that, on one side and the other, one is not in the same position. On one side, we have the universal founded on a necessary relation to the phallic function, and, on the other, a contingent relation, because woman is *pas toute*, not all.

Therefore, on the upper level I underscore that the relation that is grounded on the disappearance, the vanishing existence, of one of the partners, which leaves the place empty for the inscription of speech, is not at this level the special privilege of any one side. Only, for there to be a grounding of sex, as they say, they have to be twain. Nought and one certainly makes two. It makes two on the symbolic plane, in so far as we are in agreement that existence takes root in the symbol. This is what defines the speaking being.

The speaking being certainly *is* something. Perhaps, indeed . . . Who is not what he is? Yet this being is absolutely ungraspable. And this being is all the more ungraspable in that he is forced to go via the symbol in order to support himself. It's quite clear that a being that comes into being by the symbol alone is precisely this Beingless being in which you all partake through the mere fact that you speak. On the other hand, it's quite certain that what is supported is existence, and this is so to the extent that existing is not Being. To exist depends on the Other. All of you here, from some angle or other, do indeed exist, but when it comes to your Being, you're not so tranquil. Otherwise you wouldn't come seeking assurance for it in so many psychoanalytic endeavours.

Obviously this is something that was utterly original in the first emergence of logic. There is something quite striking in this first emergence of logic, namely the difficulty and the wavering that Aristotle displays regarding the status of the particular proposition. These are difficulties that have been underscored elsewhere. I didn't discover them myself. For those who might care to look into them, I recommend issue 10 of the *Cahiers pour l'analyse*. The leader article, by a certain Jacques Brunschwig, is excellent on this score. In it they will be able to see a flawless indication of Aristotle's difficulty with the particular. Certainly, Aristotle perceives that existence can in no way be established except outside the universal, which is precisely why he locates existence at the level of the particular, a particular which is on no account sufficient to sustain it, even though it gives the illusion of doing so by virtue of the use of the word *some*.

In formalization this is known as a *quantifier*, due to a trace left in philosophical history by the fact that a certain Apuleius – who was a writer of not especially good-taste prose, notably *The Golden Ass*, and who was a feverish mystic to boot – one day introduced the notion that, in Aristotle, whatever had to do with *all* and *some* belonged to the realm of quantity. It's nothing of the sort. On the contrary, these are simply two different modes of what I could call – if you will let this past, since it's somewhat extempore – the incarnation of the symbol.

The incarnation of the symbol, the passage into day-to-day life, the fact that there are *alls* and *somes* in every tongue, is precisely what compels us to posit that language must nevertheless have a common root. Furthermore, since all tongues are profoundly different in their structure, this common root has to be related to something that is not language. Of course, one can understand how people slip up here. What we have a sense of as what lies beyond language can only be mathematical, and, on this pretext, people imagine to themselves that, because it's number, it must be a matter of quantity. Perhaps, however, it is number, strictly speaking, in all its reality, to which language affords access, but only by being capable of locking on to 0 and 1. The real would make its entry here, this real that alone may lie beyond language, namely the only domain in which a symbolic impossibility can be formulated.

This fact of relation that is accessible to language, if it is grounded by sexual non-relation – the fact that it cannot, therefore, confront 0 and 1 – would easily ensure its reflection in Frege's elaboration of his logical generation of numbers. I have at the very least indicated what constitutes a difficulty in this logical generation, namely the wide gap that I pointed out for you in the mathematical triangle between this 0 and this 1, a gap that is duplicated by the confrontational opposition between them. Already, it is essential to remind ourselves that the fact that what may intervene is there only by virtue of it being the essence of the first couple, and that this can only be a third, is something that is far more dangerous to allow to persist in analysis than the mythical adventures of the primal Father.[4] These mythical adventures do not in themselves present any inconvenience in so far as they structure quite admirably the necessity that, somewhere, there should be *at-least-one* who transcends what is involved in the grip of the phallic function. The myth of the primal Father means just that. It is explained here quite well enough for us easily to make use of it, besides the fact that we find it confirmed by the logical structuration of what has been set out on the blackboard. On the other hand, there is certainly nothing more dangerous than the confusion over what is involved in the One.

As you know, Freud frequently invoked the One as the signifier of an essence of Eros, purported to be that of fusion. Specifically, libido would be a sort of essence that would tend towards making One from two. As one old myth has it, which is surely not good mysticism in the slightest, one of the fundamental tensions of the world tends only towards the forming of One. Truly, this myth is something that can function only on a horizon of delusion. It has strictly speaking nothing to do with anything we might meet in experience. If there is something quite patent in the relations between the sexes, and which analysis not only articulates but is designed to play out in every direction, it's that these relations between the sexes present a difficulty. Nothing in them resembles any kind of spontaneity, apart from the horizon I was speaking about earlier as being grounded, at a push, on goodness knows what animal myth. Eros is in no way a tendency towards One, far from it.

Any precise articulation of what is involved in the two levels depends on the fact that the opposition between the sexes is grounded only in discord, in that they can in no way be established on the basis of a universal. Conversely, at the level of existence, the possibility of the articulation of language harbours an opposition that consists in the annulling, in the voiding, of one of the functions, the function of the Other. This is what strikes me as being essential to bring to the fore.

Note that earlier, having spoken to you in succession of negation, conjunction, and disjunction, I didn't push on to what is involved in *implication*. Clearly, implication can function only between the two levels, between the level of the phallic function and the level that dismisses it. Now, in spite of this, nothing that is a disjunction on the lower level, the level of the insufficiency of the universal specification, *implies* that this should be so *if and only if* the syncope of existence on the upper level should effectively be produced. Nor, reciprocally, does the latter require the discord on the lower level.

On the other hand, what we see functioning once again, but distinctly and separately, is the *relationship* between the upper level and the lower level. The requirement that there should exist *at-least-one-man* is a requirement that seems to be emitted at the level of the feminine, which is specified as being a *pas-toute*, a *not-all*, a duality, the only point at which duality stands a chance of being represented. There is a requisite here that is, if I may say so, needless. Nothing imposes this *at-least-one* except the unique chance – it still has to be gambled – that something might be functioning on the other side, but as an ideal point, as a possibility that all men could reach. Reach how? Through identification. There is but a logical necessity here, which is imposed only at the level of the wager.

Observe, however, what results from this concerning the barred universal proposition. Moreover, it is in this respect that the *at-least-one* by which the Name of the Father is supported, the Name of the mythical Father, is indispensable. This is where I am offering an insight that is missing in the function, in the notion, of species or of class. It's in this respect that it was no accident that this whole dialectic was bungled in the Aristotelian forms.

In the end, where does this $\exists x$ come to function, this *There exists at-least-one* who is not the serf of the phallic function? It is merely a requisite, I would say, of a desperate type,[5] from the standpoint of something that is not even supported by a universal definition. However, note that with regard to the universal proposition written $\forall x.\Phi x$, every male is serf to the phallic function. What is meant by the *at-least-one* that functions to elude this? I shall say that it is the exception. This is indeed the one time when the proverb that says, without knowing what it says, *The exception proves the rule*, turns out to be confirmed. It's peculiar that it's only with the analytic discourse that a universal can find its veritable fundament in the existence of an exception. At any rate, this means that we can certainly distinguish the universal that is thus founded from any use that is rendered commonplace by the philosophical tradition of the said universal.

There is a peculiar thing that I have found along the path of enquiry, and because, given some training long ago, I'm not completely ignorant in Chinese. I asked one of my dear friends to remind me about something, some trace of which I had kept more or less. I had to have it confirmed for me by someone whose mother tongue is Chinese. It is certainly very odd that, in Chinese, the denomination of *all mankind* is either voiced *dōu*, which I won't write on the board because I'm weary, or, in a more ancient voicing, one says *tcha*.[6] Well, if it amuses you I will write it up for you after all.

都   *Dōu (Tcha)*

Can you imagine that one can say, for example, *all mankind eats . . .*? Well, you say, *měi gèrén dōu chī*. *Měi* insists on the fact that he is indeed there, and should you have any doubt about it, the classifier *gè* shows very well that they are countable. But this doesn't make them *all*, so one adds *dōu*, which means *without exception*. I could of course cite you other things. I could tell you that *All the soldiers have perished*, they are *dōu sǐ*, all dead, which in Chinese is *Soldiers without exception kaput*. We can see the *all* spreading out for us from within, and meeting its limit only with inclusion, by being subsumed into larger and larger sets. In the Chinese language, one never says *dōu* or *tcha* without thinking of the totality of whatever is at issue as content.

What we discover in what I have articulated for you as a *relationship*, here of unique existence in relation to the status of the universal, assumes the figure of an exception. However, isn't this idea also the correlate of what earlier I called the emptiness of the Other? We have made progress in the logic of classes by creating the logic of sets. The difference between a class and a set is that when a class is empty, there is no class, whereas when a set is empty, there is still the element of the empty set. It is indeed in this respect that, once again, mathematics leads to progress in logic.

It is here that we are able to see – because we are still keeping this up, but I assure you it will be over soon[7] – where the unilateralism of the existential function can be taken up with respect to what is involved in the other party, in the partner, in so far as here it is *without exception*. This *without exception* that is implied by the non-existence of x in the right-hand portion of the table, namely that there is no exception and that here there is something that has no parallelism, no symmetry, with the requirement that earlier I called the *desperate* aspect of the *at-least-one*, is another requirement. This other requirement hinges on the fact that, all things considered, the masculine universal may feel at home in the assurance that no woman exists who would have to be castrated, and this is for reasons that strike him as obvious. Yet in fact this has no further impact for the reason that it's an utterly needless assurance. What I called to mind earlier regarding woman's conduct shows well enough that her relation to the phallic function is an altogether active one. Here, however, as was the case earlier, while the supposition is grounded in some sense upon the assurance that an impossibility is at issue, this being the quintessence of the real, it still does not undermine the fragility of the conjecture, because in any case woman has no greater assurance of her universal essence.

The reason for this is that the contrary of the limit point, namely the fact that there is no exception, does not ensure the universal of womanhood, which already is so thinly established due to its discordance. Far from enduing consistency to any *all*, the *without exception* naturally offers even less to what is defined as *pas tout*, as *not all*, as essentially dual.

I hope that this will remain for you as a necessary peg in the steep climb that we might try to negotiate later on, if indeed we are led onto the path along which the sudden entrance of this strangest of items, namely the function of the One, has to be examined with severity. People ask themselves a great many things about animal mentality, when in the end it can only serve us as a looking-glass reference. A looking glass before which, as before any looking glass, one purely and simply disavows. There is something one could ask oneself – is there such a thing as One for animals?

The exorbitant aspect of the emergence of this One is what we shall be led to open up with Plato's *Parmenides*, which is why I've been inviting you for some time now to reread it, before I broach it.

3 March 1972

VIII

WHAT IS INVOLVED IN THE OTHER

Your fantasies derive jouissance from you
The *queue* of thoughts
Ontology is a dishonour
There is no transgression of the impossible
Woman between centre and absence

$$\exists x.\overline{\Phi x} \qquad\qquad \overline{\exists x}.\overline{\Phi x}$$

$$\forall x.\Phi x \qquad\qquad \overline{\forall x}.\Phi x$$

$$\frac{a \longrightarrow \cancel{S}}{S_2 \quad\quad S_1}$$

Since my aim this year is to speak to you about the One, I'm going to begin today by stating what is involved in the Other.

A while ago, I incurred some worry regarding this Other that I write with a capital A. It was evinced by a Marxist to whom I was then indebted for the venue where I had been able to resume my work. His worry was that this Other, this third party, when asserted in the couple's relation, could only be identified – according to him, the Marxist – with God. Did this worry develop thereafter to the extent of instilling his resolute mistrust of the trail I might leave?

This is a question that I shall leave to one side for today, because I'm going to begin by simply drawing back the veil on what is involved in this Other.

1

The Other at issue is the Other of the sexual couple, the very same. This is indeed why it will be necessary for us to produce the signifier that can be written only in so far as it bars the capital A.

Our jouissance is derived only from the Other. I'm stressing this without pausing over it because otherwise I won't move forward. It's more difficult to assert the following – inasmuch as what would seem to be vital is that what characterizes jouissance, according to what I've just said, would be evasive – our jouissance is derived only by the Other. This is precisely the gulf that is presented to us by the question of God's existence, an existence that I leave on the horizon as ineffable.

When I say that our jouissance is derived only from the Other, what is important is not the relation between what enjoys and what we might think of as our Being. What is important is that we do not derive jouissance from it *sexually* – there is no such thing as sexual relation – nor is jouissance derived from us in this way. You can see that lalingua – which I write in a single word – despite usually behaving itself, is resistant here. It gives a tight-lipped pout. It has to be said, from the Other we derive jouissance *mentally*.

There is a remark in the *Parmenides* that assumes the value of a model here, which is why I've been recommending that you go and sharpen yourselves up with it. Naturally, if you read it through the commentaries that are given in academia, you will locate it in the lineage of philosophers, where it's considered to be a particularly brilliant exercise, but then, after this brief salute, you are told that you won't get much out of it, that Plato was simply pushing to the ultimate degree of intensity what can be deduced for you from his Theory of Forms. Perhaps it needs to be read differently. It needs to be read innocently.

Note that every now and then something can touch you, if only for example when at the start of the seventh hypothesis he makes the passing remark that starts off from *if the One is not*. Very much as an aside, he says, *And what if we were to say that the non-One is not?*[1] Whereupon he sets about showing that the negation of anything whatsoever, not only the negation of the One but the negation of *non-large* or *non-small*, is as such distinguished by not negating the same term.

This is conducive to what is at issue, namely the negation of sexual jouissance, which is what I'm asking you to pause over now. The S, brackets, barred capital A, $S(\mathbb{A})$, is the same thing that I have just formulated, namely that from the Other we derive jouissance mentally. This writes something about the Other. As I have asserted, this

Other is the term in the relationship that, on account of vanishing, on account of not existing, becomes the locus where this relationship is written – written in the form of these four formulae that are written up here – so as to transmit a knowledge. Perhaps the knowledge at issue can be taught, but what gets transmitted is the formula.

It is precisely because one of the terms becomes the locus where the relationship gets written that it can no longer be a relationship, because the term changes function, because it becomes the locus at which the relationship gets written, and because the relationship *is* only on account of being written in the stead of this term. One of the terms of the relationship has to empty out to allow this relationship to be written.

Indeed, this is what radically removes any scope of idealism from the *mentally* that I have just put forward in the inverted commas that speech cannot state. Such incontestable idealism can be seen developing in remarks from Berkeley's pen, all of which hinge on the following – *nothing of what is thought is thought unless by someone.* This is the argument, or more accurately the irreducible argumentation, which would have more bite to it were it acknowledged that what is at stake is jouissance.

You derive jouissance only from your fantasies. There you have it for what sets the scope of the idealism that no one, moreover, despite it being incontestable, takes seriously. What is important is that your fantasies derive jouissance from you.

Here, I can only come back to what I was saying earlier. As you can see, even lalingua, which is well behaved, doesn't come out with this easily.

2

Idealism asserts that what is involved is *que de pensées*, nothing but thoughts. To get out of this, lalingua, which is well behaved, but not so well behaved as all that, might be able to offer you something that I won't need to write down in order to bid you have this *que* resound in a different way. Well, if I need to spell it out for you, it's q.u.e.u.e., *queue de pensées*, a *queue* of thoughts.

This is what the good behaviour of lalingua enables in French. It's the tongue in which I express myself so I don't see why I shouldn't take advantage of it. If I spoke a different one, I would find something else. What is involved here is a *queue* of thoughts, not, as the idealist says, in that one thinks them, nor even in that one thinks them *therefore-I-am*, which is still a mark of progress, but in that these thoughts really do think themselves.

It is in this respect that I include myself in the class of realists,[2] if indeed this holds the faintest interest because I don't see why I should classify myself philosophically, I through whom emerges a discourse that is not philosophical discourse, but psychoanalytic discourse, the scheme of which I have reproduced here. I qualify it as discourse because, as I have stressed, nothing takes on any meaning except from the relations between one discourse and another discourse.

Of course, this presupposes a certain practice to which I can neither say nor hope I have truly accustomed you. All this washes over you like water off a duck's back because – and this, moreover, is what constitutes your existence – you are solidly inserted in the discourses that came before, which have been there for a while, a very long while. This includes philosophical discourse, inasmuch as the university discourse transmits it to you, and in what a state! You are indeed solidly installed in all this, and this is what makes you feel quite at home.

It should not be thought that those who occupy the place of this Other, this Other that I'm bringing up to date, have been given much of an advantage over you, but even so, some furniture has been placed in their hands that is rather unwieldy.

Among this furniture there is the armchair, the nature of which has not been very well ascertained. Nevertheless, the armchair is essential because what is specific to this discourse is that it enables what is written up here in the top right, in the shape of the barred S. Like all writing, this is a very delightful shape. It is not altogether by chance that Hogarth used the S for the line of beauty. There must be some meaning to this somewhere, and surely too in the fact that it has to be barred. Be that as it may, it is curious to see that I write what is produced on the basis of this barred subject in the same way as what holds a different place, the dominant place, in the discourse of the master. This *S One*, S_1, is precisely what I'm trying to produce for you here in so far as I am speaking. As I have said several times, it is in this respect that I am in the place of the analysand, and this is instructive.

Has what is written been thought? This is the question. It might no longer be possible to say by whom it was thought. Indeed, this is what you are dealing with in everything that is written. The *queue* of thoughts that I was speaking about is the subject himself, as the hypothetical of these thoughts. Since Aristotle, people have been harping on at such length about the ὑποκείμενον, and yet it was quite clear. They made such a meal of it that a cat couldn't find her kittens. I'm going to call it a *tail*, this *queue* of thoughts, of something real that produces this comet effect that I have called *queue de pensées* and which might indeed be the phallus.

Either what occurs here is not capable of being recaptured *nachträglich* by what I have just called the *tail* – which is conceivable only because the effect that it constitutes projects out in the same way as does its advent, namely the disarray, if you will allow me so to name the disjunction of sexual relation – or else what has been thought lies open, within reach of a rethinking that consists precisely in noticing, by writing it down, that they were thoughts. Whatever one might say, the written comes after these thoughts, these real thoughts, have been produced. The repetition that is the fundament of what the analytic experience uncovers for us lies in this effort of rethinking, in this *nachträglich*. That this should be written is proof of this, but it's proof only of the effect of resumption, *nachträglich*. This is what grounds psychoanalysis.

How many times, in philosophical dialogues, have you seen the argument – *If you don't follow me this far, there's no philosophy*. What I'm going to tell you is exactly the same thing. It has to be one or the other. Either what is commonly accepted in everything that gets written on psychoanalysis, in everything that flows from the pens of psychoanalysts, is valid, namely that what thinks is unthinkable and so there is no psychoanalysis, or else, in order for there to be psychoanalysis and, to say it all, interpretation, then what the *queue* of thoughts starts off from has to be thought, thought as in real thought.

This is why I gave you all that spiel about Descartes. *I think, therefore I am* doesn't mean anything if it's not truthful. It's truthful because *therefore I am* is what I'm thinking, before knowing it and, whether I like it or not, it's the same thing.

This same thing is precisely what I called *the Freudian Thing*. It's precisely because this *I think* and *what I think* are the same thing, that is to say, *therefore I am*, that there is no equivalence. This is why I spoke about the Freudian Thing, because in a Thing there are *deux faces* – spell that how you like, *face* or *fasse*[3] – which not only are not equivalent, but cannot be replaced, one by the other, in the fact of saying. It's not equivalent. It's not even similar. This was why I only spoke about the Freudian Thing in a certain fashion.

People read what I wrote. It is even curious that this should be one of those things that compel you to reread it. It was even designed for this. And when one rereads it, one realizes that I don't speak about the Thing, because one can't speak about it. I make the Thing itself speak. The Thing in question states – *I, Truth, speak*. And of course it doesn't say it just like that, but surely this can be seen. This was even why I wrote it. It says it in all sorts of ways, and I daresay it's not a bad piece. *Only in my conundrums can I be apprehended.* What one writes of the Thing ought to be considered as what of the Thing gets written, coming from the Thing and not from whoever is writing.

This is indeed what means that ontology – in other words the consideration of the subject as Being – is, if you will allow me this, a dishonour.[4]

So, you've heard well, one has to know whereof one is speaking. Either *therefore I am* is merely a thought, demonstrating that the unthinkable is what is thinking, or it is the fact of saying that can act upon the Thing, enough for it to turn out otherwise. And it is in this respect that any thought is thought through its relations to what gets written thereof. Otherwise, I repeat, there is no psychoanalysis.

We are in the inane, which is currently what is most widespread, the inane-alysable. Saying that it is impossible is not enough, because this doesn't exclude it being practised. For it to be practised without being inane, it's not qualifying it as impossible that matters, rather it is its relation to the impossible that is at stake, and the relation to the impossible is a relation of thought. The relation will not carry any meaning if the demonstrated impossibility is not strictly an impossibility of thought, because it's the only demonstrable impossibility.

If we ground the impossible in its relation to the real, we still need to say the following, which I offer you as a gift. I got this from a charming woman, from way back in my past, who remains nevertheless marked by a delightful redolence of *savon*,[5] with her accent from the Vaud which she knew how to turn on, because even though she had purged herself of it she could still will it back. She used to say, *Nothing is impossible for man* – I can't imitate the Vaudois accent, not having been born over there – *what he can't do, he leaves.* This is to zero in on what is involved in the impossible, to the extent that this term is acceptable for anyone of sober mind.

Well, this annulling of the Other is produced only on the level at which is inscribed – in the only way it can be, namely as I inscribe it – $\overline{\Phi x}$. This means that you cannot write that what forms an obstacle to the phallic function is untrue.[6] So, what does $\exists x$ mean? Namely *There exists x*, such that it may be inscribed into this negation of the truth of the phallic function.

This deserves to be spelt out across its different moments in time. You can see that what we are going to call into question is very precisely this status of existence, in so far as it is unclear.

3

I think that you've had quite enough of people harping on about the distinction between essence and existence, drumming it into your *comprenoire*, to find it unsatisfactory.

In the meaning that the analytic discourse allows us to bring to the previous discourses, through the connection of these formulae, there is something that, at the end of the day, I will only be able to pinpoint with the term of a *motivation*. Failing to notice this motivation is what begets, for example, Hegel's dialectic. Due to this failure to notice it, Hegel's dialectic bypasses it only to consider that discourse as such rules the world.

Here I am moving into a little side note. I don't see why I shouldn't pick up this short digression, especially given that you ask nothing else, because when I go in a straight line, it tires you.

What does leave a shadow of meaning to Hegel's discourse is an absence, and very precisely the absence of surplus-value such as it is drawn from jouissance in the real of the discourse of the master. This absence does, however, note something. It notes, really, the Other, not as abolished, but precisely as the impossibility of any correlate. It is in presentifying this impossibility that it colours Hegel's discourse.

It won't cost you anything simply to reread the Preface to the *Phänomenologie des Geistes* in correlation with what I'm putting forward here. You see all the holiday homework I'm setting you, the *Parmenides* and the *Phänomenologie*, at least the Preface, because naturally you never read the *Phänomenologie*. But the Preface is damned fine. All by itself it's worth the effort of rereading. You'll see how it confirms, how it takes on meaning from what I'm telling you. I daren't promise you that the *Parmenides* will do as much, that it will take on meaning, but I do hope it will, because what is specific to a new discourse is that it refreshes what is lost in the whirling of old discourses, specifically *meaning*.

If I told you that there is something that colours Hegel's discourse, it's because the word *colour* means something other than *meaning* here. The promotion of what I'm putting forward precisely discolours it, and finishes off the effect of Marx's discourse. I should like to underscore something in this discourse that constitutes its limit. It entails a protest that turns out to consolidate the discourse of the master by completing it, not only with surplus-value, but by encouraging – I sense that this will cause a stir – the equal existence of woman.

Equal to what? No one knows, because one can also very well say that *man = 0*, since he needs the existence of something that negates him in order for him to exist as *all*. *(Lacan slams his hand on the table.)*

In other words, there is a kind of confusion. This is not unusual because we live in confusion, and it would be wrong to believe that we live *on* it. This doesn't go without saying. I don't see why a lack of confusion should prevent one from living. It is even very curious that people rush into it. Mark my word, people bolt into it. When a discourse emerges, like the analytic discourse, what it proposes is that you may hold the reins tight enough to uphold the conspiracy of truth.

Everyone knows that conspiracies come to a sudden end. It's easier to come out with so much blather that you end up spotting all the plotters. People confound, people rush into the negation of sexual division, of difference. I've said *division* because it's operational, and I've said *difference* because it's precisely what this use of the equals sign in *woman* = *man* claims to efface.

I will tell you that the wonderful thing is not all this doltishness but rather the obstacle that this doltishness claims – employing this grotesque word – to *transgress*. I have taught things that did not claim to transgress anything, but rather to circumscribe a certain number of knotty points, of points of impossibility. In view of which, there were people whom this upset, of course, because they were the representatives, the sitting officials, of the psychoanalytic discourse, who dealt me one of those blows that diminishes your voice.

I was dealt one such blow, physically, by a charming lad. He did that to me, one day. What a sweetie! He put some heart into it. He did it despite the fact that I was being threatened at the same time with a thing I didn't especially believe in – though I went along with it – a revolver. However, the fellows who cut off my voice at one point in time didn't do so *despite the fact* . . ., but rather *because* I was being threatened with a shooter, a real one that time and not a toy like the other one. It consisted in subjecting me to an assessment, that is, to the *standard* of people who wanted to hear nothing of the analytic discourse, even though they occupied the said *sitting* position. So, what would you expect me to do? From the moment I submitted to this assessment, I was condemned in advance, which naturally made it easier to cut off the voice I had.

Because a voice is something that exists. It carried on like that for several years, I must say. I scarcely had a voice at all. All the same, I did have some voice, from which the *Cahiers pour l'analyse* were born. It's a very, very, very fine literature. I commend them whole-heartedly, because I was so fully occupied with my voice that, to tell the whole story, well, I can't do everything. I can't read the *Parmenides*, reread the *Phänomenologie*, and other stuff, and then read the *Cahiers pour l'analyse* as well. I had to perk up again, which

I've now done. I've read them all, from cover to cover, and they're great.

They're great, but they're marginal, because they weren't put together by psychoanalysts. During this time, the psychoanalysts were chattering. There has never been so much talk of transgression in my ambit as during the time I had my voice cut off.

Imagine if you will that when it's a matter of the veritable impossible, the impossible that is demonstrated, the impossible such that it is articulated, well, of course, that took some time. There were the first scribblings that allowed for the birth of a logic, aided by the questioning of language, and then it was noticed that these scribblings ran into something that existed, but not in the way that had hitherto been believed, not in the way of Being, that is, not in the way that each of you believe yourselves to be, on the pretext that you are individuals. It was noticed that there were things that existed in the sense that they constitute the limit of what can hold together through the advance of articulating a discourse. This is what the real is. It is approached along the path of what I call the symbolic, which means, the modes of what is stated through this field, this field that exists, of language. This impossible, inasmuch as it is demonstrated, cannot be transgressed.

There are things that have long since performed the tracking – mythical tracking perhaps, but tracking just the same – not only of what is involved in this impossible, but of its motivation. More precisely, this is specifically the fact that sexual relation cannot be written.

As far as this tracking is concerned, no one has ever done any better than, I won't say religion – because as I'm going to explain in minute detail, one doesn't engage in ethnology when one is a psychoanalyst, blending religion into a general term, which is what engaging in ethnology amounts to – nor do I want to say that there is only one religion, but there is the one in which we are immersed, the Christian religion. Well, believe me, the Christian religion puts up with your transgressions damned well. Indeed, this is all it could wish for. It's what consolidates it. The more transgressions there are, the better it is for it.

It is precisely this that is in question. It's a matter of demonstrating where lies the truthfulness of what allows a certain number of discourses that enmesh you to stay on their feet.

Today I will end – I hope I haven't damaged my ring by banging on the table – on the same point that I opened with. I started off from the Other. I haven't got to the end of it because time has gone by, and then, after all, you shouldn't think that when the session ends I haven't had my fill of it.

So, I will wrap up what I have been saying concerning the Other, as a localized remark, leaving aside for now what might be involved in what I've put forward regarding the pivotal point on which I've set my sights this year, namely the One.

There is a good reason for my not having tackled it today, because as you will see there is nothing quite so slippery as this One. It's very curious. If there is one thing that has *des faces*, faces, in that they *se fassent*, they make themselves, not at all innumerable, but peculiarly divergent, then it's the One.

There is a good reason for my initially having to get a foothold on the Other. The Other – hear this well – is therefore an *inter*, the *inter* that is at issue in sexual relation, but displaced, and precisely on account of being *Alterposed*.[7] It's curious that in positing this Other, what I have had to put forward today only concerns woman. Indeed, she is the one who gives us an illustration of this figure of the Other, an illustration that is within our reach, on account of being, as one poet wrote, *between centre and absence*.

Between the meaning that she takes on in what I have called the *at-least-one*, where she finds it only in the state of what I have announced – announced and no more – of being nothing but bare existence, what does *between centre and absence* become for her? It becomes this second bar that I have only been able to write by defining it as *pas toute, not all*. Not all is she who is not contained within the phallic function, without being its negation either. Her mode of presence is *inter, between centre and absence*. The centre is the phallic function of which she partakes singularly, on account of the *at-least-one* who is her partner in love renouncing this function for her. This allows her to leave the very thing whereby she does not partake of the phallic function in the absence that is no less jouissance, on account of being *jouissabsence*.

I think that no one will say that what I am stating of the phallic function arises from misrecognition of what is involved in feminine jouissance. On the contrary, it's that, within the portion that makes her *pas toute*, not all, open to the phallic function, the *at-least-one* is pressed to inhabit woman's *jouissepresence*, if I may put it like that, in a radical misinterpretation as to the requirement of its existence. It is due to this misinterpretation, which means that no longer can it even exist, that the exception of its very existence is ruled out and that this status of the Other – the fact of not being universal – vanishes. Man's misrecognition is necessitated by this, and this is the definition of the hysteric.

On this point, I take leave of you today.

8 March 1972

THE ONE: NEVER THE TWAIN SHALL REACH

IX

IN THE FIELD OF
THE UNIAN

Parmenides, the One speaking
Yad'lun
Association is not free
Plato, Lacanian and feeble-minded
Existence in Aristotle

Last time, I told you something that was focused on the Other. The Other is more accommodating than what I'm going to speak to you about today, and whose relation to the Other I have already characterized by saying that it is not inscribable, which doesn't make matters any easier.

What is at issue is the One.

1

I have already indicated how its trail was blazed in Plato's *Parmenides*.

The first step towards understanding something in it is to perceive that everything that is stated about the One – as dialectizable, as developing – in any possible discourse on the subject of the One, is first and foremost, if we take it only at this level, which is to say nothing else about it, that *It is One*.

Perhaps there are a certain number of you who, on my adjuring, have opened the book and noticed that to say *One is* is not the same thing. *It is One* is the first hypothesis, and *One is* is the second. They are distinct.

Naturally, for this to deliver, you need to read Plato with a little something that comes from you. For you, Plato should not be what he is, an author. Since your childhood you've been brought up to *faire de l'auteur-stop*, to thumb a read. Ever since this became the custom, you ought to know that this way of addressing whoever they might be, the authorized ones, hasn't led anywhere, even though it can, of course, lead you far.

With these observations out of the way, I am therefore going to speak to you today about the One, due to a reason for which I shall again have to apologize, because on what grounds should I be bothering you with this? Since I'm going to speak to you about the One, I've come up with a word that will serve as a heading for what I'm going to say about it.

I didn't invent the *Unary*. In 1962, I extracted the *unary trait* from Freud by translating what he calls *einzig*. At the time this struck a few people as a small miracle. It's rather curious that the *einziger Zug*, the second form of identification singled out by Freud, had never caught their attention until then. On the other hand, the word to which I will give a special distinction in what I'm going to tell you today is utterly new.

This word is designed to be something like a precaution, because in truth there are many things that have an interest in the One. Nevertheless, I'm going to open up something straightaway that locates the interest my discourse has in going via the One, to the extent that my discourse is itself the opening up of the analytic discourse. First of all, however, take if you will the field that is broadly designated as that of the *Unian*.

This is a word that has never been uttered, and which none the less holds the interest of prompting you to stay on your toes each time the One is at stake. Taking it thus, in an epithetic form, will call to mind for you what Freud promoted, and Plato before him, namely that it is in its nature to have various aspects. I think it will not escape your notice that this gets spoken about in analysis, if you recall how it presides over this strange assimilating of Eros to that which tends towards coagulation.

It is peculiar that Freud promotes the One on the pretext that the body is very obviously one of the forms of the One, that it holds together, that it's an individual, so long as there's no mishap. Truth be told, this is precisely what is called into question by the dyad of Eros and Thanatos that he puts forward. If this dyad were not supported by another figure, which is very precisely the figure in which sexual relation fails, namely the figure of the One and the not-One, namely nought, we would be hard-pressed to make out the function that this stupefying couple might hold. It's a fact that it has contributed to a number of misunderstandings, indeed to the indiscriminate censuring of the so-called death drive. It is certain, however, that in this unruly discourse, which was established by the attempt to make a statement about sexual relation, it is strictly impossible to consider the copulation of two bodies as becoming One alone.

In this regard it's quite extraordinary that, while scholars snigger at the *Parmenides*, Plato's *Symposium* should be taken seriously as representing anything whatsoever to do with love. Perhaps some of you still remember that I made use of the *Symposium* during the academic year that preceded the one I mentioned earlier. In 1960/61, I took the *Symposium* as my practice range, and I didn't consider doing anything else with it but to use it to ground transference. Until further notice, while perhaps there is something of the twain on the horizon of transference, it cannot be passed off as a copulation.

None the less, I think that, at the time, I did indicate the mode of derision in which the scene unfolds, which very strictly speaking is designated as *Bacchic*. Aristophanes is the one who comes up with the famous bipartition of a creature that, at the start, would purportedly have been the beast with two backs that cling tightly together, and which was cleft in twain by the jealousy of Zeus. The fact that this statement comes from his lips is enough to indicate that fun is being had, and good fun too. Most incredibly, it is not apparent that she who crowns the entire disquisition, she known as Diotima, plays no other role but this, because what she teaches is that love hinges solely on the fact that the beloved, whether homo or hetero, is not to be touched. All that matters is Uranian Aphrodite. This does not exactly amount to saying that the One rules over Eros.

In and of itself, this would already be a reason to put forward a few propositions on the One – propositions which have already been opened up elsewhere – were there not also the fact that in the analytic experience the first step is to introduce, analysts that we are, the One. We bid it to step inside, whereby the first mode of the manifestation of the One is clearly when the analysand reproaches you for being merely *one among others*, though without noticing it of course. What thereby becomes manifest is very precisely the fact that he has no doings with these others, and this is why he wants to be the only one for you, the analyst, so that this may form two.

He doesn't know that what is at issue is precisely for him to realize that the twain is the One he believes himself to be, and in this it is a matter of his being divided.

2

So, therefore, there's Oneness. This ought to be spelt – I'm not really in the mood for writing today, but well, why not – *Yad'lun*.[1]

Why not spell it like this? You're going to see that spelling it like this holds a certain interest which is not without justifying my earlier choice of *Unian*. Spelt like this, *Yad'lun* brings out something propitious in the French language.

I'm not sure whether the same advantage could be drawn from [the English-language] *there is*, or from *es gibt*. Those who have a good grasp of these languages will perhaps let me know. *Es gibt* commands the accusative, does it not? You say, *es gibt einen* something, when it's in the masculine. You can say [in English], *there is one*, or *there is a* something. I know they have *there*, which is already a beginning that lies on this side, but it's not a simple form. In French you can say *y en a*.

It's very odd that there is something that I haven't managed to track down. I haven't managed to locate the historical emergence of this wording, *il y a*, as major as it is, which means *y en a*. This doesn't mean it can't be found. But, well, in my hasty fashion – I know a little something about the function of haste in logic, I have to press on because time is pressing – I didn't manage. I nevertheless consulted the *Littré*, the *Robert* while I was at it, the *Damourette and Pichon*, and even a few others, everything that a dictionary like the *Bloch and von Wartburg* is meant to afford you.

It is against a backdrop of indeterminacy that there emerges what is designated and pointed out, strictly speaking, by the *il y a*, for which, curiously, I shall say *n'y a pas*, there's no common equivalent in what we call ancient languages. It is thereby shown that, as the *Parmenides* tells and demonstrates, discourse changes.

It is in precisely this respect that the analytic discourse can represent an emergence, and that perhaps you would do well to make something of it, should it be the case that after my passing – which in the eyes of many is always a present, if not imminent, eventuality – you can expect the veritable downpour of rubbish that is already looming large. Indeed, the reckoning is that it can't be far off. On the trail of my discourse, it might be better for those who could take up this blazing of it to draw some reassurance from it. Fortunately, in one very particular place I have a few presages of this, but they are few and far between.

People spend their time nagging me and banging my eardrums to find out what relation the analytic discourse bears to revolution. It might well be this discourse that carries the seed of any possible revolution, in that revolution should not be confused with the low spirits that can seize hold of you just like that at every turn under this heading. It's not quite the same thing.

So, *y en a* stands against the backdrop of something that is formless. When one says *y en a*, it usually means *there is some* or *there are some*. Once in a while, to *il y a des* you can even add *des qui*, *some who*. There are *some who* think, *some who* say, *some who* tell. Stuff like that. This remains a backdrop of indeterminacy. The question begins with what is meant by *de l'Un*, because as soon as *l'Un* is uttered, the *de* is merely a thin pedicle onto what is involved in the backdrop.

From where does this One emerge? This is very precisely what Plato tries to push forward in the first hypothesis by saying, as best he can, not having any other words at his disposal, εἰ ἕν ἔστιν, *if One is*.[2] Here, ἔστιν clearly has the function of making up for what is not accentuated to the extent it is in French with *il y a*. I can understand the misgiving that brings the translators to a standstill here. It should surely be translated either as *if there is One*, or *if there is the One*. This is for you to decide.

What is certain, however, is that Plato does choose, and that his One has nothing to do with what surrounds it. There is even something remarkable, which is that what he demonstrates right away is that this can bear no relation whatsoever to anything of what he has passed a thousand times through metaphysical recension, namely the dyad, inasmuch as it is everywhere in the experience of thought. The largest, the smallest. The youngest, the oldest. And so on and so forth. The inclusive, the included. And anything else of the sort you might care to add.

He begins very precisely by demonstrating what happens when the One is taken as the means of a discursive questioning. Who is being questioned? It's certainly not the poor kid, the dear lad, named Aristoteles if memory serves, whom it is hard to believe is the Aristotle who has left us his legacy.[3] It's quite clear that, as in any dialogue, any Platonic dialogue, there is no trace of an interlocutor. It only seems to be called a dialogue to illustrate what I've been stating for a long time, namely that there's no such thing as dialogue. This doesn't mean that at the bottom of the Platonic dialogue there isn't a very different presence from anything to be found in a great many other things that have been written since. Let's say it – this presence is a human presence

To vouch for this we need only turn to the first inroads, to the way in which what constitutes the core of the dialogue is prepared, which I shall call the *entretien préliminaire*, the preliminary consultation. As in all the dialogues, there is one who explains to us how this madcap thing has come about, which looks nothing like anything that might be called a dialogue. This is where you can really sense, if you didn't already know it from the commonplaces of life, that no one has ever seen a dialogue amount to anything. In this literature of a certain date, in what is called a *dialogue*, it's a matter of grasping what this real is that can give the illusion that you can get to something by dialoguing with someone. So, it's worthwhile preparing the thing. It's worthwhile saying which nutcase is involved.

It's old Parmenides, and his gang, who are there. It took nothing less than that for something to be uttered that gives voice to what exactly? Well, precisely, to the One. Furthermore, once you make the One speak, it's worth taking the trouble to look at what the other one is there for, the other one who holds the floor, and who can only come out with things like

– ταῦτα ἀνάγκη
– οὐ γὰρ οὖν
– τί δέ
– αληθή
– *Oh my, it's yet three times truer than you were saying, is it not?*

That's what dialogue is when the One is speaking.

What is curious is the way Parmenides introduces him. The One puts his arm round his shoulder and says to the dear lad, *Off you go, dear little One, all this is mere gabbing.* Don't go translating ἀδολεσχίας as the idea that it has to do with adolescents. I'm saying this for those who are not conversant, especially when, on the facing page, you are told that it's a matter of behaving like innocents, like striplings, so you could get confused. This is not what striplings are called in the Greek text. Ἀδολεσχίας means *gabbing*.[4] It may, however, be considered as the prefiguration of what in our coarse language, wrought by the phenomenology that was to hand at the time, has been translated as *free association*.

Naturally, association is not free. If it were free, it wouldn't hold any interest. But it's the same thing as gabbing. This is designed to tame the sparrow. Association is, of course, tethered. I can't see what interest it would hold if it were free. It's quite certain, there can be no doubt about this, that the gabbing in question does not come from someone who is speaking. It's the One. Here you can see to what extent it is tethered, because it's highly demonstrative.

Delineating things in this way allows us to situate a number of items, and in particular the step that is taken from Parmenides to Plato.

A step had already been taken by Parmenides in this circle where, all in all, it was a matter of knowing what is involved in the real. We are still there. After they said that it was air, water, earth, and fire, and that after this you had only to start over, there was someone who became aware that the only common factor in all the substance at issue was the fact of being utterable.

Plato's step is different, however. His step is to show that as soon as one tries to say things in an articulate way, what is sketched out in terms of structure creates a difficulty. This is how we put it in what I've just called *our coarse language*. The word *structure* is worth no more than the term *free association*. But what is sketched out creates a difficulty, and it is along this path that the real is to be sought. *Εἶδος*, which is improperly translated as *form*, is something that already promises us a pinpointing of what stands as a gaping hole in the fact of saying.

In other words, to say it all, Plato was Lacanian. Naturally, he couldn't know that. What is more, he was somewhat feeble-minded, which doesn't make matters easier, but which surely helped him. What I call feeble-mindedness is the fact of being a speaking being who is not solidly installed in a discourse. This is what sets the value of the feeble-minded. No other definition can be given of them, except to be what is called *a little off beam*, that is to say, afloat between two discourses. To be solidly installed as a subject, one has to stick to one discourse, or else to know what one is doing. Either way, just because someone is on the fringes, it doesn't mean that they know what they are saying.

In Plato's case, he did have frameworks. It shouldn't be thought that in his time things weren't held in a very solid discourse. A little something of this shows through somewhere in the preliminary consultations of the *Parmenides*. After all, Plato is the one who wrote it. We don't know whether or not he's having a laugh, but in the end, to give us the dialectic of the master and the slave, he didn't wait for Hegel.

I must say that what he sets out is of a different pitch from what is put forward by the whole of the *Phänomenologie des Geistes*. Not that he comes to a conclusion, but he lays down all the material elements. He moves forward. He can do so because in his time this was no affectation. One wonders whether it was better rather than worse to allow people to imagine, which is what is affirmed therein, that the masters and the slaves can switch at any moment. And, indeed, they did switch at any moment. When masters were taken prisoner, they were enslaved, and when slaves were manumitted, well, they became masters. Thanks to this, Plato imagines, and he says as much in the preliminaries to this dialogue, the Master-essence, the *εἶδος*, and that of the Slave, may be considered to have nothing to do with what is really at issue. Between master and slave there are relations that have nothing to do with the relation between the Master-essence and the Slave-essence.[5] It's in this respect that he's somewhat feeble-minded.

We have seen the big mingle happening, have we not? It is always brought about along a certain path and, curiously enough, people don't see the extent to which it portends what comes next. In this big mingle, we are brothers, one and all. There is an area of history like this, of historical myth. I mean myth to the extent that it *is* history. This was seen once, among the Jews. We know the purpose of fraternity among them. It gave us a great model. Fraternity exists so that one can sell one's brother,[6] which didn't fail to occur in the wake of each overthrow that was said to turn around the discourse of the master.

Consider all the great effort that Hegel goes to in the *Phänomenologie* – the fear of death, the struggle for pure prestige, *and I tell you all this, and then some* – whereby the essential thing to obtain is that there is a slave. But I ask, to all those who shiver at the thought of the changing of roles, what is it that can mean that, since the slave survives, there shouldn't ensue for him, immediately afterwards, his own struggle to the death for pure prestige, and the fear of death that changes camp?

All this only stands a chance of persisting on the condition that one should see very precisely what Plato dismisses. What Plato dismisses – but in the name of what we shall never know because, good heavens, one cannot fathom the depths of his heart, and it might be mere feeble-mindedness – is what is involved in what he calls μετέχειν, partaking. This is perhaps the finest opportunity to underscore this. The slave is only ever a slave through the essence of the master. I've been calling it *essence*, but call it what you like. I much prefer to write it S_1, the master signifier. As for the master, were it not for the S_2, the slave's knowledge, what would he make of it?

3

I'm tarrying to tell you what is important about this implausible thing, that there should be Oneness. This is the point to be delineated.

Indeed, as soon as you start to examine this One, it transforms like a thing coming apart. It becomes impossible to relate it to anything beyond the series of integers, which is none other than this One.

This arises only at the end of a long elaboration of discourse. In Frege's logic, the logic that is laid out in the *Grundlagen der Arithmetik*, you will see at once the insufficiency of any logical deduction of 1, because it has to pass via 0, which cannot be said to be 1, and yet everything unfolds in such a way that the entire arithmetic sequence proceeds from the fact that 1 is missing at the level of 0. Because already, from 0 to 1, that makes two. From this point forth, it will make three, because there will be 0, 1 and 2. And so on, right on up to the first of the Alephs, which, curiously enough, yet not without reason, can only be designated as Aleph-Nought.

Of course, this might strike you as lying in some scholarly remoteness, which is why it has to be embodied, and which is why I first put *Yad'lun. Yad'lun!* The following announcement cannot be over-exclaimed, namely that a host of exclamation marks in its wake, that precisely the Aleph-Nought, will be just enough to sound out what might be involved, if you approach it sufficiently, in the astonishment warranted by the fact that there should be Oneness.

Someone in the audience lets out a loud sneeze – Ouille!

Oui! This does indeed warrant being greeted by this *ouille*, because we're speaking in the *langue d'oïl*, I mean *hoc est ille*.

Well, here, it's by grabbing the One at issue by the ears that *y en a* shows the backdrop from which it *ex-sists*. This backdrop hinges on the following, which is not self-evident, namely that, taking to begin with the first item within arm's reach, the one of feeble mind, you can then add one bout of flu, one drawer, one nose-thumbing, one puff of smoke, one *hello from your Catherine*, one civilization, and even one mismatched garter. That makes eight. However dispersed this shovel load might seem, they all come along in answer to the call, *little ones, little ones!* What is important – because I have to make things palpable for you otherwise than by using 0, 1 and Aleph, don't I? – is that this always presupposes the same One, the One that cannot be deduced, contrary to the smoke and mirrors that John Stuart Mill puts on for us simply by taking distinct things and holding them to be identical.

This is a mere something that is illustrated by the abacus, which furnishes the model thereof. However, the abacus was designed expressly for things to be counted, and, when the occasion presents, for eight dispersed things such as I have just conjured up for you to be counted. Yet what the abacus will not give you is what is deduced directly, without any abacus, from the One, namely that between these eight items, there are, because there are eight of them, twenty-eight combinations, taking them two at a time, and not one more. That's how it is due to the fact of the One.

Naturally, I hope you find this striking. You didn't know in advance that, since I've taken eight, it would make twenty-eight combinations, even though this is easy. The number of subsets of n elements in a set of m elements is effectively given by the following formula, where the exclamation mark notes the factorial, namely $m! = 1 \times 2 \times \ldots \times m$.[7]

$$\frac{m!}{n!(m-n)!}$$

This gives us 7 times 8, 56, divided by 2, equals 28. This numerical figure can be known, and this is what is at issue.

Had I put fewer of them it would have put you to work, telling me that perhaps I should also count the relations of each one to the set. Why am I not doing this? I will have to wait till next time to explain this to you. The relation that each one bears to the set precisely does not eliminate the fact of there being *one* set and that, due to this fact, this means that you are including one again. Indeed, this would lead, taking them two at a time, to a considerable rise in the number of combinations. At the level of the triangle, if I had simply noted three 1s for you, there would be just three combinations. If on the other hand you take the set as 1, then straightaway you have six combinations. What is at stake, however, is to realize that there is another dimension to the One, which I will try to illustrate for you next time with the arithmetical triangle.

In other words, the One does not, therefore, always carry the same meaning. For example, there is the meaning of the One of the empty set, which curiously enough in our numeration of elements would add two. I'm going to be demonstrating why and on what basis. Nevertheless, we are already approaching something that, in not being based at all on the One as *all*, shows us how, in its emergence, the One is not univocal. In other words, we are refreshing Plato's dialectic.

This is precisely how I can claim to lead you somewhere, by pursuing, through this bifidity of the One – we still have to see if it holds up – the One that Plato distinguishes so well from Being. Certainly Being is One, always and in every case, but in the *Parmenides* it is perfectly demonstrated that the One knows how to be as Being.[8] It is precisely from here that the function of existence arose, historically speaking. Just because *the One is not*, this doesn't mean that it doesn't pose the question.[9] Indeed, it poses it all the more given that, wherever it may be that existence has to be at stake, the question will always revolve around the One.

Aristotle only approaches this timidly, at the level of the particular propositions. He imagines that it's enough to say that *some* – just *some*, not *all* – are like this or like that, for them to be set apart. He imagines, for example, that if *these ones here* are *not like that*, then this is enough to ensure their existence. This is precisely how already, from its first emergence, existence is initiated straightaway, is stated, through its correlative inexistence. There is no existence except against the backdrop of inexistence, and inversely, *ex-sistere* only derives its support from an *out there* that is not.

It is indeed here that we have what is at issue in the One. For, in truth, from where does it arise? It arises from a *point* that Plato manages to circumscribe. It shouldn't be thought that this is – as it seems – merely a point in time. He calls it τὸ ἐξαίφνης. Translate that however you please.[10] It's the *instant*, the *sudden*, and it's the only point at which he can make it subsist. Goodness knows that the elucidation of the number has been pushed far enough to give us the idea that there are other Alephs besides the Aleph of the integers, and the said *instant*, the said *point* – which is what its true translation should be – is precisely what turns out to be decisive only at the level of a higher Aleph, at the level of the continuum.

The One seems, therefore, to get lost here, and to bring what is involved in existence to its culmination, to the extent of confining to existence as such, inasmuch as it arises from what it is most difficult to attain, from what is most elusive in the utterable. This is what led me to look up this ἐξαίφνης in Aristotle himself, noticing that actually there was an emergence of the term *to exist* in the *Physics*.

You can find it in Book IV, 222b. Aristotle defines it precisely as something that, τὸ ἀναισθήτῳ χρόνῳ, in a time that is imperceptible, διὰ μικρότητα, due to its smallness, is ἐκστάν.

I don't know whether the term ἐκστάν is uttered elsewhere in the literature of Antiquity, but it's clear that this is the past participle of the second aorist of ἵστημι, the aorist that is pronounced ἔστην. It's στάν, but I don't know if there is any verb ἐξίστημι. This will have to be checked. Be that as it may, the *sistere* is already here, to be stable, to be stable on the basis of an *out there*, ἐκστάν.

That which exists but through not being, this is what is at issue, and this is what I wanted to open up today under the general chapter heading of the Unian.

Pardon me, but I chose *Unien* [in French] because it's an anagram of *ennui*.

15 March 1972

X

YAD'LUN

From Plato to Cantor
Set and element
Impossible to denumerate
The empty set
The *nad* and the One of lack

$$\exists x.\overline{\Phi x} \qquad \overline{\exists x.\Phi x}$$

$$\forall x.\Phi x \qquad \overline{\forall x.\Phi x}$$

I'm starting right away because I've been asked, due to overriding matters in this university, to finish early, much earlier than usual.

So, to tackle what has arisen in a framework that I hope will not be a too distant memory for you, I'm going to pick up the *Yad'lun* that I have already uttered.

For those who have parachuted in from afar, I will repeat what this means, because it doesn't sound very usual. *Yad'lun* seems to have come from goodness knows where, from the One, eh? This is not a usual mode of expression. Yet this is what I'm speaking about – of the One, *y en a*.

This is a mode of expression that I hope will turn out, at least for you, to be in agreement with something that is not new for everyone here. I know that some of the ears here have been informed, thank goodness, of the fields that it so happens I have had to draw on so as to square up to what is at issue in the psychoanalytic discourse. I'm going to explain to you in what respect this mode of expression shows itself to be in agreement with what has been produced historically in set theory. You've heard about this because this is how mathematics is nowadays taught in the sixth form. Of course, it's by no means sure that this has greatly improved understanding of it.

Between a theory that has writing as one of its mainsprings – not, of course, that set theory entails a univocal form of writing, but rather, as with many things in mathematics, it cannot be spelt out without writing – and the wording *Yad'lun* which I'm trying to bring across, there lies all the difference between that which is written and speech. This is a rift that it's not always easy to bridge.

Yet this is exactly what I try to do, when the occasion presents. And you ought immediately to be able to understand why.

1

I have written again on the blackboard the four formulae in which I try to define what makes up for what I have called the impossibility of writing what is involved in sexual relation. It is to the extent that two terms confront one another in the two upper formulae, one of which is *There exists* and the other *There does not exist*, that I have been trying to make the contribution that might usefully be carried in from set theory.

It's already quite striking that the fact that there should be Oneness has never been the subject of any astonishment. It might already be somewhat brisk to word it like that, because in the end some astonishment could be accredited to what I've been speaking about – and here I call upon you to astonish yourselves – namely the famed *Parmenides* by our cherished Plato, which I have been warmly encouraging you to familiarize yourselves with, and which is still so poorly read. In any case, I have been trying to read it in a way that is not altogether the accepted one.

It's altogether striking to see the degree to which the *Parmenides* puts the university discourse in a bind. All those who proffer things sagely in academic settings do so in a tremendously awkward way, as though it were a challenge, or a kind of purely gratuitous exercise, mere manoeuvring. The sequence of the eight hypotheses on the relations of the One and of Being remains problematic, an object of indignation. Some, of course, have distinguished themselves by showing its coherence, but this coherence appears on the whole to be gratuitous, and the confrontation between the interlocutors itself confirms the ahistorical character, so to speak, of the whole.[1]

Supposing that I might be able to put something forward on this point, I would say that what I find striking is really the exact opposite. If ever something has given me the idea that in Platonic dialogue there is some kind of initial foundation of a properly analytic discourse, I would say that the *Parmenides* is indeed the dialogue that would confirm this for me.

If you recall what I set down as a structure, you will note that it's no accident that the S_1 is to be found at the level of *production* in the analytic discourse. I admit that this might not be immediately apparent for you, and I ask you not to take it as self-evident, but it indicates the opportunity of focusing the ensuing part of our examination not on the numerical figure, but very precisely on the signifier One.

$$\frac{a}{S_2} \longrightarrow \frac{\mbox{\cancel{S}}}{S_1}$$

The discourse of the analyst

That there should be Oneness does not go without saying. It *seems* to go without saying because, for example, there are living beings, and each of you here, lined up in such orderly fashion, looks in every respect to be quite independent from the others and to constitute what in this day and age is called an *organic reality*, to hold together as an individual. It was here that an entire first philosophy derived a certain support.

At the level of Aristotelian logic, in applying the principle of the same specification of the x, of the man, of the being who is qualified among speakers as masculine, if we take the term *There exists*, then *There exists at least one for whom Φx is not admissible as an assertion*. Well, from this standpoint, the standpoint of the individual, we find ourselves before a position that is markedly contradictory. Aristotelian logic is grounded on the intuition of the individual that Aristotle posits as real. Aristotle tells us that, after all, it's not the idea of the horse that is real, it's the horse that is well and truly alive, about which we are compelled to ask ourselves precisely how the idea comes about, where we draw this idea from. Aristotle, not without peremptory arguments, turns upside down what Plato stated, namely that the horse is upheld by partaking in the idea of the horse, that what is most real is the idea of the horse.

If we position ourselves from the Aristotelian angle, it's clear that there is a contradiction between the statement that *for all x, x* fulfils in Φx the function of an argument, and the fact that there is *some x* that can fulfil the place of argument only in the enunciation that is the exact negation of the former. If we are told *every horse is spirited*, and if it is added that there are *some*, or *at least one* horse that is not, in Aristotelian logic this is a contradiction.

By putting forward the two terms on the right in my group of four terms – it's no accident that there are four – I'm daring to advance something that is plainly lacking in the aforesaid logic. I am able to do so to the extent that the term *existence* has quite certainly changed meaning since then. When what is at issue is the existence of a term that is capable of holding the place of an argument in a mathematically articulated function, this is not the same existence.

So far, nothing has performed a join between the *Yad'lun* as such and the *at-least-one* that is formulated by the notation of an inverted E, *x*. The latter, *There exists an x, at-least-one*, lends a value that can be qualified as true to what is posited as a function. There is a distance between this and natural existence, which I will not name otherwise today, for want of a better word. Natural existence is not limited to living organisms. For example, we can see these Ones in the celestial bodies, which were among the first to have received properly scientific attention, and not without reason, precisely for the affinity that they have with the One. They appear as though they were inscribing themselves in the heavens as elements that are all the more easily marked out as Ones given that they are punctiform. It's certain that they did a great deal to lay the accent on the point, as a form of passage. In the interval between the individual and what is involved in what I shall call the *real One*, the elements that are signified as punctiform have played an eminent role as far as their transition is concerned.

Is it not palpable for you – and surely this has caught your ear in passing – that I'm speaking about the One as a real, a real that may equally have nothing to do with any reality whatsoever?

I use the word *reality* for the reality of your existence, for example. This is a mode of support that is assuredly material, and first and foremost because it is corporeal. However, it's a matter of knowing what is being spoken of when one says *Yad'lun*. On the path along which science has been travelling, I mean the path it has been travelling since the great turning point when it started to trust in number as such, the Galilean turning point, it's clear that from this scientific perspective, the One that we can qualify as *individual*, and then something that is stated in the register of the logic of number, there is no real cause to wonder about the existence, about the logical support, that can be given to the unicorn, given that no animal is conceived of in a more appropriate manner than the unicorn itself. It is indeed from this perspective that one can say that what we call reality, natural reality, can invariably be taken, at the level of a certain discourse, as fantasy. I do not recoil from claiming that this discourse is the analytic discourse.

The analytic discourse is designed to remind us that the real I've been speaking about is accessed via the symbolic. We access this real in and through the impossible that is defined only by the symbolic. I'm coming back to this at the level of Pliny's *Natural History*. I don't see what differentiates the unicorn from any other animal that is perfectly existent in the natural order. The perspective that examines the real in a certain direction compels us to state matters in this way.

Even so, on no account am I speaking to you about anything that might resemble progress. What we have gained on the scientific plane, which is incontestable, absolutely does not increase our critical sense in matters of political life, for example. I have always stressed how what we gain on one side is lost on the other, in that there is a certain inherent limitation to what may be called the field of adequation in speaking beings.

Just because we have made some progress since Pliny regarding biology, this is not an absolute progress. Were a citizen of Rome to see how we live – unfortunately it's out of the question to conjure one up in person on this occasion – he would likely be overcome with horror. Since we can only envisage this on the basis of the ruins that this civilization has left behind, the idea we may form of it is to see, or to imagine, what the remains of our civilization will be like after a similar lapse of time, if this is supposable.

This is not to get you riled up, so to speak, over the matter of some confidence that I might have in science in particular. The analytic discourse is not a scientific discourse, but rather a discourse of which the material is provided by science, which is quite different.

The grasp that speaking beings have of the world is to conceive of it as something into which they have been immersed. This scheme already smacks of fantasy, does it not? It's quite clear, therefore, that this grasp will only increase to the extent that something is elaborated, and this is the use of number. I claim to be showing you here that this number boils down quite simply to *Yad'lun*.

So, we have to see what has enabled us, historically speaking, to know a little more about this *Yad'lun* than what Plato makes of it, by laying it out flat, so to speak, alongside what is involved in Being.

It's quite certain that this dialogue is extraordinarily suggestive and fruitful, and that if you would care to look into it closely, you will already find the prefiguration of my being able to state, on this basis, on the theme of set theory, that *Yad'lun*.

2

Simply begin if you will with the statement of the first hypothesis – *if the One*. It should be taken for its signification – *if the One is one*.[2]

What will we be able to make of this? The first thing that Plato sets down by way of objection is that this One will not be anywhere,[3] because if it were somewhere, it would be in an envelope,[4] in a limit,[5] and this is quite in contradiction with its existence of One.

(*Protests from the audience*). What's the matter? Am I speaking quietly? Too bad, that's how it is today. I can doubtless do no better.

The One was able to be developed in its existence of One in the way that is grounded by *Mengenlehre*. This has been translated into French, not unprofitably, as *la théorie des ensembles*, but certainly with an accentuation that does not correspond entirely to the meaning of the original term in German, which, from the standpoint of what we're aiming at is no better. This set theory only came on the scene late in the day, and only came about at all by virtue of the entire history of mathematics itself. Of course, there is no question of my tracing out even the briefest of synopses, but, in this history, one needs to take into account the following, which has taken on its full accentuation, its full scope, namely what I might call the extravagances of number.

Clearly this began very early on, because already in Plato's time irrational numbers were posing a problem. It turned out that he inherited – Plato sets out all these developments for us in the *Theaetetus* – the Pythagorean scandal of the irrational character of the diagonal of a square, the scandal being that you never get to the end of it. This can be demonstrated in a figure. It was the most favourable thing there was in that era by which to bring to light the existence of what I am calling *numerical extravagance*. I mean, something that moves out of the field of the One.

What came next? In Archimedes' method known as *exhaustion* there is something that we may consider to be the avoidance of what came along so many centuries afterwards in the form of the paradoxes of infinitesimal calculus, in the form of the statement of what is called the *infinitesimally small*. This is something that takes a very long time to work through, by positing some finite quantity about which it is said that, either way, a certain mode of operating will reach a yet smaller quantity. At the end of the day, this amounts to saying that one makes use of the finite in order to define a transfinite.

And then, my word, one cannot fail to mention the appearance of Fourier's trigonometric series, which certainly poses all sorts of problems for theoretical foundation. All of this is conjugated with the reduction to the perfectly finitist principles of the calculus that was called infinitesimal, which was being pursued at the same time, Cauchy being the great representative.

I am giving this extremely brisk reminder simply to date what is meant by the resumption in Cantor's writings of what the status of the One amounts to. From the moment it becomes a matter of grounding it, the status of the One can only start off from its ambiguity, namely that the mainspring of set theory hinges entirely on how the One – that *there is* – of the set is distinct from the One of the element.

The notion of *set* leans on the fact that there is a set even with just one element. This is not the usual way of putting it, but what is particular to speech is that it advances clumsily. Besides, opening any old exposé of set theory is enough to put your finger on what this entails, namely that if the element posited as fundamental to a set is this something that the very notion of the set allows us to posit as an empty set, well, this means that the element is perfectly admissible. A set can have the empty set as its constituent element, and in this capacity it is absolutely equivalent to what is conventionally called a *singleton*, not to announce straightaway the card of the numerical figure 1. This is so in a perfectly well-founded fashion, for the good reason that we can define the numerical figure 1 only by taking the class of all the sets that are of one single element, and by highlighting their equivalence as what constitutes the grounding of the One properly speaking.

Thus, set theory is designed to restore the status of number. What proves that it does indeed restore it, within the perspective that I have been laying out, is that, setting out as it does the grounding of the One, and making number lean on this as a class of equivalence, set theory thereby manages to highlight what it calls the *non-denumerable*, which is very straightforward, as you are about to see. It's readily accessible, but to translate it into my vocabulary, I call it, not the *non-denumerable* – an object that I would unhesitatingly qualify as mythical – but the *impossible to denumerate*.

I apologize for not being able to give an illustration directly on the blackboard of how it is crafted, but then, after all, what's stopping those of you who are interested from opening a simple handbook called *Naive Set Theory*? You will see that through the Diagonal Method one can be led to put one's finger on how there is a means of laying out the sequence of integers in a series of different ways. In truth, one can lay out this sequence in umpteen thousand different ways. It will be immediately accessible to show that, irrespective of how you might have ordered it, simply by changing each time the values on the diagonal in keeping with a rule determined in advance, there will be yet another way of denumerating them.

It is very precisely in this that the real attached to the One consists.

3

If I am indeed able today to push the demonstration of this fairly far, within the time to which I promised I would limit myself, I am nevertheless going to accentuate now what is entailed by this ambiguity that lies at the foundation of the One as such.

Contrary to appearances, this ambiguity hinges precisely on the fact that the One cannot be grounded on sameness. On the contrary, it has been marked out, by set theory, as having to be grounded on pure and simple difference.

What governs the grounding of set theory consists in the following. Let's say, to go straight to the basics, that when you note down three elements, each separated by a comma – so, there are two commas – if one of these elements appears to be in any way the same as another, or if it can be united to it by any sign of equality, then it is purely and simply *all-at-one* with it. On the first level of assembly that constitutes set theory lies the Axiom of Extensionality, which means that, here at the outset, it cannot be a matter of the *same*. It is a matter of knowing at what point in this construction sameness emerges.

Not only does sameness emerge as a latecomer in this construction, and, if I may say so, on one of its edges, but I may also assert that this sameness as such is counted in number, and therefore the emergence of the One, inasmuch as it may be qualified as the same, only emerges in an exponential way, so to speak. I mean that, as soon as the One that is at issue is none other than this Aleph-Nought – which symbolizes the cardinal of the numerical infinite, this infinity that Cantor calls *improper*[6] and which is made up of elements of what constitutes the first proper infinite, namely the $\aleph_0$ in question – in the course of constructing this $\aleph_0$ there appears the construction of the *same*, and this *same* is itself counted as an element in the construction.

It is in this respect that it is, let's say, *inadequate* in the Platonic dialogue to make anything whatsoever of the *existent* participate in the realm of the *like-for-like*. Without the crossing-through whereby the One is initially constituted, the notion of *like-for-like* would not appear in any way whatsoever.

This is what we are going to see. If we don't see it here today, because I've been limited to a quarter of an hour less than I usually have, I will pursue this elsewhere. Indeed, why not at the forthcoming Thursday appointment at Sainte-Anne, because a certain number of you here know the route? Nevertheless, what I do want to stress is what results from this point of departure of set theory and from what I will call, why not, the *Cantorization* of number.

This is what is at issue. To ground cardinality in any way, there are no other paths but those of what is called the one-to-one mapping of one set onto another. When they want to illustrate this, they find no better, nothing else, but alternatively to evoke goodness knows what primitive potlatch ritual, where the prevailing competitor will emerge to be established at least temporarily as leader, or more straightforwardly the table-laying of the headwaiter, who matches each of the elements of a set of knives with a set of forks. Whether it's a matter of herds that each of the two competing chieftains send across a certain brink, or the headwaiter counting out his cutlery, what will appear? Well, it appears that the One begins on the level at which there is one missing.

The empty set is, therefore, strictly legitimized in that it is, so to speak, the gate that has to be gone through in order to constitute the birth of the One. This is the first One that is designated through an admissible experience. I mean mathematically admissible, in a way that can be taught, because this is what *matheme* means, and not one that appeals to any kind of coarse figuration. What constitutes the One and very precisely justifies it, which is designated only as distinct, and not through any other qualificative ascertainment, is that it only begins with its lack.

This is indeed what becomes apparent to us in the reproduction of Pascal's triangle that I have given here, namely the necessity of distinguishing each of these rows. I think you've known for a little while now how they are constituted. Each row is made by adding what stands above to what is in the same row, which is then notated to its right. Each of the rows is constituted as follows –

1	{1}	{1}	{1}	{1}	{1}
	1	2	3	4	5
		1	3	6	10
			1	4	10
				1	5
					1

What is important is to notice what each of the rows designates.

In Book VII of his *Elements*, lines α΄ and β΄, Euclid defines the monad thus – Μονάς ἐστιν, καθ᾽ ἣν ἕκαστον τῶν ὄντων ἓν λέγεται. Ἀριθμὸς δὲ τὸ ἐκ μονάδων συγκείμενον πλῆθος. *The monad is that by which each entity may be said to be one*, and *number*, ἀριθμὸς, is very precisely *this multiplicity composed of monads*. This definition sets out the error, the lack of grounding.

Pascal's triangle is not here just for the sake of it. It is here to figure what are called in set theory, not the elements, but the *parts* of these sets.[7] At the level of the parts, the parts of a set laid out monadically are the second row. The monad is second. What shall we call the first row, the row that is, in sum, constituted of this empty set, the crossing of which is precisely what constitutes the One? Why not make use of the echo that Spanish gives us, and call it the *nad*? What is at issue here in the One that repeats across the first row is very specifically the *nad*, namely the entrance porthole that is designated by lack.

On the basis of what is involved in the place where a hole is made, in this something that, if you want a figuration, I would represent as being the foundation of *Yad'lun*, there can only be Oneness in the figure of a bag, which is a bag with a hole in it. Nothing is One that doesn't come out of this bag, or which does not go back into the bag. This is the original grounding, to take it intuitively, of the One.

Given what I've promised, I can't push what I have brought any further today, and this I regret. Let me tell you simply that we are going to be examining the most straightforward figure, which I have already designated, namely the triad in which the parts, the subsets formed of the parts of the set, can be figured in a way that is satisfactory for us, then to move back up to the level of the dyad, and to the level of the monad.

You will see that by examining these primal numbers – not prime numbers – a difficulty will arise. I hope that the fact that this is a figurative difficulty will not prevent us from understanding what the essence of the One is, and from seeing what is involved in its grounding.

19 April 1972

XI

AN ISSUE OF ONES

A TALK AT SAINTE-ANNE

The twain, the structure of real sex
The One, an effect of lack
Disputing the non-denumerable
Equivalence between the element and the empty set
The two levels of the One

It's a funny old way to spend one's time, but in the end, why not? It so happens that over the weekends I sometimes write to you. In a manner of speaking. I write because I know we're going to see each other during the week. So, last weekend, I wrote to you. Naturally, in the meantime, I had all the time it took to forget this piece of writing. I've just reread it over dinner, a hurried dinner so that I could be here on time. I'm going to begin with this. It's a bit difficult, so perhaps you will take notes. Afterwards I'll say the things that I've thought since then, with you more really in mind.

I wrote the following – which, of course, I would never submit for *poubellication*, I don't see why I should swell the contents of libraries – *There are two horizons of the signifier.* Then, I've put a curly bracket. Since it's written, you'll have to pay attention. I mean that you mustn't believe you comprehend. After the bracket, there is *the maternal*, which is also *the material*, and then there is written, *the mathematical*.

I know I will have to, but, in the end, I can't start speaking straightaway. Were it not for this, I would never read you what I have written. Perhaps in the next part I will have to come back to this distinction, which I am underscoring as a horizon.

Articulating them as such in each of these two horizons – this is a parenthesis, I haven't written this – is therefore – this I have written – *to proceed in accordance with these two horizons themselves, because any mention of their beyond . . .* beyond the horizon *. . . is supported* *only by their position* . . . when this starts to bore you, let me know and I'll tell you the items that I have to tell you this evening . . . *by their position in a de facto discourse. For the analytic discourse, this* de facto *implicates me sufficiently in its effects for it to be said that this is my* fait, *my doing, for it to be designated by my name. The amur* . . . – what I have designated as such here – . . . *reverberates this diversely with the available means of what is rightly called* le bord, *the rim, of this* bord-homme.[1] This *bord-homme* inspired me to write *brrom-brrom-wap-wap*. This was the discovery of a person who in times gone by mothered my children. It's an indication concerning *l'a-voix*, th'a-voice, which, as everyone knows, *aboie*, barks, and also *l'a-regard*, th'a-gaze, not to take so close *a-look*, and *l'a-t'suce*, a-stutely licking you into shape, and then *l'a-merde* as well, th'a-crap that from time to time forms the somewhat injurious graffito directed at my name on the pages of newspapers. In short, *c'est l'a-vie!* As somebody who is having fun for the moment would say, it's cheerful. In the main, this is true.

These effects have nothing to do with the dimension that is measured against my doing. This is to say that it is from a discourse that is not my own that I make the necessary dimension. It is from the analytic discourse, which, not yet having been . . . – and for good reason – . . . *properly instituted, finds itself in need of a few facilitations, to which I employ myself.* On the basis of what? Solely on the basis that, in fact, *my position is determined by it.*

Let's speak, now, about this discourse and about the fact that the position of the signifier as such is essential to it. Given the audience that you constitute, I would like to make a remark. This *position of the signifier* takes shape in an experience, which is within reach of every one of you, so that you may see what's at issue and how essential it is.

When you speak a language imperfectly, and you read a text, well, you comprehend, you still comprehend. This ought to put you a little on alert. You comprehend in the sense that you know in advance what is being said in it. Of course, this can result in the text contradicting itself. When you read, for instance, a text on set theory, the text explains what constitutes the infinite set of all integers. On the next line, you are told something that you comprehend, because you keep reading – *It would, however, be a fundamental mistake to deem this set infinite because the integers* . . . *increase infinitely.* Since it's just been explained to you that this is the reason that it is so, this gives you a start. When you take a closer look, however, you find the term *deem*. In other words, this is not the reason why you should deem it so, because they know that the series of integers doesn't stop, that it is infinite. It's not that the series is *indefinite*.

You realize that either you've skipped over *deem*, or you're not sufficiently familiar with English, and therefore you have comprehended too quickly, that is, you have skipped over this essential element, the element of a signifier that makes this change of level possible, this change of level that, for a moment, gave you the sense of a contradiction.

One should never skip a signifier. It's to the extent that the signifier doesn't halt you that you comprehend. Now – *comprehending always amounts to being comprehended oneself within the effects of discourse, a discourse that, as such, gives an order to the effects of knowledge that have already been precipitated through the formalism of the signifier alone. What psychoanalysis teaches us is that any naïve knowledge* . . . this is written, which is why I'm reading again . . . *is associated with a veiling of the jouissance that is realized therein, and poses the question as to what is betrayed therein of the limits of power, that is to say –* what? – *of the* tracé, *the layout, imposed on jouissance.*

As soon as we speak – this is a fact – *we suppose something of what is spoken, this something that we imagine as having been pre-posited, even though it is quite sure that we only ever suppose it after the event. That which speaks . . . –* whatever it is – *. . . is that which derives jouissance from the self as a body. The fact of speaking . . . –* in the current state of our knowledge – *. . . refers only to this. It derives jouissance from a body that it experiences as* tuable, *that is, as a body that it can address in the* tu *form and a body to which it can say* tue-toi, *kill yourself, in the same line. What is psychoanalysis? It is the tracking of what is comprehended by way of obfuscation, of what is obfuscated in comprehension, due to the fact of a signifier that has marked a point of the body.*

Psychoanalysis is what reproduces . . . – here you will find the usual guardrails – *. . . a production of neurosis. Everyone agrees on this point. There is not a single psychoanalyst who has not perceived this. This neurosis that is attributed, not unreasonably, to the action of the parents can be reached only to the extent that the action of the parents is articulated precisely . . . –* this is the term with which I started the third line – *. . . from the position of the psychoanalyst. To the extent that neurosis converges towards a signifier that emerges from it, neurosis will take on an order in accordance with the discourse whose effects produced the subject. Every traumatic parent is, in sum, in the same position as the psychoanalyst. The difference is that the psychoanalyst, from his position, reproduces the neurosis, whereas the traumatic parent produces it innocently.*

What is at issue is to reproduce it – this signifier – *on the basis of whatever its initial flowering had been. All in all, the operation of the analytic discourse is to fashion a model of the neurosis. Why? Well, to the extent that it takes out the rib of jouissance. Indeed, jouissance demands this special privilege. There are not two ways of doing this for each subject. Every reduplication kills jouissance. Jouissance only survives in that its repetition is of no avail, that is to say, it is always the same. It is the introduction of the model that completes it –* this repetition of no avail. *A completed repetition dissolves it, in that it is a simplified repetition.*

Of course, when I speak of Yad'lun, *I am still speaking of the signifier. To lay out this* d'lun *in keeping with the extent of its empire, because it assuredly is the master signifier, it has to be approached right where it has been left to its talents, so as to box it into a corner.*

There you have it for what renders the point I have got to this year useful as an incidence, having no choice but this, . . . *or worse.* This incidence is the mathematical reference, so called because it is the realm in which the matheme governs, that is to say, that which produces a knowledge that, being merely a product, is bound to the norms of surplus jouissance, that is, of the measurable. A matheme is that which alone is taught, and strictly so. No teaching but of the One. We still have to find out what is at issue. And this is why I am examining it this year.

I'm not going to read any further. The text is rather difficult, but I think I've read it slowly enough for a few questions to be left hanging regarding each of the terms I have spelt out. I will now speak more freely.

The other day, as I was leaving the latest session up at the Panthéon, someone questioned me – he might be here again – on the subject of whether I believed in freedom. I told him he was being funny. And then, as I am always fairly weary, I broke off. But this doesn't mean I wouldn't be prepared to confide in him personally on this matter. The fact is, I seldom speak about freedom, and so this question was his initiative. Knowing why he asked me this would not be unwelcome to me.

So, what I would like more freely to say is that, in alluding in my written text to how I find myself in the position of facilitating the analytic discourse, clearly I consider it to constitute, at least potentially, this sort of structure that I have been designating with the term *discourse.* Through discourse, which is the pure and simple effect of language, a social bond is precipitated. Yet this was noticed without any need of psychoanalysis. This is even what is conventionally known as *ideology.*

The way in which a discourse takes on order in such a way as to precipitate a social bond entails, conversely, that everything that is articulated within it takes on an order through its effects. It is indeed in this way that I understand what I have been articulating for you about the discourse of psychoanalysis. Were there no psychoanalytic practice, what I might articulate thereof wouldn't have effects that I might anticipate. I didn't say, *wouldn't have meaning*. What is particular to meaning is that it is always confusional, that is, it believes it forms a bridge between one discourse – in so far as a social bond is precipitated therein – and what, in another realm, stems from another discourse.

What is annoying is that whenever you proceed – since I have just said in this written text that it is a question of *proceeding* – that is, whenever you target, from one discourse, what holds the function of the One within it, what am I doing in such an instance? If you will allow me the following neologism, I am engaging in *henology*.[2] Given what I have been articulating, anyone could turn it into an ontology, in keeping with what he presupposes beyond these two horizons that I have marked out as being defined as the horizons of the signifier.

In the university discourse, one may set oneself to drawing the model from my construction by presupposing, at some arbitrary point, goodness knows what essence that would become – though who knows why? – the supreme value. This is particularly conducive to what is offered to the university discourse, in which what is at issue, according to the diagram I have designed for it, is to put S_2 at the place of semblance.

$$\frac{S_2}{S_1} \longrightarrow \frac{a}{\text{\$}}$$

University discourse

Before a signifier is truly put in its place, that is, picked out by the ideology for which it has been produced, it always has effects of circulation. In these effects, signification precedes the acknowledgement of its place, its instituting place. The very nature of teaching gives confirmation of the fact that the university discourse is defined by knowledge being put in the position of semblance. What can we see there? It is a false ordering of what has fanned out, so to speak,[3] over the course of the centuries by way of diverse ontologies. Its summit, its culmination, is what is gloriously termed *the history of philosophy*, as though philosophy didn't have its remit – and this has been amply demonstrated – in the adventures and misadventures of the discourse of the master, which does indeed need to be overhauled once in a while. The cause of philosophy's shimmerings lies elsewhere, as has been affirmed sufficiently on the basis of points from which the notion of ideology has emerged, as though the cause at stake did not lie elsewhere. What is difficult, however, is that any process of articulating a discourse, above all if it has not yet been ascertained, offers a pretext for a certain number of new *beings* to swell up prematurely.

I know full well that none of this is easy, and that I shall have to tell you some more amusing things, in the fine tradition of what I have been doing here. So, let's speak about the analyst and love.

People speak about love in analysis. And, of course, this is due to the position of the analyst. All things considered, people don't speak about it any more here than elsewhere since, after all, this is what love is for. This is not what is most gratifying, but in the end, in mundane terms people speak about it a great deal. It is even tremendous that people still go on about it after all this time, because they might have noticed, after all this time, that this hasn't made it any the more successful. It's clear, therefore, that it's by speaking that one makes love. So, what is the role of the analyst in this? Can an analysis really make a loving relationship successful? I have to tell you that, as far as I'm concerned, I have no such example. And yet I did try. For me, not having quite come down in the last shower, this was a challenge.

I once took on someone on the basis of a request, though thank goodness I knew beforehand that he was in need of a psychoanalysis – you realize the dirty tricks I'm capable of pulling to verify my affirmations – the request being that he should at any cost obtain *conjugo* with the lady on whom he had set his heart. Naturally, of course, this failed – thank the Lord – and very quickly too. I do hope he's not here. I'm almost certain he isn't.

Let's put an end to this, because all this is anecdotal. One day, when luck is going my way, and I venture to do a little La Bruyère, I'll deal with the question of the relations between love and semblance. But this is not where we are this evening. There's to be no lingering over these knick-knacks. It's rather a matter – I'm returning to this because it seems to me that I did open this up – of knowing what the relation is between everything that I've been restating, which I'm recalling by briefly touching on the truths of experience, and the function of sex in psychoanalysis.

I think that on this score I have even got through to the tin ears with a statement that deserves to be commented on – that *there is no such thing as sexual relation*. Of course, this deserves to be spelt out.

Why does the psychoanalyst imagine that sex forms the base of his reference? That sex is real is not to be doubted in the slightest. Its very structure is the *dual*, the number *duo*. Whatever one may think, there are two of them. Men. Women. So they say. And they insist on adding Auvergnats.[4] That's an error. At the level of the real, there are no Auvergnats.

What is at issue when sex is involved is the other, the other sex, even when one prefers the same. Just because I said a moment ago that the aid psychoanalysis can bring is precarious when it comes to the success of a loving relationship, it shouldn't be thought that the psychoanalyst doesn't give a stuff, if I can put it like that. The psychoanalyst cannot be indifferent to the fact that the partner in question is of the other sex, and that what is in play is something that bears a relation to his or her jouissance – I'm speaking of the other, the third party, about whom this gab around love is voiced – because the one that is not there is, for the analyst, the real.

This jouissance, the jouissance that is not in analysis, if you will allow me to put it like this, holds the function of the real for the analyst. On the other hand, what *is* in analysis, that is to say, the subject, the analyst takes for what it is, namely for an effect of discourse. I ask you to note in passing that he doesn't subjectify it. This doesn't mean that all this is his own little idea, but rather that, as a subject, he is determined by a discourse from which he has long originated, and this is what is analysable.

I will specify that the analyst is on no account a nominalist. He does not think of his subject's representations. Rather, he has to intervene in his discourse by procuring for him *un supplément de signifiant*, an additional signifier. This is what is called *interpretation*. When it comes to what is not within his reach, which is what is in question here, namely the jouissance of the one who is not there in analysis, he takes it for what it is, that is, of the order of the real, because he can do nothing about it.

No one has ever dared, not even Bishop Berkeley, to state that sex, as real – I mean as dual, I mean that there are two of them – was a little idea that each person had in their head, that it was a representation. It is highly instructive that no one in the entire history of philosophy has ever ventured to extend idealism this far.

For a while now we have been able to see what sex is under the microscope. I'm not talking about sexual organs. I'm talking about gametes. Can you imagine that they had nothing of this prior to Leeuwenhoek and Swammerdam? They were reduced to thinking that sex was everywhere. Nature, νοῦς, the whole racket, all that was sex. *And the female vultures made love with the wind.* From the pretext that, long before it was known that there are two kinds of gamete, we have known for certain that sex is to be found in two small cells that do not resemble one another, psychoanalysts believe that there is such a thing as sexual relation. We have been seeing psychoanalysts, in their literature, in an area that cannot be said to be highly controlled, find in the intrusion of the male gamete – of the *spermato*, as they say, and then the *zoon* – through the girdle of the ovum, the model of goodness knows what formidable breach. As though there were the faintest relation between this reference – which doesn't bear the slightest relation to what is involved in cop-ulation, except through the coarsest of metaphors – and anything whatsoever that might be referred to what is in play in *love relations*, which, as I said at the start, amounts to a great many words.

The whole question lies here, and it is indeed here that the evolu-tion of the forms of discourse is far more indicative for us of what is at issue. What are at issue are effects of discourse, even if it is quite sure that the sexes are twain. This is far more indicative of what is at issue than any reference to what remains entirely in abeyance, namely whether what discourse is capable of articulating compre-hends, or not, sexual relation. This is what deserves to be called into question.

The small items I have already written up on the blackboard for you include an opposition between $\exists x$ and $\overline{\exists x}$, between a *There exists* and a *There exists not*, on the same level of *it is not true that* Φx. Then, there is another level, that of *all x complies with the function Φx*, and of *pas tout, not all* – which is a new form, in the right-hand column – *and nothing more, is apt to satisfy the phallic function*.

As I shall strive to explicate in the forthcoming lessons of my Seminar, that is, somewhere else, what deserves to be pointed out is a series of gaps which are diverse, which are not the same in each case, between each of these points, the four points stated above, in order to give its rightful status to what is involved in sexual relation at the level of the subject.

This shows well enough to what extent language traces out, in its very grammar, the said subject-effects. It intersects sufficiently with what was first discovered in logic for us to be able, now, to set about hearing a signifier, as I have been doing since these reminders that I have been issuing, so that I might try to give it a meaning. For this is the only case, and rightly so, in which the term *meaning* is justified when stating *Yad'lun*, because there is one thing that must neverthe-less be apparent to you, which is that if there is no relation, then each of the two remains One.

What is incredible is that, whereas psychoanalysts' mythology has been condemned, more or less justifiably, oddly enough the mythology that people have failed to condemn is precisely the one that lies closest to hand. When the gametes conjoin, this does not result in their fusion. Before this can come about, there has to be a severe elimination, known as meiosis. The newly formed One is made from what we may call, quite rightly, I won't say the debris of *chacun d'eux*, the debris of each of them, but a *chacun deux*, an each twain, that has extruded a certain amount of debris.

From the pen of Freud we find the idea that Eros *se fonde* – in the subjunctive, you can see the equivoque between *fonder* and *fondre*, I don't see why I shouldn't exploit the French language[5] – that Eros should be founded by making One from two. Clearly this is a strange idea from which there stems, of course, the absolutely exorbitant idea that is embodied in the sermonizing that dear Freud nevertheless abhorred with all his being. He expresses in the plainest terms, in *The Future of an Illusion*, and in many other places besides, in *Civilization and Its Discontents*, his repugnance at the idea of universal love. And yet the founding force of life, of the *life instinct*, as he puts it, would fall squarely into the Eros that is purportedly behind the principle of union. It is not only for didactic reasons that I would like to furnish you, on the subject of the One, with what can be used to fight back against this coarse mythology, aside from the fact that it might enable us to exorcize not only Eros – I mean the Eros of Freudian doctrine – but dear Thanatos too, which people have been boring us with for quite long enough.

At this juncture it is not unhelpful to make use of something that came to light some time ago, and not by chance. I have already introduced – I introduced it last time – an account of what has been identified as *la théorie des ensembles*, set theory. Men and women – we can laugh a little as well – are also *ensemble*, together. This doesn't stop them from being each on their own side. It's a matter of knowing whether we might be able to draw some light from the *ensemble* – from a *set*, of course, which was never designed for this – to shed on the *Yad'lun*. So, since I too release trial balloons, I propose simply to try to see with you what in all this might be of service, not as an illustration, for it's about something quite different. It's about what the signifier has to do with the One.

The One didn't come on the scene just yesterday. But, even so, it arose with regard to two quite different things, with regard to a certain use of instruments of measure, and at the same time something that bore absolutely no relation to this, namely the function of the individual.

The individual, this is in Aristotle. Aristotle was struck by these beings that reproduce, always the same ones. This had already struck someone else, a certain Plato. Actually, I think that this was because he didn't have anything better to offer by which to give us an idea of form. He managed to state that form is real. He did indeed have to illustrate his idea of *Idea* as best he could. The other fellow, of course, remarked that, even so, form is all very nice, but what singles it out is simply that form is what we recognize in a certain number of individuals that resemble one another.

Here we find ourselves sliding off down various metaphysical slopes. This is of no degree of interest to us when it comes to illustrating the One, whether by the individual or by a certain practical usage of geometry. Irrespective of the developments that you might be able to add to this geometry, considering the proportions of the manifest difference between the length of a stake and the length of its shadow, it's been a good while since we first noticed that the One poses other problems, and this is for the simple fact that mathematics has progressed somewhat. I'm not going to go back over what I stated last time, about differential calculus, about the various trigonometric series, and in a more comprehensive way about the conception of number as defined by a sequence. What appears very clearly is that the question of what is involved in Oneness is posed altogether differently there, because a sequence is typified as being composed in the same way as the sequence of integers. It's a matter of accounting for what an integer is.

I am not, of course, going to lay out for you the theory of sets. I want simply to point out that we first had to wait until rather late in the day, the end of the last century, not even a hundred years ago, before there was an attempt to account for the function of the One. It is remarkable that the set should be defined in such a way that its first apparent aspect should be that of the empty set, and that, on the other hand, this constitutes a set, namely that of which the said empty set is the only element. This makes a set with one element. This is where we begin. Last time – I'm saying this for those who weren't up at the Panthéon when I started to tackle this slippery subject – I underscored how the grounding of the One turns out, by virtue of this fact, to be strictly constituted by the place of a lack.

I referred to pedagogical use in order to give a broad illustration of what it is a matter of getting across in set theory, in order to give you a sense of how this theory has no other direct object besides that of making it apparent how the specific notion of cardinal number can be generated through one-to-one correspondence. The illustration I used was that, at the moment at which, in the two compared series, a mate is missing, the notion of the One arises. There is one missing.

Everything that is said about the cardinal number stems from the fact that, if the sequence of numbers always necessarily entails one, and only one, successor, and provided that what is at issue in cardinality is realized in the order of number, then this is strictly the cardinal sequence in that, by starting from zero, it extends up to the number that immediately precedes the successor. By stating it thus, in an extempore manner, I have made a small mistake, which is to speak of a sequence as though it were already well-ordered. Take from this the following, which I didn't assert – it's simply that each number corresponds cardinally to the cardinal that precedes it by adding to it the empty set.

What is important in what I would like to give you a sense of this evening is that while the One arises as the effect of lack, taking the sets into consideration lends itself to something that I believe worthy of mention, and which I would like to highlight, in reference to how set theory has enabled us to distinguish two types of set. It has enabled us to admit the finite set and the infinite set. In this statement, what typifies the infinite set is that it can be posited as equivalent to any one of its subsets. As had already been remarked by Galileo, who didn't have to wait for Cantor for this, the sequence of all the square numbers is in one-to-one correspondence with each of the integers. Indeed, there is no reason ever to consider any of the square numbers to be too large to be in the sequence of the integers. This is what constitutes the infinite set, whereby it is said that it can be *reflexive*. On the other hand, the chief property of the finite set is that it is conducive to the specifically mathematical reasoning, which makes use of it, known as *induction*. Induction is admissible when a set is finite.

What I would like to say is that there is a point in set theory that I deem problematic. This point stems from what is called the non-denumerability of the *parts* – to be understood as the *subsets* – such as they can be defined on the basis of a set.

This is quite straightforward if you start off from the cardinal number. For example, you have one set composed of five elements. You call *subset* the subsuming of each of these five elements into a set. Next, taking the groupings that are formed by two out of these five elements, it will be easy for you to calculate how many subsets this makes. There will be exactly ten. Then you can take them three at a time. There will again be ten of them. Then take them four at a time. There will be five. In the end, you get to the set of which there is only one, the present set, containing five elements. To this should be added the empty set, which, in any case, without being an element of the set, can be indicated as one of its parts. The parts are not an element.

The ordering can be written as follows.

$$1$$

$$5$$

$$10$$

$$10$$

$$5$$

$$1$$

What have we written down as parts of the set? The empty set is here. The five elements, α, β, γ, δ, and ε, for example, are here. What comes next is $\alpha\beta$, $\alpha\gamma$, $\alpha\delta$, $\alpha\varepsilon$. You can do the same starting with β. You can do the same with γ, and so on. You will see that there are ten. Next, here, you have $\alpha\beta\gamma\delta$, with ε missing. By missing out each of these five letters, you can obtain the number 5 that is necessary for the grouping as parts of elements.

1	$\varnothing$
5	α, β, γ, δ, ε
10	$\alpha\beta$, $\alpha\gamma$, $\alpha\delta$, $\alpha\varepsilon$, $\beta\gamma$, $\beta\delta$, $\beta\varepsilon$, $\gamma\delta$, $\gamma\varepsilon$, $\delta\varepsilon$
10	$\alpha\beta\gamma$, $\alpha\beta\delta$, $\alpha\beta\varepsilon$, $\alpha\gamma\delta$, $\alpha\gamma\varepsilon$, $\alpha\delta\varepsilon$, $\beta\gamma\delta$, $\beta\gamma\varepsilon$, $\beta\delta\varepsilon$, $\gamma\delta\varepsilon$
5	$\alpha\beta\gamma\delta$, $\alpha\beta\gamma\varepsilon$, $\alpha\beta\delta\varepsilon$, $\alpha\gamma\delta\varepsilon$, $\beta\gamma\delta\varepsilon$
1	$\alpha\beta\gamma\delta\varepsilon$

In view of which, you find that it would be enough for me to complement this statement of a set of cardinality 5 with the sequence – which we shall put alongside – that refers to a set of four elements.

1	1
4	5
6	10
4	10
1	5
	1

In other words, imagine this as a tetrahedron. You will see that you have one tetrad, that you have six sides, that you have four vertex corners, that you have four faces, and that you have one empty set. I have only alluded to this other case to show you that in both cases the sum of the parts is equal to 2^n, n being precisely the cardinal number of the elements of the set. This is not something that undermines in any way whatsoever the theory of sets. What is stated regarding denumerability has all its applications, for example in the remark that nothing changes with respect to the categorization of a set as *infinite* if any denumerable sequence is dropped from it. Nevertheless, with regard to the contribution that is made of non-denumerability, in that assuredly and in every case one cannot map onto a finite set the sum of its parts defined in the above manner, I ask, is this the best way to introduce the non-denumerability of an infinite set?

What is at issue here is a didactic introduction. I dispute it from the moment that the property of *reflexivity*, such as it is assigned to the infinite set, and which entails that it lacks the *inductiveness* that is characteristic of finite sets, allows it nevertheless to be written, as I have seen in some places, that the non-denumerability of the parts of the infinite set would emerge *by induction* due to the fact that these parts would be written just as the infinite set of integers is written, $2^{\aleph_0}$. I dispute this.

How do I dispute it? There is some artifice involved when the parts of the set are taken on the mounting scale, the addition of which does effectively give 2^n. It is clear, however, that if on one side you have a, b, c, d, e – to Romanize the Greek letters I wrote on the blackboard, which I did for a reason – and if you bring what corresponds to them, namely, a, b, c, d corresponds to e, while a, b, d, e corresponds to c, you can see that the number of parts, if you substitute a *partition* here, leads to a very different formula, the number 2^{n-1}. You will see why this is of interest to me.

Given the time, and then the fact that this is not of interest to absolutely everybody here, I cannot develop this now. However, I welcome contributions, as I usually do, in my helpless way. I solicit grammarians once in a while, to give me a little pointer. They do, but they're always poor ones. I've solicited mathematicians, a great many already, to respond to me on this matter, and the truth is they turn a deaf ear. I have to tell you that they cling to this non-denumerability of the parts of the set like fleas to the skin of a dog.

None the less, I propose the following, which holds its own small interest. I shall go straight to one point, which will leave to one side another point to which I should like to return afterwards. By replacing the notion of *parts* with that of *partition*, it is necessary – in the same way that we have admitted that the parts of the infinite set would be $2^{\aleph_0}$, the smallest of the transfinites, the one that is constituted by the cardinal of the set of integers – that instead of getting $2^{\aleph_0}$, we get $2^{\aleph_0 - 1}$.

I suspect that this will give anyone an inkling of the misuse that consists in presupposing the bipartition of an infinite set. If, as the formula itself bears the trace, what is called *the set of the parts* leads to a formula that contains the number 2 raised to the power of the elements of the set, is this altogether admissible, above all from the moment we call induction into question when the infinite set is at issue? How is it admissible that we should accept a formula that shows so plainly that it's a matter, not of *parts* of the set, but of its *partition*?

To this I will add something that possesses its own special interest. Of course, $\aleph_0$ is merely an index. It's an index that has not been taken at random in that it has been wrought to perform a designation. There is the whole series of integers that can, in principle, serve as the index of what is involved in the set inasmuch as it grounds the transfinite. Nevertheless, as soon as what is at stake is the exponential function, and now that it seems we have misused induction by allowing ourselves to find therein the test of the non-denumerability of the parts of the infinite set, would we not find here, on closer inspection, another function for this nought, the nought in exponential power, namely that, whichever the number, designating its power with the exponent 0 makes it equal to 1? To reiterate, any number to the power of 1 is itself, but a number to the power of 0 is always 1, for the very simple reason that a number to the power of minus 1 is its inverse. Therefore, 1 serves as the pivotal element here.

From this moment forth, the partition of the transfinite set leads to the following. If in this instance we make $\aleph_0$ equal to 1, then what seems to be altogether admissible for the partition of the set is that the sequence of integers is supported by nothing other than the reiteration of the One, the One that came out of the empty set. It is in reproducing that it constitutes what I gave last time as the principle displayed in Pascal's triangle, at the level of the cardinality of the monads. Behind the supports – I'm saying this for the deaf ones who have been wondering what I said – you have what I call the *nad*, that is to say, the One that has come out of the empty set, which is the reiteration of the lack.

I stress that the One at issue is specifically what set theory replaces only with the reiteration of the empty set, whereby this theory shows the true nature of the *nad*.

Indeed, this is affirmed, from Cantor's own pen, in the principle of the set – which is certainly *naïve*, as one says – when he is opening up this truly sensational path. What Cantor's pen asserts is that the elements of the set can be as diverse as one might please, on the sole condition that we posit that each of them are what he will go so far as to call *objects of our intuition or of our thought*.[6] This is how he expresses it. Indeed, why deny him this? It means nothing more than something as eternal as one may wish. It's utterly clear that as soon as you mix intuition with thought, you get signifiers, which of course is made manifest by the fact that this is written *a, b, c, d*. What is said, however, is specifically that what is ruled out when it comes to the membership of an element in a set is that any element should be repeated as such. Therefore, any element of a set subsists qua *distinct*. When it comes to what is involved in the empty set, it is affirmed as a founding principle of set theory that it can only be One. This One – the *nad* that is the principle behind the emergence of the numerical One, of the One from which an integer is made – is thus something that is posited as lying at the origin of the empty set itself.

This notion is important because we are examining this structure to the extent that for us in the analytic discourse the One suggests itself as the principle behind repetition. Therefore, it is a matter, here, precisely of the sort of One that finds itself marked out as never being anything but a lack, an empty set.

However, now that I have introduced the function of the *partition*, there is a point of Pascal's triangle that you will allow me to examine. With the two columns I have just made, I have enough to show you what my question marks.

If it is true that as the number of the partitions we have only the number that was previously assigned to the set *n*–1, the set whose cardinal number is one unit less than the cardinal of a set, see how, on the basis of this number that corresponds to the presumed parts of the set that we shall call, more briefly, *lower by one*, the parts – which will find themselves in a bipartition – will compose the higher set, in accordance with the first statement. Each time, we have to add together the two numbers in the column to the left, one immediately to the left and the other above it. Here we obtain the figure 10, from the figure 4, here, and the figure 6.

1	1	1	1	1	1
	1	2	3	4	5
		1	3	6	10
			1	4	10
				1	5
					1

What does this mean? It means that we obtain the first figure, that of the monads of the set, of the elements of the cardinal number of the set, solely from the fact of having put, by means of what I would call a necessary misuse, the empty set on the row of the monadic elements. In other words, it is by adding the empty set to each of the four monads from the previous column that we obtain the cardinal number of the monads, of the elements, of the higher set.

To make this figurable, let's simply try to see now what this yields in a diagram. To make things more straightforward, let's take the column before, the three monads, and not the four. We figure the set by means of a circle. But we figure the empty set as follows. It's not important for it to be in the centre.

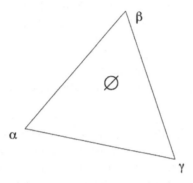

We have said, when it's a matter of forming the tetradic set, that this empty set will come to the preceding row of monads. To represent it with a tetrahedron – of course, it's not about tetrahedra, it's about numbers – if this is designated by the Greek letters α, β, γ, we will have, here, the empty set as a fourth single-member element in the order of these subsets.

However, it no less remains that the empty set still exists at the level of this new set. At the level of this new set, we shall give a different term to what has just been extracted from the empty set. Since we already have α, β, γ, we shall call it δ.

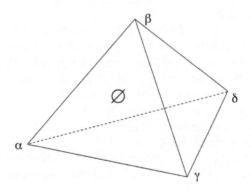

What does this lead us to see? At the level of the elements of the antepenultimate subsets, we can see, to remain in intuition, the five quadrangles that can be highlighted in a polyhedral with five vertices.[7] There, too, what do we have to take up? We have to take up the four triangles of the tetrad in so far as we are going to be able to perform three different subtractions. This will be added together here, and constitutes it as a set, or more precisely as a subset. How can we make up our count, unless at this same level, where we will only have three subsets, each comprising three elements, we add to them the *single* elements of the set? Thus, α, β, γ, δ, in not having been subsumed into a set, that is, in being defined as *elements* – they are not *sets* – but in being isolated from what includes them in the set, they must be counted in order for us to have our count of four. To yield the partial aggregate of the figure 5 at the level of the five-element set, we have to bring in the elements that are four in number qua simply juxtaposed, and not as subsumed into a set, a subset in this instance.

We notice that, in set theory, every element is worth any other. And it is indeed in this way that unity can be generated. It is precisely in that the said concept of *distinct and definite*[8] on this occasion represents the fact that *distinct* can only mean *radical difference*, since nothing can resemble itself. There are no sorts. All that is distinguished in the same way is the same element. This is what this means.

By taking only the element of pure difference, we can also see it as the sameness of this difference. I mean, to illustrate this, that in set theory, one element is absolutely equivalent – as has already been demonstrated on the second line – to an empty set, because the empty set can also come into play as an element. Everything that is defined as an element is equivalent to the empty set. However, taking this equivalence, this sameness of absolute difference, as isolable – and not as subsumed into this aggregative inclusion, which would make it a subset – means that sameness as such is, at one point, counted.

This strikes me as having great importance, and very precisely, for example, at the level of what is played out in Plato, where similitude is turned into an idea of substance, a universal in the realist perspective, in so far as this universal is reality. What we see is that the idea of *like-for-like* is not introduced at the same level. This is what I alluded to in my most recent disquisition up at the Panthéon. The sameness of the elements of the set is, as such, counted as playing its role in the parts of the set.

This certainly holds importance for us, because what is at issue at the level of analytic theory? Analytic theory sees the One rearing its head at two of its levels. At a first level, the One is the One that repeats. It lies at the foundation of this major incidence in the analysand's speaking, which he decries as a certain repetition with regard to a signifying structure. On the other hand, considering the diagram that I have provided for the analytic discourse, what is produced when the subject is placed at the level of the jouissance of speaking? What is produced, and which I have designated at the storey of surplus jouissance, is S_1. This is a signifying production that I propose to acknowledge, even if it means setting myself the task of giving you a sense of its incidence, but in what exactly?

What is the sameness of difference? What does it mean that something that we designate in the signifier by means of diverse letters can be *these same*? What might *these same* mean, if not that this is unique, based indeed on the hypothesis that the function of the element starts with in set theory? The One at issue, which the subject produces – an ideal point, let's say – in analysis, is, contrary to what is at issue in repetition, the One as One by itself. It is the One inasmuch as, whatever difference might exist, all differences are worth as much as another. There is only one of them, and this is *difference per se*.

It is with this that I wanted to bring this disquisition to a close this evening, besides the fact that it so happens that the time and my weariness are hurrying me to it. In the coming sessions I will give you an illustration of the function of the S_1 in the way I have positioned it in the formula that gives its rightful status to the analytic discourse.

4 May 1972

XII

KNOWLEDGE ABOUT TRUTH

Wisdom is knowledge of jouissance
They peel away and go astray
The analyst does not affect a semblance
The poverty of the phenomenology of love
The inaccessible cardinals

It's hard for me to blaze a trail for you in a discourse that is of interest to not all of you. I shall say, that is of interest to you *as not all*, and I shall even add, *only as not all*.

1

One thing is clear, and this is the key character of the *tous*, of the *all*, in Freud's thinking. The notion of the crowd that he inherited from that imbecile called Gustave Le Bon served him in entifying this *all*. It comes as no surprise that he discovered in this the necessity of a *There exists*. On that occasion, the only aspect of it that he was able to see was what he translated as the unary trait, *der einziger Zug*.

The unary trait has nothing to do with the *Yad'lun* that I've been trying to tighten up this year, on the grounds that we don't have better things to do, which I've been expressing as . . . *or worse*. It wasn't just for the sake of it that I said to say it adverbially.

I shall say right away that the unary trait is what repetition as such is marked by. Repetition doesn't ground any *all*, nor does it identify anything, because tautologically, so to speak, there cannot be a first of them.

It is in this respect that all the psychology of something that is translated as *des foules*, crowd psychology, misses what stands to be seen here with a bit more luck, namely the nature of the *pas-tous*, the *not-all* that grounds this psychology, a nature that belongs precisely to *woman*, in inverted commas, which for father Freud constituted a problem right to the end, the problem of what she wants. I've already spoken to you about this. Let's come back to what I'm trying to spin out for you this year.

Anything whatsoever can serve to write the One of repetition. It's not that it's nothing, it's that it can be written with any old thing so long as it's easy to repeat in figures. For the being who finds himself in charge of making sure that, in language, *it speaks*, nothing lends itself more easily to figuration than what he is designed to reproduce naturally, namely, as they say, his *like* or his *type*. Not that he knows from the start how to produce his figure, but this figure marks him, and this he can give back to it. He can give back the mark that is precisely the unary trait. The unary trait is the support of what I started off from under the heading of the *mirror stage*, that is, *imaginary identification*.

However, this checking off of a support that is *typical*, that is to say, imaginary, the mark as such, the unary trait, does not constitute a judgement of value. It occurred to me that people said I used to make value judgements of the type – *imaginary*, poo, *symbolic*, yum-yum. But everything that I said, wrote, and inscribed in the graphs – which I schematized in the optical model where the subject is reflected in the unary trait, and where it's on this basis alone that he gets his bearings as an *ideal ego* – all of this insists precisely on how imaginary identification operates through a symbolic mark. So, whoever decries Manichaeism in my doctrine – the judgement of value, *bah!* – simply demonstrates what this is, on account of having heard me thus since the start of my disquisition, which is nevertheless coeval with it. A pig that rears back on its hind legs to become a standing pig is still the pig that it was of origin, but the pig is alone in imagining that anyone remembers this.

To come back to Freud, thus far I have only commented on the function that he introduced under the heading of narcissism. The unbelievable aspect of the institution for which he envisaged what he calls the *economy of the psyche*, namely the organization to which he deemed he should entrust the re-launch of his doctrine, stems indeed from the error he made when tying the ego, without any relay, to his *Massenpsychologie*.

Why did he want it to be so? He wanted to establish the safeguarding of a kernel of truth. This is what Freud thought it would be, and this is also how those who have proven to be the products of this conception express themselves in order to draw consideration thereof to themselves, even if they declare this kernel to be modest. Given the point things have reached in present-day opinion, this is comical. To make this apparent, it's enough to indicate what is implied in the sort of guarantor that is known as a school of wisdom. This is what it has always been called. Is this what it is?[1]

As is plainly stated in the very book of patience, of sapience, that the Ecclesiastes is, wisdom is the knowledge of jouissance. Everything that is posited as such is characterized as esotericism, and it may be said that there is no religion, besides the Christian religion, that doesn't *s'en pare*, in the two senses of the word. In all religions, the Buddhist and the Mohammedan, not to mention the others, there is this *parading* and this way of *parrying*, I mean, of marking out the place of this knowledge of jouissance. Need I mention the tantras, for one of these religions, and the Sufis for the other? This is what the pre-Socratic philosophies also authorized for themselves, and it was what Socrates broke with. He replaced it – and we may say nominally – with the relation to the object *a* that is none other than what is called the *soul*.

The operation is illustrated well enough by the partner he is given in the *Symposium* in the guise of the perfectly historical Alcibiades, in other words, in the guise of sexual frenzy, which is the normal culmination of the discourse of the absolute master, if I may say so, which produces nothing but symbolic castration. I remind you of the mutilation of the hermai, which I mentioned in its time when I was using the *Symposium* to spell out transference. From Socrates onwards, this knowledge of jouissance was only to survive on the fringes of civilization, not without thereby feeling what Freud discreetly calls *its discontents*.

Once in a while some crackpot goes bellowing on, falling in with this undermining. It only goes down in history when he's capable of making it heard in the very discourse that produced this knowledge, Christian discourse, to get things perfectly straight, because, make no mistake, it's the heir to Socratic discourse. It's the up-to-date discourse of the master, the latest model of the master, and the young women who are model models are its offspring. I am assured that, within this kind, the one I'm calling *model model*, which now parades under various initials but which invariably starts with an M, they are aplenty.[2] I know because I've been told. Indeed, from where I'm standing, for me to be able to see them, it's not enough just to look at you, because to begin with, they are *pas toutes*, not all, model models.

Clearly this produces an effect when the remark that there has been an undermining – I said that it goes down in history – is proffered by the likes of Nietzsche. I simply note that he can only proffer it – I mean, make himself heard – by voicing it in the only audible discourse, namely the one that determines the up-to-date master as his progeny. Naturally, all these lovely people are delighted by this, but it changes nothing. Everything that has been produced has been part and parcel of it from the start. Of course, the fact that the initials themselves, which were at issue just now, have also been there from the start is only discovered *nachträglich*.

I don't think it will be unhelpful to underscore here that the *pas-tous* has just slid quite naturally to *pas toutes*. That's what it's there for. Today I'm merely showing how all this blather can highlight one movement or another in the emergence of discourse, underscoring how its meaning remains problematic. In particular, it remains problematic on account of what ought not to be heard in what I have just said, namely a sense of history, because, like any other meaning, it only assumes clarity through what comes to pass, and what comes to pass depends only on fortune. This does not mean, however, that it isn't calculable. On what basis? On the basis of the One that is found therein. You mustn't be mistaken, however, as to which One you find. It's never the one you're seeking.

This is why, as I once said in echo of another who was in my situation, *I don't seek, I find*. The way, the only way, to avoid being mistaken is to start from the finding, to question oneself about what was there – if one so wanted – for the seeking.

What is the formula with which, once upon a time, I articulated transference? It was the now famous formula of the *subject supposed to know*. My artefacts of writing demonstrate a pleonasm here. *Subject* may be written with a barred S, which calls to mind how a subject is only ever supposed, ὑποκείμενον.

I only use this redundant form given the deafness of others. It's clear that knowledge is that which is supposed, and no one has ever made any mistake about it. Supposed of whom? Certainly not of the analyst, but of his position. On this point, you can consult my Seminars, because this is what's striking when you reread them. There are no blunders, unlike my *Écrits*.

Yes, that's how it is. It's because I write quickly. I'd never told myself that before, but I noticed it because it so happened that I recently spoke to someone, since the last time that some of you heard me at Sainte-Anne.

2

At Sainte-Anne, I put forward some items on the basis of set theory, which has been drafted in here to call into question the One I was speaking about just now.

I always take my risks, and it can't be said that I didn't this time, with all the necessary humour, by writing *two to the power of Aleph subscript nought minus one*.

$$2^{\aleph_0-1}$$

I think I've sufficiently underscored for you the difference that lies between the subscript 0 and the function of 0 when it is used in an exponential scale. Of course, this doesn't mean that I didn't tickle the sensitivity of any mathematicians who might have been in my audience that evening. What I wanted to say was in the expectation that I might receive some reaction. It was an appeal. What I wanted to say is that, subtract the One, and this entire edifice of numbers – when understood as the product of a logical operation, in particular the operation that proceeds from the position of 0 and the definition of the successor number – would come undone from the entire chain, until it comes back to its starting point.

It's curious that I had to summon someone expressly in order to hear from her lips the legitimacy of what I also uttered last time, namely that this entails not only the One that is produced from nought, but also another that, as such, I marked out as ascertainable in the chain, in passing from one number to another, when it's a matter of counting its parts. It is with this point that I should like to conclude.

Right now, however, I shall content myself with noting that the person who confirmed this to me is the same who, in a dedication that she honoured me with in connection with an article, herself expressed her perception that I wrote quickly. This idea had not occurred to me because what I write, I rewrite ten times. But it's true that the tenth time round, I do write very quickly. This is why blunders remain, because it's a text. A text, as the name indicates, can only be woven by tying knots. When one ties knots, there is something that remains and is left dangling.

I apologize for this. I have only ever written for people who were supposed to have heard me, and when, as an exception, I did write beforehand – a congress report, for example – I only ever gave an address on my report. Have a look at what I said in Rome, for the congress that went by the same name. I wrote the written report that people know about, and it was published in its time. In my written piece, I didn't take up what I said, but you shall certainly be more at ease with what I said than in the report itself. So, those for whom, all told, I carried out this work of logical recovery, which had the Rome Address as its point of departure, as soon as they give up the critical line that results from this work, to return to those beings – whom I show precisely that this address should forgo – and to make them the support of the analysand's discourse, they do no more than go back to chattering. This is why these people who gave the Address a wide berth, no sooner said than done, utterly lost the sense of it.

In peeling away from the line into which I was guiding them, it ensued that they came out with – indeed, what is more, that they even published in cold print – things that showed they no longer knew anything about my *subject supposed to know*. They went so far as to say that to suppose this knowledge in the position of the analyst was quite dreadful because it amounts to saying that the analyst affects a semblance. There is just a small hairline crack in this, which I already pointed out earlier, which is that the analyst does not affect a semblance, he occupies the position of semblance.

The analyst occupies the position of semblance legitimately because there is no other tenable position in relation to jouissance such as he has to grasp it in the remarks of the one who, in the capacity of analysand, is supported by the analyst in his enunciation as a subject. It is from here alone that it may be perceived how far the jouissance of this authorized enunciation can be led without wreaking overly manifest havoc. But semblance does not feed on jouissance. Those who fall back into the discourse of this same old rut would have it that semblance scorns jouissance. This semblance lends its loudhailer to something other than itself, and precisely by showing itself as a mask, one that is openly worn, as on the Greek stage.

Semblance takes effect by being manifest. When an actor wears a mask, he is not pulling a face. He is not a realist. The pathos is reserved for the *chœur*, the choir, who give themselves over to it *à cœur joie*, wholeheartedly. What for? So that the spectator, the spectator of the stage in Antiquity, may find there his own communitarian surplus jouissance. This is indeed what for us constitutes the value of cinema. There, the mask is something else. It is the unreal aspect of the projection. But let's come back to us.

It is in giving voice to something that the analyst can demonstrate that this reference to the Greek stage is opportune. For what is he doing in occupying as such this position of semblance? Nothing other than demonstrating, than being able to demonstrate, that the terror that is felt in relation to the desire by which neurosis is organized, which we call *defence*, is, in regard to what is produced there as a labour of sheer loss, merely a conjuration to arouse pity. At either end of this sentence you can find what Aristotle designated as the effect that tragedy has on the listener.

Where did I say that the knowledge from which this voice originates would be semblance? Need it even appear to be so? Need it even assume an inspired tone? Nothing of the sort. Neither walking the walk nor talking the talk of semblance is suited to the analyst. Yet, there you have it. Since it's clear that this knowledge is not the esoteric aspect of jouissance, nor merely the *savoir faire* of making a face, one must resolve to speak of truth as a fundamental position, even if not all is known about this truth, since I define it by its half-saying, by the fact that it cannot come more than midsay.

But what, then, is the knowledge that is assured by truth? It is nothing but what stems from what is noted as a result of the fact of positing truth on the basis of the signifier. This poise is rather tough to sustain, but is confirmed in yielding a non-initiatory knowledge, because it proceeds – no offence to anyone – from the subject who is subjected as such, by a discourse, to production. This is the subject that mathematicians can be found qualifying as *creative*,[3] specifying that a subject is indeed what is at issue, which corroborates the subject in my logic, exhausting himself to be produced as an effect of the signifier while of course still remaining just as distinct from it as a real number is from a series of which the convergence is assured rationally.

Saying *non-initiatory knowledge* is tantamount to saying *knowledge that is taught by other paths besides the direct paths of jouissance*. These paths are wholly conditioned by the founding failure of sexual jouissance. By that, I mean this whereby the constitutive jouissance of the speaking being is differentiated from sexual jouissance. The efflorescence of this separation and differentiation is certainly brief and limited, and this is why it has been possible to draw up a catalogue thereof, precisely on the basis of the analytic discourse, as an absolutely finite list of drives.

The finitude of this list is concomitant with the impossibility that is demonstrated in the veritable questioning of sexual relation as such. More exactly, it is in the very practice of sexual relation that the link – which as speaking beings we claim lies entirely elsewhere – between the impossible and the real is affirmed. The real is attested to by this alone.

All reality is suspect. It is not to be suspected of being imaginary, as is imputed to me, for in truth it's fairly patent that the imaginary such as it emerges in animal ethology is an articulation of the real. What we have to suspect of any reality is that it might be fantasmatic. And what allows of an escape from this is that an impossibility in the symbolic formula that we are enabled to draw from it demonstrates what is real therein. It is not for nothing that here, to designate the symbolic in question, the word *term* shall be used.

Love, after all, could be taken as the object of a phenomenology. The literary expression of what has been ventured on love is profuse enough for it to be presumed that something may be gleaned from it. Even so, it is curious that, apart from a few authors, Stendhal, Baudelaire, . . . and let's ditch the phenomenology of love in Surrealism, the moralism of which makes us go to pieces – forgive the pun – this literary expression comes up so short that it cannot even be apparent to us. The only thing that would interest us is its strangeness.

While this suffices to designate everything that is set down in this regard in the nineteenth-century novel, the opposite is the case for everything that came before. Look at *L'Astrée*, which for its contemporaries was no small matter. We comprehend so little of what it might have been for these contemporaries that we feel nothing more than boredom on reading it, and thus it is rather difficult for us to constitute this phenomenology. Taking up its inventory, one can only deduce the poverty of what it draws on.

Psychoanalysis went venturing into this quite innocently. Of course, what it encountered at first was not especially cheerful. It has to be acknowledged that it didn't limit itself to this, and what remains of what it initially opened up by way of example is the model of love as furnished by the mother's care of her son. This is also inscribed in the Chinese character *Hǎo*, which means *good*, or *that which is good*.

It is composed of this, which means *son*, *Zǐ* –

And this, which means *woman*, *Nǚ* –

Stretching this out from the daughter who cherishes the senile father, and even up to what I allude to at the end of my *Subversion of the Subject*, namely the miner whose wife gives him a rubdown before he fucks her, is not what will afford any great clarification of sexual relation.

Knowledge about truth is useful for the analyst to the extent that it allows him to widen a little his relation to these subject-effects, which I said he authorizes by leaving the field open to the analysand's discourse. Indeed, that the analyst ought to comprehend the analysand's discourse strikes me as preferable. But as to *whence* he ought to comprehend it, this is a question that doesn't seem to force itself on people's vision in merely noting that he should be occupying the position of semblance in this discourse.

Of course, it needs to be accentuated that he occupies this position of semblance as *a*. The analyst cannot comprehend anything except in respect of what the analysand says, namely in seeing himself not as the cause, but rather as the effect of this discourse, which does not prevent him by rights from recognizing himself therein.

This is why it is advisable for him to have gone through this in his didactic analysis, which can only be dependable when it has not been undertaken under this heading.

3

There is one facet of knowledge about truth that derives its strength from entirely neglecting its content.

This hammers home how the signifying articulation is its time and its place, and it does so to such an extent that something is shown which is nothing but this articulation.

The *monstration* of this articulation, in the passive sense, finds itself assuming an active sense and imposing itself as a *demonstration* to the speaking being who, in this instance, can only acknowledge, for the signifier, not merely inhabiting it but being no more than its mark. The freedom to choose one's axioms, that is to say, the point of departure chosen for this demonstration, consists solely in undergoing its consequences as a subject, consequences that, for their part, are not free.

Truth can be constructed on the sole basis of 0 and 1. This came about only at the start of the last century, somewhere between Boole and De Morgan, with the emergence of mathematical logic.

It should not be thought that 0 and 1 here stand for the opposition between truth and falsehood. This was the revelation by Frege and Cantor, which only assumes its value *nachträglich*. This 0 was said to be falsehood, which encumbered the Stoics for whom it was just that. This led to the charming folly of material implication. Not without reason did some refuse this. It posits that the implication that would be true is the one that makes formulated truth result from formulated falsehood. The falsehood that implies truth is a true implication.

There is nothing of the like in the following position, in mathematical logic –

$$(0 \rightarrow 1) \rightarrow 1$$

That 0 should imply 1 is an implication of 1 – that is, of the true – that can be noted down. For 0 carries just as much veridical truth as 1, because 0 is not the negation of the truth, 1, but the truth of the lack that consists in 1 being missing at 2. This means that, on the plane of truth alone, truth can only speak occasionally to affirm itself, as was done for centuries, as *double truth*, but never as the whole truth.

0 is not the negation of just anything, especially of any multitude. It plays its role in the construction of number. As everyone knows, it is altogether accommodating. Were there only noughts, O how smoothly things would coast along. What it indicates, however, is that when there would have to be two of them, there is only ever one of them, and this is a truth. *That 0 implies 1, the whole implying 1*, is to be taken not as falsehood implying truth, but as two truths, one implying the other. But it can additionally be taken as affirming that the true only ever occurs in missing its mate.

The sole thing to which the 0 is opposed, but resolutely so, is that there could be a relationship with 1 such that 2 would result from it. It is not true – which I will mark with the bar that befits it – that *0 implying 1, implies 2*.

$$\overline{(0 \rightarrow 1) \rightarrow 2}$$

How, then, are we to grasp what is involved in this 2, without which it is quite clear that no number whatsoever can be constructed? I haven't been speaking about numerating them, but about constructing them. It is for precisely this reason that last time I led you as far as the Aleph. It was to give you a sense, in passing, of how in the generation from one cardinal number to another, in the counting of the subsets, something somewhere is counted as such that is another One. I marked this out using Pascal's triangle, noting that each number that, to the right, stands as the number of parts, is made by adding together what corresponds to it as parts in the previous set.

1	1
3	4
3	6
1	4
	1

Counting the subsets

It is this 1, the 1 that I characterized when it was a question of 3, for example, namely *ab* in opposition to *c*, and of *ba* which comes from the same. For there to be 4 of them, to *ab*, to *ba*, and to *ac*, we have to put *abc*, the juxtaposition of the elements from the previous set – their juxtaposition as such – which come into account in the simple capacity of 1.[4] This is what I called the sameness of difference, since it is through no other property but that of their difference that the elements that here support the subsets are themselves counted in the generation of the parts that will ensue.

I insist. It is a question of what is at issue with respect to what has been tallied. It is the *One-to-boot*, in so far as it is counted as such in what has been tallied in the Aleph of its parts with each passage from a number to its successor. In counting difference as such as a property, what does the multiplication that is expressed in the exponential 2^{n-1} of the parts of the higher set, of its bipartition, bear out? What is borne out in the Aleph when put to the test of the denumerable? It is here that it is revealed that, given a One, the One at issue, what is at issue is another One. What is constituted on the basis of 1 and 0 as the inaccessibility of 2 is only delivered at the level of the $\aleph_0$, that is to say, the actual infinite.

To bring this to a close, I'm going to give you a sense of this in a form that is quite straightforward. It has to do with what can be said with respect to what is involved in the integers concerning a property that would be one of accessibility.

Let's define this property as follows – a number is accessible when it can be produced either as a sum or as an exponentiation of numbers that are smaller than it. In this respect, the start of the numbers is confirmed as not being accessible, and very precisely up to 2. This is of interest to us most especially with respect to this 2, because I have underscored sufficiently that in the relation between 1 and 0, the 1 is generated in that 0 is the mark of lack.

With 0 and 1, whether you add them, or raise one to the other, or even to itself, in an exponential relation, 2 is never reached. For the number 2, in the sense I have just set it out, the test as to whether it can generate smaller numbers, whether through a summation or an exponentiation, proves to be negative. There is no 2 that can be generated by means of 1 and 0.

A side-note from Gödel is instructive in this regard, that the $\aleph_0$, the actual infinite, turns out to realize the same case.

Meanwhile, for what is involved in the integers upwards of 2, there is no number that cannot be realized by one of the two operations using smaller numbers. Start with 3. It can be made of 1 and 2. And 4 can be made by raising 2 to its own exponentiation, and so forth.

At the level of $\aleph_0$, the rift that I'm calling inaccessibility is reproduced. There is strictly no number that ever gains access to the Aleph, irrespective of whether one uses a number by adding it to itself indefinitely, or even to each of its successors, or else by raising it to a power however high you like.

It is quite striking – and this is what I must leave aside for today, perhaps to resume it in a smaller circle should this be of interest to some of you – that from Cantor's construction it results that there is no Aleph, starting from $\aleph_0$, that may be held to be accessible. It is no less true that in the opinion of those who have pushed forward this difficulty in set theory, it is only through the supposition that, in these Alephs, there is inaccessibility, that what I shall call *consistency* may be reintroduced into the integers.

In other words, without this supposition of inaccessibility being produced somewhere in the Alephs, what is at issue, and which was my starting point, is what is designed to suggest to you the usefulness of there being Oneness, should you manage to hear what is involved in this bipartition, this one-to-one between man and woman, which slips away from one instant to the next.

Is everything that is not man, woman? This is what tends to be accepted. However, since woman is *not-all*, why would all that is not woman be man?

The fact that in this one-to-one it is impossible to apply, in this matter of gender, something that would be the principle of contradiction, the fact that it takes nothing less than the acceptance of the inaccessibility of something beyond the Aleph for non-contradiction to be consistent, and the fact that it is valid to say that which is not 1 is 0, and that which is not 0 is 1, this is what I am indicating to you as what ought to enable the analyst to hear, a little further than through the spectacle lenses of the object *a*, what is produced by way of effect, what is created by way of One, by a discourse that hinges only upon the grounding of the signifier.

10 May 1972

XIII

THE FOUNDING OF SEXUAL DIFFERENCE

The geniality of strike action
The ancillary position of truth and meaning
Wavering in the sharing-out of the sexes
Theory of hunting
Difference and attribute

Analysis leads us to formulate the function Φx. What is at issue is to find out whether there exists an x that would satisfy this function. So, naturally, this presupposes that we spell out what *existence* might be.

It is fairly certain that, historically speaking, this notion of existence only emerged with the intrusion of the mathematical real as such. This proves nothing, however, because we are not here to set out the history of thought. There can be no history of thought. Thought is, in itself, an evasion. Under the name *mémoire*, it projects the misrecognition of its moire.

This does not prevent us from being able to try to map something out by starting from what I have written down in the form of a function.

1

I started to utter something that I hope will be of service to you. This something is a fact of saying. If I write it down, it goes in one direction, in the sense that it's a function that bears no relation to anything that *fonde d'eux*, that from *eux*, from them, founds One.

You can see that the whole trick is in the subjunctive, which belongs both to the verb *fonder* and to the verb *fondre*.[1] *D'eux* has not founded into One, nor is One founded by *d'eux*. This is what Aristophanes tells in a very nice tale in the *Symposium*. They were cleft in twain, for at first they were shaped as a beast with two backs, or as a beast *à dos d'eux*, with the back of them both. Of course, if the fable were thought in the least to be something other than a fable, that is, to be consistent, on no account would this imply that they should produce offspring with two backs, *à dos d'eux*. No one remarks on this, and fortunately so, because a myth is a myth, and this one says quite enough.

I first envisaged this myth in a more modern form, in the form of Φx. All in all, this is what, concerning sexual relations, presents itself to us as a kind of discourse. I'm speaking about the mathematical function. At the very least, I propose this to you as a model that in this regard would allow us to ground something else – semblance . . . *or worse*.

This morning, I got off to the worse start. In spite of it all, I don't think it will be extraneous to let you know about this, if only to see where it might lead.

It was due to the brief power cut we had. I don't how long it lasted for you, but for me it went on until ten o'clock. It was a royal pain in the arse, because this is the time of day when I usually gather together these little notes and think them over. The power cut didn't help matters. What's more, this same power cut caused someone to smash a tooth mug of which I was particularly fond. If there are people here who love me, they can send me a new one. Then I might have several, which would allow me to smash all of them save the one I might prefer. I have a little courtyard that is there just for that.

So, I told myself that this power cut wasn't the doing of just anyone, but was a workers' decision. For my part, you cannot imagine the respect I have for the geniality of this thing known as a strike, industrial action. What sensitivity, to go no further than that. A strike is the most social thing there is in the whole world. It represents fabulous respect for the social bond. On this occasion, however, this power cut that had the purport of a strike carried a slight overtone.

At that time of day, when I was cooking up what I would be saying to you now, how bothersome it must have been for she who, being the worker's wife, is called, from the lips of the worker himself – despite everything, I do rub shoulders with them – the *bourgeoise*.[2] It's true that this is what they call them.

So, my mind started to wander, because all of this holds together. They are the workers, the exploited, precisely because they still prefer this to the sexual exploitation of the *bourgeoise*. That's worse. It's the . . . *or worse*, you understand?

What does this lead to, laying out articulations concerning things about which one can do nothing? It cannot be said that sexual relation presents itself solely in the form of exploitation. It's prior to that. It's because of this that exploitation is organized, because we don't even have this kind of exploitation. There you go. This is worse. It's the . . . *or worse.*

It's not serious. It's not serious, even though we can see that this is precisely where a discourse that would not be a discourse of semblance ought to be. But it's a discourse that would end badly. It wouldn't be a social bond at all, in the way that a discourse needs to be.

So, now, what is at issue is the psychoanalytic discourse. It's a matter of making sure that he who functions as the *a* in this discourse should hold the position of semblance.

Of course, I explained this to you last time, and naturally it washed over you like water off a duck's back, though in the end some of you did seem to have got a little damp. I've had some feedback. Those of you who took an interest in it were moved by it. There are some psychoanalysts who have something that torments them, that anguishes them every so often.

This is not why I'm saying this, why I'm insisting on the fact that the object *a* should hold the position of semblance. It's not to get them all anxious. I would even prefer them not to have any anxiety. Well, that it should make them anxious is not a bad sign because it means that my discourse is not entirely superfluous, that it can take on a meaning. But this is not enough. That a discourse should have meaning guarantees absolutely nothing, because this meaning has at least to be ascertained. If you do that, well, Brownian motion means that from one instant to the next, it has a meaning. This is precisely what makes the psychoanalyst's position difficult, because the function of the object *a* is displacement.

It wasn't in connection with the psychoanalyst that I first fetched the object *a* down from the heavens. I started to circumscribe it, at a point from which it couldn't budge, in a little graph that was designed to provide the skeleton, or the bearings, of the formations of the unconscious. In the position of semblance, it's not so easy to stay put, because the object *a* will just slip through your paws in two shakes of a lamb's tail. As I explained when I started speaking about this, in connection with language, it's that *il court, il court, le furet*, in everything you say.[3] It is somewhere else from one instant to the next.

This is why we are trying to grasp *whence* something could be situated that would lie beyond meaning, beyond the meaning that also means that I can obtain no other effect but anxiety, when this wasn't remotely my aim. It is in this respect that we are concerned for this real to be anchored.

I say, and not without reason, that this real is mathematical, because given the experience as a whole, the experience of what is at issue, of what gets formulated, of what in this instance gets written, we are able to put our finger on how there is something here that resists. I mean that this is something of which one cannot say just any old thing. One cannot give just any old meaning to the mathematical real.

This is even quite striking among those who, in a recent age, got close to this real with the preconceived idea of making it account for its meaning on the basis of truth. There was one great eccentric, whose reputation you are aware of because he made quite a splash in the world, by the name of Bertrand Russell. He was at the heart of this enterprise, and it was in fact he who said something along the lines of mathematics being something that is articulated in such a way that, in the end, we don't even know if it's true, or if it has a meaning. This doesn't prevent – indeed this proves – the fact that it cannot be given just any meaning or just any truth, and that it resists to the point of culminating in a result, which I consider to be a success. This success, the way in which it imposes its realness, is precisely due to the fact that neither truth nor meaning dominates here. They are secondary.

This ancillary position of these two thingummies called truth and knowledge remained uncustomary for those people. It made their heads spin a bit when they took the trouble to ponder it. This was the case for Bertrand Russell. He was a thinker. It was an aristocrat's fixation, you see. There's really no reason to view this as an essential function.

Yet those who have been constructing set theory – I'm not trying to be wry – have had quite enough to do in this real to find the time to do some thinking on the side.

The way they have committed themselves to a path which not only can they not leave, but which leads somewhere with a necessity, and then with a fecundity to boot, has meant that they have touched on how this has to do with something altogether different from what is nevertheless employed, which was the step taken in the *initium* of this theory.

2

This initial step consisted in examining everything that was involved in this real. This is where they started because they couldn't fail to see that number was the real, and because for some time there had been some exchanging of fisticuffs with the One.

None the less, it was no mean feat to realize that it could be called into question as to whether real numbers had anything to do with the One, the 1, the first of the integers, known as the natural numbers. They'd had time, since the seventeenth century, and up to the beginning of the nineteenth century, to approach number very slightly differently from how they did in Antiquity. If this is my point of departure it's because this is what is essential.

Not only *Yad'lun*, but this can be seen in that the One, for its part, does not think. In particular, it does not think *therefore I am*. I hope you remember that even Descartes doesn't say that. He says, *Ça se pense, It thinks itself, 'therefore I am'*, in inverted commas. The One does not *think itself*, even all alone, but it says something, and this is even what distinguishes it.[4]

The One didn't wait for people to ask in its regard the question of what this means from the standpoint of truth. It didn't even wait for logic. For this is what logic is. Logic is a matter of ascertaining in grammar what takes shape as the position of truth, which in language makes it suitable for forming truth. *Suitable* does not mean that it will invariably succeed. So, in carefully seeking out its forms, one believes one is approaching what is involved in truth. However, before Aristotle became aware of this relation to grammar, the One had already spoken, and not to say just anything. The One says what it has to say. In the *Parmenides*, it is the One that *se dit*, that *says itself*. It *says itself* – it has to be said – in aiming to be true, hence the tizzy that naturally arises from it as a result.

Among those who cook up knowledge, there's not one who hasn't felt this to be quite a smash. It smashes your tooth mug. Even though there are some who put some goodwill into it, some courage, by saying that after all it could be admitted that this is somewhat far-fetched, we haven't yet got to the bottom of this thing that was nevertheless so straightforward, and which consists in realizing that the One, when it is veridical, when it says what it has to say, leads in every case to the total rejection of any relation to Being.

When the One *s'articule*, when it articulates itself, the only thing that arises from it is that *y en a pas deux*.[5] I said so – it's a fact of saying. You can even find in this, in arm's reach, the confirmation of what I've been saying when I say that truth can only go midsay. You just have to break up the wording. In order to say this, it can only say either *y en a*, *there is*, and, as I say, *Yad'lun*, or else, *pas deux*, *not twain*, which for us is immediately interpreted – there is no such thing as sexual relation. So, as you can see, this is already within our arm's reach.

Of course, it's not within reach of the unian arm of the One to make something of it, in the sense of meaning. Indeed, this is why I recommend to those who want to hold the position of analyst – with all that this entails in terms of knowing how not to slip out of this position – that they should get up to speed with what could be read simply by working through the *Parmenides*.

But, all the same, this would come up a bit short. We hit the wall with the *Parmenides*, instead of something else happening, which – if, of course, we persevere a little, if we break ourselves in to it, and even if we break ourselves up on it – makes absolutely clear the distinction that there is between a real that is a mathematical real and anything whatsoever of the banter that starts off from this *je ne sais quoi* that is our queasy position, called *truth* or *meaning*.

This doesn't mean, of course, that this reading will not have an effect, an effect of massage, of reinvigoration, a breath of fresh air, a purging, in connection with what will become apparent to us as a requisite with regard to truth or indeed to meaning. But this is precisely what I expect from it. Training oneself to distinguish what is involved in the One, and relating it to this real which is at issue in that it supports number, will already afford the analyst a great deal. I mean that it may come to him from the angle where it is a matter of interpreting, of regenerating meaning, of saying things which are thereby a little less circumvented, a little less shimmering, than all the damned stupidity that can occur to us.

Earlier I gave you, ... *or worse*, a sample of this on the mere basis of this morning's aggravation. I could have embellished, just like that, on the worker and his *bourgeoise*, and drawn a mythology from it. Besides, it got a laugh out of you, because when it comes to this sort of thing, the field is vast. There is no shortage of meaning and truth. It has even become the academic feeding trough, there is so much of it.

There is such a wide range of it that one day someone will come along to make an ontology out of it, as I told you, an ontology to say that I said that speech was an effect of filling in the open gap that I've been articulating as – *there is no such thing as sexual relation*. That can be rattled off smoothly just like that, a subjectivist interpretation, because it cannot be brought round to the fact that it requires some spiel. It's all quite straightforward.

What I've been trying to do is something different. It's to ensure that in your discourse you include less of this damned stupidity – I'm speaking about the analysts – and, to do so, that you try to air meaning a little with elements that would be somewhat novel.

Yet this is not a requirement that fails to impose itself, because it's quite clear that there is no means of sharing out any two series of attributes – *any*, I say – that would form a male series on one side and on the other the woman series.

To start with, I've avoided saying *man* so as not to lead to any confusion, because I'm going to be elaborating further on this, so as to stay in the worst. Clearly it's tempting, even for me. I amuse myself. And I'm sure to amuse you by showing you the inanity of what is called *active*, if this is what you ground yourselves on to distinguish man from woman.

This is common currency – man, the dear lad, is active. However, in the sexual relation, it seems to me that it's rather the woman who gets a wriggle on. Indeed, you have only to look at the positions that we shall on no account label as primitive, though it's not because they are to be found in the *tiers monde*, in the third world, which is the world of Monsieur Thiers, is it not? It's plain to see that in normal life – and of course I'm not speaking about those blokes from the Gas and Electricity Board, who have taken their distance, who have set on labour, but rather about a life that we shall simply describe as it is, as it is everywhere, except where our great Christian overhaul has occurred – man twiddles his thumbs while woman does the milling, the grinding, the sewing, the errands, and, in those solid civilizations that have not been lost, she still finds the wherewithal to twirl her rump for the exhilarating satisfaction of the chap beside her. I'm speaking about a dance, of course. So, as far as active and passive are concerned, allow me to . . .

It's true that he does go hunting! And this is no laughing matter, my little ones. This is very important.

Since you're goading me, I'm going to carry on amusing myself. It's unfortunate, because this way I shall never get to the end of what I had to say to you today concerning the One. Since this is making you laugh, however, this matter of hunting, I don't know whether it wouldn't be entirely superfluous to see in this precisely man's virtue. When hunting, there is a virtuous display of what is finest about him, namely to be passive.

I don't know if you're aware of this, because of course all of you here are layabouts. There are no country folk here. None of you go hunting. But even if we did have some country folk here, they don't hunt well. For the country folk – they are not necessarily men, whatever one might say – the game is flushed out into the open. Whack, whack! All the game is driven towards them. That's not what hunting is.

You only have to look at the trance that hunting, when it exists, used to put people in. We have some faint traces of everything they used to offer to the thing in propitiation, which nevertheless was a thing that was no longer there. You understand that they were no more doolally than we are. A slain beast is a slain beast. Only, if they managed to slay the beast it was because they had submitted themselves so fully to everything that goes to make up its moves, its trace, its boundaries, its territory, its sexual preoccupations, by having substituted themselves for that which does not belong to all that, for the wide-openness, for the unenclosedness, for the unboundedness, of the beast. We have to say the word – for *life*. And when, after having become this life so fully, they had to take it away, we can understand that they found not only that this was unpleasant, but also that it was dangerous, and that it could happen to them as well.

This might be one of those things that made a few people think, because one can still have a sense of such things. I heard this formulated in a curious way by someone who is inordinately intelligent, a mathematician. He said that it might well be that an organism's nervous system is nothing other than what results from its identifying with its prey. The fellow is extrapolating here, but even so, I'm giving you this because it's stimulating. I'm slipping you the idea, and all the more readily in that it's not mine. It was passed on to me, too. You can make what you will of it, of course. But on this basis one can knock together a new theory of evolution that will be a bit more of a hoot than the previous ones. I'm sure this will stimulate the ontological grey matter.

The same is true of the fisher, and, ultimately, of everything whereby man is woman. Think of the way a fisher rubs the underbelly of the trout beneath its rock. There must be some trout ticklers here. There is every chance of that. They would know what I'm talking about. It's quite something.

In the end, all of this does not afford us, on the subject of active and passive, a clear-cut sharing-out. I won't go on and on, because it suffices to compare each of these customary couples with an attempt at any sort of bisexual sharing-out to arrive at results that are every bit as farcical.

So, then, what might that be?

3

Even so, I do have to clean up my own backyard. I don't see why I shouldn't stick with this, because I'm going to be speaking to you on Thursday, 1 June. Can you imagine that? I'm forced to come back from my few days of holiday so as not to miss Sainte-Anne.

When I say *Yad'lun*, this doesn't mean that there is something of the individual. It seems to me that for many of you this is something you already know, but why not? This is precisely why I've been asking you to embed this *Yad'lun* right where it arises. That is to say, *there is no other existence of the One but mathematical existence.*[6] There is One something. One argument that satisfies a formula. And an argument is something that is completely devoid of meaning. It's simply the One as One.

This is what at the start I had intended to mark out for you in set theory. Perhaps, even so, I shall be able to give some indication of this before taking leave of you.

First, however, we need to put paid to an idea. Even the idea of the individual in no case whatsoever constitutes the One. A number of people imagine that sexual relation is grounded on there being, in principle, as many individuals on one side as on the other, at least for the being who speaks. The number of men and women evens out, save exceptions, slight exceptions I mean – the British Isles, for example, where there are slightly fewer men than women. Large massacres of men also occur. But in the end, this doesn't stop each Jill from having her Jack. Well, their going one-by-one is not remotely sufficient to account for sexual relation.

It's all the same rather odd that there is a kind of impurity here in set theory with respect to this idea of one-to-one correspondence. You can see how the set has its roots in the class and how the class, like everything that is pinpointed with an attribute, is something that has to do with sexual relation. Yet what I am asking you to come to apprehend thanks to the function of the set is that there is a One that is distinct from what unifies a class as an attribute.

There is a transition through the intermediary of this one-to-one correspondence. There are as many on one side as on the other, and some people ground the idea of monogamy on this. One wonders why this is tenable, but in the end it's in the Gospel. There are as many on either side until a social catastrophe happens, which is what apparently occurred midway though the Middle Ages in Germany. It seems they were able to decree at that time that sexual relation would not have to be bi-univocal.

It's fairly amusing that people posed themselves the problem as such of the sex ratio, namely *are there as many males as there are females?*

There was a literature on this that has great zest, because all in all the problem is one that is most frequently resolved by what we shall call chromosomal selection. The most frequent case is clearly the sharing-out of two sexes into a quantity of individuals reproduced in equal number in either sex. But it's really very nice that they should have asked the question of what might happen should a skew start to occur. It is very easy to demonstrate that in some cases of such skewing, it can only grow, if we stick with chromosomal selection. We won't say that this is random, because what is at issue is a sharing-out. However, the altogether elegant solution they found was that this must be compensated for by natural selection.

Here we can see natural selection for what it is. It may be summarized by saying that the strongest are necessarily the fewest, and since they are the stronger, they thrive, and so they become as numerous as the others. The connection between this idea of natural selection and sexual relation is one of those cases in which it is clearly shown that the risk one runs whenever one tackles sexual relation is that one remains at the level of quips. Indeed, everything that has been said about it is of this order.

It is important that one should be able to voice something other than what gives rise to laughter because we are striving, in order to ensure the position of the analyst, for something different from what it appears to be in many cases, namely a gag.

In set theory, the starting point can be read in the function of membership. To be an element of a set is to be something that has no business belonging to a register that could be qualified as universal, that is to say, to something that falls within the scope of the attribute. What set theory attempts is to dissociate, to disarticulate, in a definitive fashion, the predicate from the attribute.

Prior to this theory, what characterized the notion in question in what is involved in the sexual type, inasmuch as this type might prefigure something of a relation, was precisely that the universal should be grounded on a common attribute. Moreover, there is a faint prefiguration here of the logical distinction between attribute and subject, and on this basis the subject is grounded. It is through this that something that is distinct can be called *attribute*.

From this distinction of the attribute there quite naturally results the following – you do not put in one same whole both apples and oranges, for example. In contrast to this category that is called *class*, there is the category of *set*, in which not only are apple and orange compatible, but in a set as such of each of these two kinds, there can be only one. In a set, if there is nothing to distinguish one apple from another, there can only be *one* apple, just as there can only be *one* orange. The One qua pure difference is what distinguishes the notion of the element. The One qua attribute is thus distinct from this.

The difference between the One of difference and the One attribute is that when you make use of the latter to define a class, in any attributive statement the attribute will not be supernumerary in the definition.

If you say *man is good*, positing that *man is good* does not rule out your having to account for how man does not always correspond to this appellation. Who is not compelled to say such a thing? Besides, plenty of reasons are invariably found to show that man is capable of not corresponding to this attribute, of evincing a failure to fulfil it. This is the theory that has been made, and with all the range of meaning you have at your disposal to contend with it, you set about explicating how, though once in a while he can admittedly be *bad*, this changes nothing about his attribute. You could then tot up the balance from the standpoint of number by asking how many of them hold to this attribute and how many do not correspond to it. It's still the case that the attribute *good* will not come into the balance on top of each of the good men.

This is very precisely the difference compared with the One of difference. When it comes to articulating its consequence, this One of difference has to be counted as such in what is stated about what it grounds, which is a set and which has parts. Not only is the One of difference countable, but also it must be counted among the parts of the set.

My time is up. Indeed, it's now two. Therefore, I can only indicate what the next part will be to what, as usual, I'm having to cut off, more or less any old how, due precisely to another cut, this morning's power cut, with the consequences it had.

So, I'm led to give you a mere indication of what I will be picking up from the following pivotal affirmation.

It has to do with the relation that this One, which has to be counted on top of the rest, bears to what is specified – in what I describe not as a stand-in, but as being deployed in a locus *in the stead of sexual relation* – as *There exists*, not Φx, but the fact of saying that this Φx is not the truth.

$$\exists x.\overline{\Phi x}$$

It is from here that arises the One that means that this formula has to be put on the side of what founds man as such. And this is the only characteristic element.

Does this mean that this founding specifies him sexually? This is very precisely what is going to be called into question in what comes next, because it is still no less the case that the relation Φx is what defines man, attributively this time, as *all man*.

$$\forall x.\Phi x$$

What is this *tout*, or this *tous*? What is this *all men* inasmuch as it founds one side of the articulation of supplementation?

This question of what a *tous* is needs to be entirely posed anew on the basis of the function that is articulated as *Yad'lun*.

17 May 1972

XIV

THEORY OF THE FOUR FORMULAE

A TALK AT SAINTE-ANNE

The analyst's relation to knowledge
Freethinkers in the Vatican
Thinking only by means of the One
The modalities of the formulae
The family wowed by the father is a thing of the past

You know that here I say what I think. It's a feminine position, because all things considered, thinking is highly peculiar. So, since I write to you once in a while, I've set down in writing, during a short trip I've just taken, a number of propositions. The first of these is that it has to be acknowledged that the discourse that conditions the psychoanalyst puts him in a position that is, let's say, difficult. Freud said *impossible, unmöglich*. That's perhaps pushing it a bit. He was speaking for himself.

Second proposition. However little practised he may be in psychoanalysis, the psychoanalyst knows from his experience that he bears a common measure with what I've been saying. This is quite independent of whether he might be informed of what I've been saying, because what I've been saying culminates in locating his knowledge. This is the matter of knowledge about truth.

$$\frac{a \longrightarrow \text{\$}}{S_2 \qquad S_1} \qquad \frac{\text{semblance} \longrightarrow \text{jouissance}}{\text{truth} \qquad \text{surplus jouissance}}$$

$$\text{Terms} \qquad\qquad\qquad \text{Places}$$

The place of truth is on the bottom left. On the top left is the place of semblance. On the top right is the place of jouissance. On the bottom right is the place of surplus jouissance, which I'm writing in an abbreviated form as + *de-jouir*. For jouissance, we shall put a capital J.

What is difficult is the psychoanalyst's relation to knowledge, and not, of course, his relation to what I've been saying, because across the psychoanalytic no-man's-land as a whole they don't know that I've been saying this. It doesn't mean that they don't know anything about what I've been saying, because it comes from experience, but they abhor what they know about it.

I can say quite simply that I comprehend them. *I can say* means *I can say, if pressed.* I comprehend them. I can put myself in their place, and all the more easily in that this is where I am. I comprehend it all the more easily in that, like everyone else, I hear what I say. Nevertheless, this doesn't happen to me every day, because I don't speak every day. In reality, I hear what I say during those few days, say one or two, that come just before my Seminar, because that's the time when I start writing to you. On the other days I'm inundated with the thought of those I've been attending to. I have to confess this because right now I'm dominated by the restlessness of what in *Scilicet* I called my *failure*. That's what I called it, and I can still call it that, because seldom do I backtrack. There you have it.

Indeed, they know. I'm calling this to mind because the title of what I'm dealing with here is *Le Savoir du psychanalyste*. In this case, *du* connotes *le*, the definite article in French. Well, it's what is known as *definite*. Why not *des psychanalystes*, after what I've just told you? This would be in closer conformity with my theme this year, that is to say, *Yad'lun*. There are some who say they are such. I'm that much less inclined to dispute their saying so given that there are no others. Why am I saying *du*? Because I'm speaking to them, despite the presence here of a very large number of people who are not psychoanalysts.

The psychoanalyst, then, knows what I've been saying.

As I said, they know it from experience, however little they may have, even if this is restricted to the didactic aspect which is the minimum requirement for psychoanalysts to say they are such. Even if they miss out on what I've called *the Pass*, it will be restricted to their having had a didactic psychoanalysis, but at the end of the day this is enough for them to know what I've been saying. When I say that the Pass has been missed out on – all of this is also in *Scilicet*, which is the appropriate place – it doesn't mean that they haven't gone forward for the experience of the Pass. As I have often underscored, the experience of the Pass is simply what I've been proposing to those who are dedicated enough to expose themselves to it, with the sole purpose of affording information on a very delicate point, which is affirmed in the most certain fashion, namely that it's altogether a-nomalous – object *a-nomalous* – that someone who has been through a psychoanalysis should want to be a psychoanalyst. This really requires a sort of aberration, which it was worthwhile taking the trouble to offer up to all that might be gathered by way of testimony. This is precisely why I set up this trial run, on a provisional basis, so as to know why someone who knows what psychoanalysis is, through didactic analysis, can still want to be an analyst.

I won't say any more about what is involved in the psycho-analysts' position, simply because I chose *The Psychoanalyst's Knowledge* as the title I would propose for my return to Sainte-Anne this year. On no account is this designed to make things easy for the psychoanalysts. They have no need of me when it comes to feeling the vertigo of their position, but I'm not about to intensify it by telling them so. Something that could be done – and perhaps I will do so on another occasion, with zest, using a reference that I shall only call *historical* in inverted commas – is to speak about the word *temptation*. I'm saying this for the wily ones.

Here, I'm going to speak only of knowledge, and I note that it's not a matter of the truth about knowledge, but of knowledge about truth. Knowledge about truth is articulated by means of the touch that I've been putting forward this year in connection with *Yad'lun*. *Yad'lun* and nothing more. It's an altogether particular One, the same that separates 1 from 2, and it's a gulf. I repeat, truth only comes midsay. When the free time is over, which will allow me to respect the alternation, I will speak about the other facet, that of the *mi-vrai*, the half-true. One ought always to *séparer le bon grain et la mivrai*, to winnow the wheat from the half-true.[1]

I've just got back from Italy, where I can never be anything but pleased with the welcome I receive, even from my psychoanalyst colleagues. Through one of them I met a third, who is quite up to speed – to my speed, anyway. He has been using Dedekind, and he came across it quite without my influence. I can't say that at the date he first got down to it I wasn't on to it already, but in the end the fact is that I spoke about it much later than he did, because I'm only speaking about it now whereas he'd already written a piece on it. In sum, he realized the value that mathematical elements could possess when it comes to making something emerge that genuinely concerns our experience as analysts.

As he is very highly thought of – he did everything it took for that – he managed to make himself heard in the upper echelons of what is called the IPA. I would translate it as the *Institution psy-chanalytique avouée*, the Avowed Psychoanalytic Institution. He managed to make himself heard, but what is most curious is that they wouldn't publish his piece. They declined to publish, saying – *you do understand, no one will understand.* I must say that this comes as a surprise to me, because they're always so eager to fill the *International Journal* with a bit of Lacan, in inverted commas, and other items in the same vein that I'm supposed to represent for the botchers of a certain linguistics. Naturally, the more stuff there is in the bin, the less of it can be discerned. So, why the devil did they think they should stymie this case? As far as I am concerned, this is a stymie, and saying that the readers wouldn't understand is secondary. It's not necessary for all the articles in the *International Journal* to be understood. There's something in it, therefore, that they don't take kindly to.

Since the fellow I just mentioned – I haven't said his name, because you're utterly unfamiliar with his name given that he still hasn't managed to publish anything – is perfectly identifiable, I don't despair of seeing him published in the wake of what will filter through of today's remarks, especially if they find out that I haven't said his name. It seems that his heart is sufficiently set on this for me to help him quite willingly in this matter. Should it fail to appear, I'll speak about it a little more.

So, the psychoanalyst has a complex relationship with what he knows. He renounces it, he represses it – to employ the term that is used in English to translate *refoulement, Verdrängung* – and it can even happen that he may not want to know anything about it. And why not? What could this confound? Psychoanalysis, you will tell me. In this I hear the blather of someone who has not the faintest idea about psychoanalysis. In response to what might arise from this floor, I reply – is it knowledge that cures, whether the subject's knowledge or the knowledge that is supposed in the transference, or is it transference, such as it is produced in any given analysis? Why should knowledge – the knowledge which I say every psychoanalyst possesses a dimension of – be *avowed*, as I put it earlier?

It was from this question that Freud took *Verwerfung*. He calls it *a judgement which,* in choosing, *rejects.* He adds, *which condemns,* but I'm abridging. Just because *Verwerfung* makes a subject go mad when it is produced in the unconscious, this doesn't mean that the very same, and under the very same name, which Freud borrowed, doesn't rule the world as a rationally justified power.

Psychoanalysts in the plural, in contradistinction to *the* psychoanalyst, are the preference, the self-preference, you see. They're not the only ones. There is a tradition of this – the medical tradition. When it comes to self-preference, no one's ever done any better, except the saints. S-A-I-N-T-S. I'm spelling it out because people go on so much about the others.[2] The saints also exercise self-preference. They think only of that. They are consumed by finding the best way for self-preference, when there are such simple ways, as shown by the *méde-saints*, too. Well, the *médecins*, the doctors, are not saints. This goes without saying. Few things are so abject to leaf through as the history of medicine. It could be recommended as a purgative or an emetic. It works as both. When it comes to knowing that knowledge has nothing to do with truth, there is really nothing more convincing. It might even be said that this goes so far as to turn the doctor into a sort of provocateur. This doesn't mean that the doctors didn't see to it that psychoanalysis would be brought to their heel, and for reasons that had to do with how the platform that the doctors shared with the discourse of science was becoming more confined. They were dab hands at this, and all the more so given that the psychoanalyst, who was in a terrible bind with his position, felt that much more disposed to receive counsel from experience. A purposeful article by Freud, on *Laienanalyse*, took a stand against this plotting.

I insist on underscoring this point in history, which was an altogether key moment as far as my affair is concerned. Due to the plotting that happened shortly after the war, I had lost the match before even making my first move. I declare, however, that it was very precisely on account of knowing full well at the time that I had lost the match that I made my move. I'm bearing witness this evening, and I'd like you to believe me on this matter. It's no accident that I'm doing so at Sainte-Anne because I told you that here I say what I think. A whole load of matches get played out in such conditions. There's nothing heroic about it. It's even one of the fundaments of what they call the human condition, and it doesn't come off any worse than any other enterprise. The proof is right here. The only drawback – though not for me alone – is that it doesn't afford you much liberty. I say this with a passing thought for the person who questioned me on whether or not I believed in freedom.

When I say I'd noticed perfectly well that the match was lost, I ask you to believe me. After all, I wasn't so shrewd. Perhaps I thought I should plough into it, and that I could mess up the Avowed Psychoanalytic International. But I have another declaration to make, and this time no one can dispute what I'm about to say. It's that I never dropped any of the people I knew were going to leave me, before they left of their own accord. And this is true also of the period to which I alluded a moment ago, when the match was lost for France, the little brouhaha amid the plotting by the medically qualified psychoanalysts, which gave rise to the start of my teaching in 1953.

On those days when I don't harbour the idea of pursuing this teaching, that is to say a certain many, needless to say I get the idea, like any imbecile, of what it might have been for French psychoanalysis if I had been able to teach where, for the reason I've just mentioned, I wasn't remotely disposed to let anyone drop. I mean that however scandalous were my propositions on the *Function and Field . . .* and yackety-yak . . . *of Speech and Language*, I was minded to smooth out the wrinkles even for the hardest of hearing, and, at the point we've now reached, no one among the psychoanalysts would have lost out.

By the way, someone sent me a tooth mug. I'm saying this for those who were up at the Panthéon last time. I'd like to know who it was, in order to thank them. I'd like to thank them all the more extensively given that it's not a tooth mug. It's a marvellous little red glass, tall and curved, in which I shall place a rose, whoever it was who sent me it. But I only received one, I have to say. Anyway, let's move on.

I told you that I'd made a little tour of Italy. There are people who like me a bit in practically every corner, even in the wings of the Vatican. Why not, after all? There are some great people there. For the person who questioned me about freedom, I shall say that the only freethinkers I know are in the Vatican. For my part, I'm no freethinker. I'm forced to stick to what I've been saying, but over there in the Vatican, what ease they have! You can understand how the French Revolution was helped along by the abbots. If you knew what liberty they have, my dear friends, it would send a shiver down your spine. I try to bring them back to the hard line, but there's no way. They outflank me. For them, psychoanalysis is old hat. You can see what use freethinking has. They're clear-sighted.

Yet it was a good profession, don't you think? It had a good side. When they say that it's old hat, they know what they're talking about. They're saying, *It's shot, because one really ought to do a bit better*. I'm saying this to forewarn those people who are not behind the times, and particularly of course those who follow me, that you should have a second think before getting your descendants involved, because it's quite possible that, given the way things are going, it will come to a sudden stop. Well, this is just for those who would get their descendants involved. I advise them to be prudent.

I've already spoken about what is happening in psychoanalysis. Some points that I've already broached really need to be specified, and consequently, now that we've come this far, I think I can look briefly at the discourse of the analyst. It's the only discourse among the four that I have catalogued – and in this we may pay homage to it – that is such that knavery necessarily culminates in foolery.[3] If you were to know straightaway that someone who comes to ask you for a didactic analysis is a knave, you would tell him – *No psychoanalysis for you, dear fellow, you'll become simplicity itself.* But you cannot know this. It's carefully dissimulated. One does come to know, however, after a certain while of psychoanalysis. Knavery is not hereditary. It's not a matter of heredity, but rather of the desire, the desire of the Other, from which the one in question has arisen. It's not always his parents' desire. It might be his grandparents' desire. But if the desire from which he was born is the desire of a knave, then he is inevitably a knave. I've never seen an exception to this. This is even why I have always been so tender with the people I knew would leave me, at least in those cases where I was the one who had psychoanalysed them, because I knew they had become utter fools.

I can't say I did this on purpose. As I've told you, it's necessary. It's necessary when a psychoanalysis is pushed to the end, which is the least that ought to be done for a didactic analysis. If the analysis is not didactic, then it's a question of tact. You have to leave the fellow enough knavery for him thereafter to fend decently for himself. This is therapeutic in the proper sense. You should let him stay afloat. But for didactic psychoanalysis, you can't do that, because goodness knows what that would lead to. Imagine a psychoanalyst who has remained a knave. This haunts everyone's thoughts. Rest assured, contrary to what one might believe, psychoanalysis is always didactic in the true sense, even when practised by a fool, and, I would even say, all the more so in such cases. Anyway, the only risk is to have foolish psychoanalysts. As I've just told you, however, at the end of the day there are no drawbacks, because the object *a* in the place of semblance is a position that can be held. People can also be fools to begin with. It's very important to distinguish between the two.

As for me, I have found no better than what I've been calling *matheme* to approach something that concerns knowledge about truth, because all in all it's in psychoanalysis that we have managed to give it a functional scope.

It's far better when Peirce deals with it. He sets down the functions 0 and 1 to designate the two truth values. On the other hand, he doesn't imagine that one can write capital T or capital F for *True* and *False*. Up at the Panthéon, I've already indicated in a few sentences that there are two stages in relation to *Yad'lun*. There is the *Parmenides* and, then, set theory. They had to get to set theory in order to pose the question of a knowledge that takes truth as a mere function, which is far from contenting itself with this, and which also entails a real that has nothing to do with truth. None the less, we have to believe that for centuries mathematics bypassed any question of this because it was only late in the day, and through the intermediary of a logical examination, that it led a step to be taken towards this question, which is crucial for what is involved in truth, namely how and why *Yad'lun*.

You will excuse me. I'm not alone in this.

Around this One revolves the question of existence. I've already made some remarks in this regard, namely that existence had never been tackled as such before a certain age, and that it took a long while to extract it from essence. I've spoken of the fact that, strictly speaking, there is nothing in Greek that would commonly mean *to exist*. Not that I'm unaware of ἐξίστημι, ἐξίσταμαι, but rather that I observe that no philosopher ever made use of it. Yet this is where something gets under way that might interest us. It's a matter of knowing what exists. *Il n'existe que de l'Un*. There is no existence but on the basis of the One.

Set theory is the examination of why *Yad'lun*. Whatever you may think, the One is not a dime a dozen, including the utterly illusory certitude, which has long been such – this doesn't stop people from holding to it – that you are One of them as well. You just have to raise your little finger to perceive that not only are you not One, but that you are, alas, innumerable. You are each innumerable for yourself. You are innumerable right up to the point that you will be taught – which might be one of the good results of the psycho-analytic contribution – that you are, depending on the case, either quite *finis*,[4] for the men, it's clear, you are *finis, finis, finis*, or, for the women, denumerable. I'm saying this rather briskly because I don't know for how much longer I'll be able to carry on. I shall try briefly to explain to you something that is starting to clear a path for you, because of course this is not one of those things that is blindingly obvious, especially when you don't know what *finite* and *denumerable* mean. However, if you follow my indications a little, you will read anything and everything, because this abounds in all the books on set theory these days, even to take an opposing stance.

There is a certain someone who is very kind, whom I hope to see later in order to apologize for not having brought back a book that I did everything I could to find, and which is out of print. He passed it on to me last time, and it's called *Cantor a tort*. It's a very good book. It's clear that Cantor *a tort*, that Cantor is wrong, from a certain standpoint, but he is incontestably right for the simple fact that what he put forward has given rise to innumerable descendants in mathematics. It all comes down to whatever allows mathematics to advance. This is enough for it to stand up for itself.

Even if Cantor is wrong from the standpoint of those who have claimed – we don't know why – that they know what number is, the entire history of mathematics, well before Cantor, demonstrated that there is no place where it is more true that the impossible is the real.[5] This began with the Pythagoreans, who one day were struck by the patent fact – which they must have known full well because they should not be taken for infants either – that the square root of 2 is not commensurable. This was taken up by the philosophers. However, just because this has come down to us by way of the *Theaetetus*, it shouldn't be thought that the mathematicians of the time were not up to it, or incapable of responding. Indeed, having realized that the incommensurable existed, they started to pose the question of what number is.

I'm not going to go over the whole history. There is a certain business of the square root of minus one, which has since been labelled – we don't know why – *imaginary*. There is nothing less imaginary than the square root of minus one, as was proved by what came in the wake of its discovery, because this is where what are called *complex numbers* emerged from. Complex numbers are among the most useful and productive things that have ever been created in mathematics. In short, the more objections that are levelled at what is involved in this entry via the One, that is, via the integer, the more it is demonstrated that the real is generated in mathematics precisely from the impossible. It is precisely in so far as something was able to be generated by way of Cantor, which was nothing less than Russell's entire life's work, and indeed infinitely many other points that have been extremely productive in function theory, that it is quite certain that, with regard to the real, Cantor is the one who is wholly on track in what is at issue.

If I'm suggesting to you, the psychoanalysts, to get a bit up to speed with this, it's because there is something to be got from it, in your guilty pleasures, of course. I'm saying this because I'm dealing with beings who ponder – who ponder, of course, because they can't do otherwise – who ponder, like Telemachus, or at least like the Telemachus described by Paul-Jean Toulet, who *pense à la dépense*. They ponder expending. Well, it's a matter of knowing whether you analysts, and those whom you steer, spend your time in vain or not.

In this regard, the pathos of pondering, which for you may result from a short initiation in set theory – though it shouldn't be too brief – is of such a nature as to make you reflect about notions like existence, for example. It's clear that only once there had been a certain reflection on mathematics did existence take on its meaning. Everything that had previously been said about it, through a sort of presentiment, in particular a religious presentiment, namely that

God exists, strictly speaking only holds meaning in that it lays the accent on the following point – I have to *mettre l'accent*, to lay the accent, because there are people who take me for a *maître à penser* – whether you're a believer or not, bear the following in mind. With God, you have to count. I don't believe in Him, but no one gives a stuff. For those who do believe it's the same thing. Whether you believe in Him or not, it's absolutely unavoidable.

This is why I'm writing once again on the blackboard the formulae around which I've tried to make what is involved in what is claimed to be sexual relation revolve.

$$\exists x.\overline{\Phi x} \qquad\qquad\qquad \overline{\exists x}.\overline{\Phi x}$$

$$\forall x.\Phi x \qquad\qquad\qquad \overline{\forall x}.\Phi x$$

Here, $\exists x.\overline{\Phi x}$ means there exists an x determined by having said no to the phallic function. The phallic function dominates sexual relation. I write it Φx. You can already see the question of existence being linked to something that we cannot fail to recognize as a fact of saying. It's a *saying no*, and even, I would say, a *naysaying*. This is crucial. It is what indicates for us, for our analytic training, the exact point at which we must take up what is stated by set theory – *there is at-least-one who naysays*.

This is a marker.[6] But it's a marker that doesn't hold up even for an instant, that is neither instructive nor teachable, if we do not conjoin it to another quantifier that is set down within the four terms, namely the quantifier that is said to be universal.

Thus, $\forall x.\Phi x$ is the point from which it may be said, as is stated in Freudian doctrine, that the only desire, the only libido – it's the same thing – is masculine. In truth, this is an error, but it is still the case that it's an error that has all its worth as a marker.

Next, $\overline{\exists x}.\Phi x$ means that no x exists to say that it is not true that the phallic function is what dominates sexual relation.

Meanwhile, at a level that is complementary to these three terms, we ought to write – I'm not saying that we *can* write – $\overline{\forall x}.\Phi x$, the function of *pas-tout, not-all*, as the function that is essential to a certain type of relation to the phallic function, inasmuch as the latter founds sexual relation.

This is what turns these four inscriptions into a set. Without this set, it is impossible to orient oneself correctly in what is at issue in the practice of analysis, inasmuch as it has to do with something that is commonly defined as *man*, on the one hand, while on the other the corresponding term is generally qualified as *woman*, which leaves it on its own.[7] If it is left on its own, this is not the fault of the corresponding term. It's the fault of man.

However, fault or no fault, this is not a matter that we should settle immediately. I shall say in passing that what we need to examine for the time being is the meaning that these four functions might have inasmuch as their quantic coupling diversifies them. For the four are merely two, one being the negation of the function and the other the opposite function.

It is clear that what is meant by $\exists x.\overline{\Phi x}$ reaches far enough back to the origin for it to be said that Freud's ignorance of it is utterly confounding. This $\exists x$ negation of Φx, this *at-least-one*, this One all alone,[8] which is determined as the effect of naysaying the phallic function, is very precisely the corner beneath which we need to place everything that has so far been said about *Totem and Taboo*, so that it can be something other than a myth.[9]

This holds all the more interest in that it is not a matter of genesis, nor of history, nor of anything whatsoever that might resemble an event, even though this is what Freud seems to have called it at some moments. It could not be an event in that it is represented for us as standing prior to all history. There is only an event when connoted as such in something that is stated. It's a matter of structure. The myth of *Totem and Taboo* is designed in the most patent fashion so that one may speak of *tout homme*, of man one and all, as being subject to castration.

Is it really necessary to start reverting to mytheme-atical functions to set out a logical fact? Namely that, if it is true that the unconscious is structured like a language, then the function of castration is necessitated by it. Indeed, this is exactly what is implied by something eluding it. And whatever it is that eludes it is not inevitably something human. Why should it be? This is in the myth. Why not see the father of the primal murder as an orang-utan? A number of items coincide in this regard in the Judaic tradition, from which, all the same, it has to be said that psychoanalysis arose. The year when I didn't care to deliver more than the first session of my Seminar on the Names-of-the-Father, I still had time to accentuate that in

Abraham's sacrifice, what is sacrificed is effectively the father, which is none other than a ram. As in any self-respecting human lineage, its mythical descent is animal.

All things considered, what is at issue is what I said to you the other day about the function of hunting in man. I could have told you more about the fact that the hunter loves his quarry, just like the sons in the said primordial event in the Freudian mythology who kill the father, like those you can see traces of in the Lascaux caves. They killed him, my goodness, because they loved him, of course, as the ensuing part proved. The ensuing part is woeful. The ensuing part is very precisely that all the men, $\forall x$, the universality of men, is subject to castration.

At the point from which we are speaking, we shall not call the fact that there is an exception *mythical*. This exception is the inclusive function. What is to be stated of the universal, besides that the universal is enclosed by negative possibility? More exactly, existence here plays the role of the complement, or to speak more mathematically, of the boundary. Thus, somewhere there is an *all x*. This *all x* becomes the upside-down A of $\forall$ whenever it is embodied in what may be called *One Being*, one being at least that posits itself as Being, and specifically in the capacity of man.

This is very precisely what means that it is in the other column, and with a type of relation that is fundamental, that something may be articulated – for anyone who knows how to think with these symbols – in the capacity of woman. Simply by articulating it thus, $\overline{\exists x}.\overline{\Phi x}$, it gives us a sense of how there is something remarkable, remarkable for you, in what is thereby stated, namely that in the statement that it is not true that the phallic function dominates what is involved in sexual relation, there is not one who would take exception to it. To allow you to find your way here by means of references that will be a little more familiar to you, I shall say, my goodness, since I spoke earlier of the Father, that this *There does not exist any x that is determined as a subject in the statement of naysaying the phallic function*, concerns the virgin, properly speaking. You know that Freud reports on the taboo of virginity, and other outlandishly folkloric stories about this business, and the fact that in times gone by the virgins were not to be fucked by just anyone. It had to be a high priest or a local lord. Anyway, no matter. This is not the important thing.

What is important is what we may say in connection with this function of the *vir*, which is so striking in that, at the end of the day, people only ever say of a woman that she is virile.[10] Should you have ever heard anyone say of a guy that he is virile, you will point him out to me. It would be of interest to me. Here, however, while the man is anything you please of this sort, a *vir*-tuoso, *vir*-ing to the portside, make ready to *vir*, *vir* whatever you like, the virile is on the side of woman.[11] She's the only one who believes in it. She thinks. This is even what characterizes her. In a short while I'm going to explain to you in detail why the *virgo* is not denumerable. It's because she is located between the 1 and the 0, contrary to the One which is on the side of the Father. It is well known that what lies between 0 and 1, even when one *a tort*, when one is wrong, is demonstrated in Cantor's theory, and in a way that I find absolutely marvellous.

There are at least a few people here who know what I'm talking about, such that I shall give a brief indication of it. What lies between 1 and 0 is altogether demonstrable. It can be demonstrated with decimals. We use decimals in the system that goes by the same name. Let's suppose – you have to suppose – that this system is denumerable. The method known as the Diagonal Method can allow you always to forge a new decimal sequence such that it is certainly not inscribed in what has been numerated. It is strictly impossible to construct this denumerable, to provide even a way, however meagre, of lining it up, which is the most straightforward operation because the denumerable is defined by its correspondence with the sequence of integers.

We begin, therefore, with a pure and simple *let's suppose*. In this respect, we will quite readily accuse Cantor, as is done in the book *Cantor a tort*, of having quite simply forged a vicious circle. A vicious circle, my good friends, but why not! The more vicious a circle is, the more fun it is, especially if you can get something to emerge from it, something like this little bird called the non-denumerable, which is one of the most pre-eminent and one of the most ingenious things ever invented, and which tallies most closely with the real of number. Well, let's move on. *The 11,000 virgins*, as is said in the *Legenda aurea*, is the way to express the non-denumerable, because 11,000 is an enormous figure for virgins, and not only in this day and age.

Having pointed up these facts, let's try now to understand what becomes of this *pas-toute*, this *not-all* [in the feminine], which is truly the vital point, the original point, in what I have written up on the blackboard, because until now the function of the *pas-tous* has never been put forward as such in logic.

In so far as the pattern of thinking is, so to speak, undermined by the lack of sexual relation, we think only by means of the One. The universal is something that results from the envelopment of a certain field by something of the order of One, with the proviso that the veritable signification of *set* is precisely that it is the mathematical notation of this something in which, alas, I am not without responsibility, which is a certain definition that I have noted as barred S. This barred S is the subject, the subject inasmuch as it is nothing other than the effect of the signifier. In other words, it is what is represented by a signifier for another signifier. Some fellows – who were the least equipped to bring to light what is involved in the subject – found themselves, at a certain turning point in history, *necessitated*, as it were, in this respect. The set is nothing other than the subject. This is precisely why it cannot even be handled without the addition of the empty set.

I would say that up to a certain point the empty set is differentiated in its necessity in that it can be taken for an element of the set. Without inscribing the brackets that designate the set that has the empty set as its element, $\{\varnothing\}$, any handling of this function is absolutely unthinkable. I believe I've already indicated this sufficiently, but I will repeat that this function was devised very precisely at a certain turning point in order to examine, from the logical standpoint, but at the level of *common* language – the language of everybody, because on no account does *meta*language govern here – what is involved in the impact of number in language itself. Number is something that has nothing to do with language. Number is more real than anything, and the discourse of science has amply revealed this.

The *pas-tout*, *not-all*, is very precisely what results from the fact, not that nothing bounds it, but that the bound is located in a different way. To go quickly, I will say that contrary to the inclusion in $\exists x.\overline{\Phi x}$ – namely, there exists the Father whose saying no situates him in relation to the phallic function – it is in so far as there is the void, the lack, the absence of anything whatsoever that denies the phallic function at the level of woman that, conversely, there is nothing but this something that the *not-all* formulates in woman's position with regard to the phallic function. For her, this function is, in effect, *pas-toute*, *not-all*. This doesn't mean that she negates this function, in any capacity whatsoever.

I won't say that she is Other, because the mode whereby she does not exist in this function, which is very precisely the mode of negating it, is that she is the same as what is inscribed on my graph by the signifier of the Other as barred, S(Ⱥ). Woman is not the locus of the Other. More to the point, she is inscribed as *not being the Other* in the function that I give to the capital A, namely the locus of truth. Just as I translated here, in $\exists x.\overline{\Phi x}$, the existence of the naysaying using the function of the empty set, what is inscribed here, in $\overline{\exists x}.\Phi x$, in the non-existence of what might negate the phallic function, is the fact of absenting oneself, and even of being this *jouis-centre*. This *jouis-centre* is conjugated to what I shall call, not an absence, but a *de-sense-cy*. Woman is posited for the signifying fact, not only that the big Other is not here – since it's not her – but that it is altogether elsewhere, in the locus where speech is located.

Since you have had the patience to carry on listening to me – it's already eleven o'clock – I still have to designate the gap that separates each of these terms in so far as they are statements. This is crucial among the number of crystallizing themes that I'm pressing forward for you now that we're at the end of the year.

Between *There exists*, $\exists x$, and *There does not exist*, $\overline{\exists x}$ – there's no need to garble this – lies *existence*.

Between *There exists one who does not* . . ., $\exists x.\overline{\Phi x}$, and *There is not one who is not* . . ., $\forall x.\Phi x$, there lies *contradiction*. When Aristotle highlights particular propositions to contrast them with universal propositions, he establishes contradiction between a particular affirmative and a universal negative. Here, it's the contrary. The particular is negative and the universal is affirmative.

Between the $\overline{\exists x}.\Phi x$, which is the negation of any universality, and this $\overline{\forall x}.\Phi x$, we have the *undecidable*. This is just an indication. I'll be accounting for it afterwards.

What is at issue between the two universal quantifiers, $\forall x$ and $\overline{\forall x}$? I think that all of our experience of this situation shows that this is not so straightforward. We will call it lack. We will call it a rift. We will call it, if you like, desire. And to be more rigorous, we shall call it the object *a*.

$\exists x.\overline{\Phi x}$	existence	$\overline{\exists x}.\Phi x$
contradiction		undecidable
	lack	
	rift	
	desire	
$\forall x.\Phi x$	object *a*	$\overline{\forall x}.\Phi x$

It's now a matter of finding out how, in the midst of all this, something functions that may resemble a circulation. For this, we have to ask ourselves about the mode in which these four terms are posited.

The $\exists x$ on the top left is literally the *necessary*. Nothing is thinkable. It is absolutely not our function – for the rest of us men – to think. Well, when it comes to a woman, there is thinking. This is even from time to time the thought *therefore I am*. In which, of course, she deceives herself. But as far as the *necessary* is concerned, it is absolutely necessary, to think about anything whatsoever to do with relations that are called human relations – we don't know why – within the experience that is established by the analytic discourse, to posit that there exists one for whom castration is told to scram. This is what Freud tells us in the cock-and-bull story of *Totem and Total Bull*. What does castration mean? It means that it leaves everything to be desired. It means nothing but that. To think this through, that is to say, to think this through on the basis of woman, there has to be one who leaves nothing to be desired. This is the story of the Oedipus myth, but it's absolutely necessary.[12] If you lose sight of this, I really don't see what would allow you to find your bearings in any way whatsoever. It's very important to find your bearings.

I've already told you that this $\exists x$ is the *necessary*. Necessary on what basis? Precisely on the basis of what, my word, I wrote just now – the *undecidable*. In the end, we can say absolutely nothing that resembles anything that might constitute a truth function if we do not admit the necessity of *there being at-least-one who says no*. I'm insisting a little because this evening, due to the disturbances outside, I haven't been able to tell you all the niceties that I would have liked to be able to tell you on this score. I do have one, however, which is very nice indeed, and since I'm being teased, I'll come out with it. It's the function of *l'é-pater*.

People have been wondering a great deal about the function of the paterfamilias. What we may require of the function of the father needs to be better focused. How people indulge in these stories of paternal shortcoming! It's a fact that there is a crisis. This is not completely false. *L'é-pater ne nous épate plus.* His wowing us is a thing of the past. This is the only genuinely decisive function of the father. I've already marked out how it was not the Oedipus complex, how it was shot, how if the father was a legislator, the child this would produce is President Schreber. No more no less. On any plane, the father is the one who ought to wow the family. If the father no longer wows the family, something better will be found. It's not inevitable that he should be the father in flesh and blood. There is always one who will wow the family, which as everyone knows amounts to a herd of slaves. There are others who will wow them.

You can see how the French language can serve many things. I explained this to you last time by starting with *fondre* or *fonder*, founding, *d'eux*, from them, a One. In the subjunctive it's the same word. To *fonder* you have to *fondre*. There are some things that can only be expressed in the French language. This is precisely why there is an unconscious, because equivoques are what *found*, in both senses of the word. Indeed, this is all there is. If you take *tous* and try to see how it is expressed in each language, you will find heaps of things, some absolutely terrific things. For my part, I have been looking into Chinese, because I can't make a catalogue of the languages of the whole world. Also, through the intermediary of the charming treasurer of our School, I questioned someone who got her father to write down how they say *tous* in Yoruba. It's crazy. I do this for the love of the art, but I know full well that, either way, I will find in every language that there is a means to say *tous*.

What is of interest to me is the signifier as One. This is what is used in every language. The only interest that the signifier holds is the equivoques that can emerge from it. That is to say, something of the order of *fonde d'eux un Un*, and other such messing about. This is the only interesting thing because what for us is involved in *tous* – you will always find this expressed – is unavoidably semantic. The mere fact that I may say that I would like to examine *all* the languages resolves the question because *les langues*, precisely, *ne sont pas toutes*, they are *not all*. This is their definition. On the other hand, when I ask you about *tous*, you understand. There you have it. In the end, semantics comes down to translatability. What else could I offer as a definition of this? It is thanks to semantics that a man and a woman comprehend each other only when they do not speak the same language. I'm telling you this to give you some exercises, because that's what I'm here for, and also perhaps to open up a little your *comprenoire* on the use I've been making of linguistics.

I want to wind this up.

With respect to what is involved in what necessitates existence, our point of departure is the gap of the *undecidable* [*i*], that is, between the *not-all* and the *pas-une*, the *not-one* [*ii*]. After, this goes to *existence* [*iii*]. Then, it goes to *all men are under the might of castration* [*iv*]. It goes to the *possible*, because the universal is never anything but that. When you say *all men are mammals*, it means all the possible men might be so.

And after that, where does it go? It goes to the object *a* [*v*]. It is with the object *a* that we are in relation. And where does it go after that? It goes here, where woman is distinguished in not being unifying [*vi*]. All that remains is to complete this, here, in order to go towards *contradiction* [*vii*]. We're coming back from the *pas-toute*, from the *not-all* which is, in sum, nothing other than the expression of *contingency*.

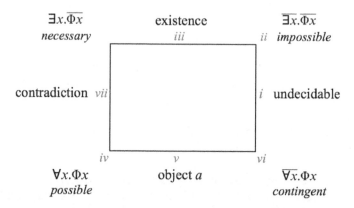

As I pointed out in its time, the alternation between *necessity*, the *contingent*, the *possible* and the *impossible* is not in the order that Aristotle gives, because what is at issue here is the impossible, that is to say, all things considered, the real.

So, follow this little path carefully, because it will be of use to us in the near future. You will be seeing something of it. The four triangles in the corners need to be indicated, too, along with the direction of the arrows.[13]

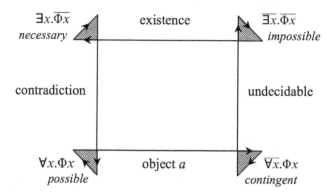

There you have it. I feel I've had enough for this evening. I have no desire to end with a show-stopping peroration. It's a matter of clearing the way. Let me check – *necessary, impossible, possible,* and *contingent.* Yes, it's written correctly enough. You will hear the rest when I give the next session of my Seminar up by the Panthéon. I'm not sure whether this is to be the last.

1 June 1972

CODA

XV

THE DESIRE TO SLEEP

Creating the verb *unigate*
Dreams according to Freud
The body's access to jouissance
Pollution represented in existence
The objection against *argumentum ad absurdum*

Given what I shall call the mixing, the communicating, that has occurred between my audience here and the audience at Sainte-Anne, I'm supposing that they have now become unified, this being the operative word. Last time at Sainte-Anne you saw that we have passed from what one day I labelled here, using a predicate specially formed for your use, the *Unian*, to a term of another fashioning, which may be promoted in the verb form *unier, to unigate*.

What I put forward last time, at Sainte-Anne, is the pivotal point that is taken in this order that is founded by the One. Put *fonde*, indeed *fondez-le*, in order for it to be *fondé-fondu*, a founded founding. All in all, I was pressing home that this founding should not appear to you as something overly fundamental. This is what I'm labelling as *le laisser dans le fondu*, to leave this founding *unigate* in a founded state.

There exists one who naysays. It's not quite the same thing as negating, but from this forging of the term *unigate*, as a verb that can be conjugated, we may assert that for what is involved in the function that is represented in analysis by the myth of the Father, it *unigates*.

This is what was there for the hearing for those who managed to hearken through the bangers reverberating around Sainte-Anne, and this is what today I should like to enable you to accommodate, let's say.

1

So, the Father *unigates*.

In the myth, he has the correlate of *toutes*, of all the women. If we follow my quantic inscriptions, there is cause to introduce a modification here. Certainly he *unigates* them, but precisely *pas toutes*, not all.

Something is touched on here that is not my own invention, namely the kinship between logic and myth. It simply marks out how the former can rectify the latter.

This is the work that lies ahead of us. For the time being, I will remind you that with what I permitted myself in terms of approximations of the Father, with what I inscribed using *l'é-pater*, you can see that the path that occasionally leads myth to meet up with derision is no stranger to us. In no respect does this touch on the fundamental status of the structures concerned.

It's amusing that there are people who are discovering, somewhat late in the day, terms like *signifier*, *sign*, *signification* and *semiotics*. From where I'm standing I can say that all the buzz and excitement that is being produced around these terms is a bit non-specific. It's on the centre stage, right now. The peculiar belatedness that is being shown in this respect is quite curious.

There is a little journal that is rather good, well, no worse than any other, in which, under the heading *L'Atelier d'écriture*, I've seen an article that, my goodness, is no worse than any other, called 'L'Agonie du signe'. Agony is always very touching. *Agony* means *struggle*, but it also means that someone is about to pass out. So, there is pathos in the agony of the sign. I would have preferred all this not to be revolving around pathos.

The article begins with a delightful invention, the possibility of forging a new signifier, that of *fourmidable*. Indeed, the whole article is *fourmidable*, and it begins by asking what the status of this *fourmidable* might be.

This is very much to my liking. All the more so given that it's someone who for a good while now has been fully abreast of a number of things that I have been putting forward. Yet at the start of the article he feels compelled to play the innocent, namely to hesitate over whether *fourmidable* should be classified as metaphor or as metonymy. He also feels compelled to say that there is something that has been neglected in Jakobson's theory, the theory that purportedly consists in running words into one another. But I explained this ages ago. I wrote *L'Instance de la lettre* expressly for this purpose. Capital S over lower case *s*, with the result of 1 effect of signification [ɪ over s]. It's displacement, it's condensation, it's very precisely the path along which one can create *unigate*, which is all the same a little bit more amusing and useful than *fourmidable*.

Then, *unigate* can be used for something else. It can be used to explain, along another path, what I completely relinquished tackling along the path of the Name-of-the-Father. I relinquished this because at a particular moment I was prevented from doing so. And then, the people who prevented me were precisely the ones to whom it might have been of service. It might have been of service to them in their private lives. These are people who are particularly implicated on the side of the Name-of-the-Father. There is in this world a very special clique, which can be pinpointed as a religious tradition. They are the ones whom this might have aerated, but I don't see why I should devote myself especially to them.

So, I've been explaining the story that Freud broached as best he could, precisely to avoid his own story. El Shaddai, in particular. This is the name to designate the one whose name is not uttered. Freud turned to the myths, and then he produced something very proper, something that was a little aseptic. He didn't push it any further, but this is very much what is at issue.

Opportunities were missed to look again at what was steering him, and which should have meant that psychoanalysis would now be at its rightful place in its discourse. The chance has been missed.

2

On the aeroplane back from Milan yesterday evening, I came upon a really very nice article in a thing called *Atlas*, which is handed out to Air France passengers. I don't have it with me. I forgot to bring it, and fortunately so because that would have led me to read you some passages from it and there's nothing so tiresome as to hear people read aloud. Anyway, it informs us that there are high-flying psychologists in America who have been investigating dreams. Because people investigate dreams, don't they?

They've been investigating, and they've found that, in the end, sexual dreams are very few and far between. These people dream about everything. They dream about sport. They dream about a whole load of josh. They dream about falling. But, in the end, there is not an overwhelming majority of sexual dreams. Since the widely held conception of psychoanalysis, so we are told in this text, is to believe that dreams are sexual, the general public, which comprises the psychoanalytic propagation – you are a general public as well

– is naturally going to be peeved. The whole soufflé is going to collapse, just like that, to sink to the bottom of the dish.

Among this supposed general public – because all this is supposition – it's true that there is a certain resonance according to which Freud is purported to have said that all dreams are sexual. Except that he never, ever, said that. He said that dreams were dreams of desire. He never said it was sexual desire.

It took me some time to broach the relation between, on the one hand, the fact that dreams are dreams of desire and, on the other, this realm of the sexual that is characterized by what I have been putting forward.

I had to avoid throwing the spirit of these nice people into disorder, the same people who after ten years of my recounting them stuff thought only of returning to the bosom of the International Psychoanalytic Association. They were very nice exercises that I recounted, exercises in style, but these fellows were getting down to serious business. The serious business is the International Psychoanalytic Association. Which means that now I can assert, and it can be heard, that there is no such thing as sexual relation.

It is for this reason that this amounts to a whole order that is functioning in the place where this relation would be. It is here, in this order, that something has a consequence as an effect of language, namely desire. One could perhaps take a small step forward and ask, *when Freud said that the dream is the satisfaction of a desire, in what sense is satisfaction to be taken?*

When I think that I'm still here, and that among all these people who have set themselves to obfuscating what I say, to turning it into noise, no one has ever dared to assert the very thing that is nevertheless the strict consequence of everything I articulated in the most precise fashion, in 1957 if memory serves – no, even earlier, in '55 – in connection with the dream of Irma's injection.

To show how one ought to treat a text of Freud's, I carefully explained to them what was ambiguous. I explained that it is here, at the level of his present preoccupations, and not at all in the unconscious, that Freud interprets this dream, this dream of desire that has nothing to do with sexual desire, even if there are all the implications of transference that suit us down to the ground.

I put forward the term *immixing of subjects* in 1955.[1] Can you imagine? Seventeen years ago. I will have to publish that Seminar. I haven't done so already because I was absolutely sickened by the way it was taken up in a book that came out under the title *L'Autoanalyse de Freud*. It was my text, but added to in a way that no one would understand anything of it.

What does a dream do? It doesn't satisfy desire, for reasons that are fundamental, and which I won't start developing today because it would require four or five sessions. It's for the simple reason that Freud says that the only fundamental desire when asleep is the desire to sleep.

It's making you laugh because you've never heard this. Fair enough. Yet it's in Freud.

How is it that this fact of what sleeping consists in doesn't occur straightaway to your gumption? It consists in suspending what is in my tetrad – semblance, truth, jouissance, and surplus jouissance. Anyone can just take a look at any sleeping animal to realize that sleep is designed to suspend the ambiguousness that there is in the body's relation to itself, namely the deriving of jouissance therefrom.

The body's possibility of gaining access to deriving jouissance from itself is plain to see everywhere. When it bumps into something. When it gets hurt. That's what jouissance is. So, here, mankind has some small ports of entry that the others don't have. He can turn it into a goal. In any case, when he sleeps, it's over.

When one sleeps, it's a matter of making the body coil up. It rolls itself into a ball. To sleep is not to be disturbed. After all, jouissance is disturbing. Naturally, the body gets disturbed, but so long as it's asleep, it can hope not to be disturbed. This is why, from then on, all the rest vanishes. Nor is it a question any more of semblance, nor of truth – because all of this holds together, it's the same thing – nor of surplus jouissance.

Except, there you have it. What Freud says is that, during this time, the signifier is still on the go. This is indeed why, even when I'm sleeping, I'm preparing my seminars. Monsieur Poincaré was discovering the Fuchsian functions.

3

[*Various noises*]

What's going on?

A MAN IN THE AUDIENCE – *Pollution!*[2]

Who said that? This precise term? I'm especially glad to hear you choose this term. You must be particularly intelligent.

I have already expressed in public how delighted I was that someone I analysed, who is here today somewhere – she's a particularly sensitive person – spoke about my discourse as *intellectual pollution*.

Pollution is an altogether fundamental dimension, you see. I probably wouldn't have pushed things quite that far today, but you seem to be so proud of having come out with this term *pollution* that

I suspect you might understand nothing of it. Nevertheless, you will see that not only am I going to make use of it, but also I'm glad a second time that someone should have come out with it, because this is precisely the difficulty of the analytic discourse.

I'm picking up on this interruption, seizing on it, taking on board something that, in the urgency of the end of the year, I find myself having occasion to say.

It is precisely in so far as the analytic discourse is characterized by locating the object *a* in the place of semblance that – can you imagine, sir, thinking you'd pulled quite a stunt – you've gone exactly in the direction of what I have to put forward, namely that the pollution that is most characteristic in this world is the object *a*, from which man takes his substance, you included.

In having to turn himself, in his body, in his existence as an analyst, into the representation of this pollution, which is the most certain effect across the surface of the globe, he has to take more than one look at this. It's made the little darlings ill, and I must tell you that I'm no more at ease in this situation than they are.

What I'm trying to demonstrate to them is that it's not entirely impossible to do so with a little decency. Thanks to logic, if they would kindly allow themselves to be tempted by it, I've managed to make this position bearable for them, the position that they occupy as *a* in the analytic discourse. It would allow them to conceive of how raising this function to a position of semblance, which is the key position in any discourse, is clearly no small matter. Here lies the mainspring of what I have always been trying to make you feel as the analyst's resistance – which is only too understandable – to truly fulfilling his function.

It oughtn't to be believed that the position of semblance is easy for anyone and everyone. It is tenable only at the level of scientific discourse. This is for the very simple reason that what is carried to the command position here is something that belongs utterly to the order of the real inasmuch as all that we touch on by way of the real is the *Spaltung*, the split, in other words, the way that I define the subject. This is because in scientific discourse it is the barred capital S that holds this key position.

For the university discourse, it is knowledge. The difficulty is yet greater here due to a kind of short-circuit, because in order to turn knowledge into semblance one has to know how to affect a semblance. And this soon wears thin.

In Milan, from which I have just returned, obviously I had a far less numerous audience than here, about a quarter of the number of you, but there was a throng of young people who are what is known as *in the movement*. There was even one most respectable character, of fairly high stature, who happens to be the representative of the movement down there. Only afterwards was I told that he was there. I didn't want to question him, but does he know or doesn't he know that, by being posted at this outcrop, what he wants, like all those who are a little involved in the movement, is to restore to the university discourse its value? As the noun indicates, this culminates in units of value, in *credits*. They would like to know a little better how to affect a semblance of knowledge. This is what guides them.

Well, indeed, this is respectable. And why not? The university discourse has a status that is just as fundamental as any other. However, what I'm pointing out is that it's not the same as the psychoanalytic discourse. The place of semblance is held differently there.

Good gracious, how is one to manage with a new audience, and above all if they might be confused? I tried to explain to them a little what my place is in the story. I started by saying that my *Écrits* are a *poubellication*, and that they shouldn't believe that they could take their bearings from them. The word *Seminar* did nevertheless crop up thereafter. Of course, I was forced to confess that the Seminar is not a seminar. It's me wittering on all by myself, my good friends, as I have been for years now. Though there was a time, back in the day, when it lived up to its name, and there were other people who contributed.

So, being forced to come to that put me beside myself. And since on the return flight there was someone who was pressing me to know how it was that there once was a time when it was like a seminar, I told myself that today I would say that, for this penultimate session, good Lord, someone should come along to say something.

Whereupon I received a letter from Monsieur Recanati. I won't tell you the story just yet. I'm not pretending that I'm conjuring up a contribution from the floor. I'm simply saying that I received a letter, which moreover was a reply to one of mine. To my great surprise, my correspondent, who is here beside me, proved to me that he had understood something of what I've been saying this year. So, I'm going to give him the floor.

He has something to say to you that bears the closest relation to what I've been trying to open up, notably to set theory and mathematical logic. He's about to tell you which.

[*François Recanati's exposé revisits Lacan's thematic from the perspective of Peirce's logic. Lacan printed the exposé in the journal* Scilicet 4 (1973): 55–63, *followed by Recanti's commentary on his own exposé, addressed to Lacan in the form of a letter, pp. 64–73. The following four paragraphs are drawn from Lacan's responses.*]

I think it should be underscored here that the bar placed over both terms, $\exists x$ and Φx, which are each negated, is an *It is not true that . . .* which is frequently used in mathematics, because this is the key point to which the so-called proof by contradiction leads. All in all, it's a matter of knowing why it is accepted in mathematics, but only in mathematics, that one can ground something affirmable upon an *It is not true that . . .* How could you do this anywhere else?

It is precisely here that the objection comes, within mathematics, to using the *argumentum ad absurdum*. The question is how, in mathematics, the *argumentum ad absurdum* can ground something, which as such proves not to lead to contradiction. This is where the specific domain of mathematics is specified.

So, under this *It is not true that . . .* , it's a matter of furnishing the status of the negative bar that I've been using at one of the points on my chart, in order to say *There does not exist an x to satisfy a negated Φx.*

I had to go to Milan to feel the need to get a response. I feel that the one I've just had is quite satisfactory enough for you to be able to be satisfied by it too, for today.

14 June 1972

XVI

BODIES CAPTURED BY DISCOURSE

The affable Umberto Eco
Self-cognizance is hygiene
The bodily support in analysis
Jurisprudence and fine sentiments
Racism and fraternity

Qu'on dise comme fait reste oublié derrière ce qui est dit,

dans ce qui s'entend.

This statement, assertive in its form, belongs to the modal for

issuing what it does by way of existence.

Today, I will be taking my leave of you, of those who've been coming along and then of those who haven't been coming but have come along for this leave-taking. There's no need to strike up the band.

What can I do? Summing myself up, as they say, is absolutely out of the question. So, I shall mark something, a point, a suspension point. Of course, I could say that I've continued to circumscribe this impossibility in which, for us in the analytic discourse, everything that can be founded as real is gathered.

At the last minute and, my word, by a stroke of luck, I received testimony that what I've been saying is being heard. I received it by virtue of the person who, to his great merit, was kind enough to speak at this final moment of the year, proving to me that indeed for some, for more than one, for happenstances that come about from angles that I can on no account predict, they found some interest in what I've been trying to set out. I thank, therefore, the person who bore me this testimony, and not only to me. I hope that there are enough people for whom this created an echo, and who were able to realize that it can yield something. Naturally, it's always hard to know how far this reaches.

On this score, I don't think it beside the point to bring up the meeting I had with someone in Italy, whom I find to be a very affable fellow. He's in art history and is involved in the idea of the *Work*. It's not known why, though we might come to understand, he is interested in what is being set out under the heading of *structure*, and specifically in what I have been able to produce in this respect. He is interested in it on account of personal issues.

This idea of the Work, this art history, this vein, tends to enslave. There's no doubt about that. It can be seen quite clearly when one beholds what someone who was neither a critic nor a historian, but a creator, formed as an image of this vein, namely the slave, the captive. A certain Michelangelo showed us this. So, on the margins, there are the historians and the critics who pray for the slave. This is mummery like any other. It's a kind of divine service that can be practised. It's a way of making you forget what is in command, because the Work is always in command, even for Michelangelo.

The one in command is what I first tried to produce for you this year under the heading *Yad'lun*. The One is in command. The One makes Being. I asked you to go to look this up in the *Parmenides*. Some of you perhaps complied. The One maketh Being just as the hysteric maketh the man. Obviously, the One that maketh Being is not itself Being. It *maketh* Being. This is what is unbearable for a certain creativist infatuation.

The person I'm speaking about, who was really very affable with me, explained how he has got caught up on what he calls my *system*, in order to speak out against its barbs. This is why I'm making a big deal of this today, so as to avoid a particular confusion. He has got caught up on what in his mind is my practising too much ontology.

This is rather odd. I know that of course there are not just open ears in this audience. I think there are a certain number of deaf ears, as there are everywhere. But to say that I practise ontology is all the same fairly odd. And positioning this ontology in the big Other, which I show as having to be barred, and to which I pin the signifier of this barring, is curious indeed.

What has to be seen in the reverberations, in the response that one obtains, is that, after all, people respond to you with their own issues. His issue is that ontology, and even Being, has got stuck in his craw. This is due to the fact that, if ontology is simply the puckering of the One, then obviously everything that is done on command becomes suspended from the One, and, my goodness, this is a nuisance for him. So, what he would like, all in all, is for structure to be *absent*.

Indeed, this would be more convenient for the *hey presto*. What is wanted here is that the sleight of hand that takes place, which is the work of art, should have no need of cups and balls. You have only to behold this in a painting by Hieronymus Bosch, who was an artist far above this. He doesn't hide how it's done, the captivation of gawkers.

This is not what we are busying ourselves with here. We are dealing with the analytic discourse.

1

Regarding this analytic discourse, I thought all the same that it might not be a bad idea before leaving you to punctuate something that would give you the idea not only that this is neither ontological nor philosophical, but indeed that it is only necessitated by a particular position. This particular position is the one in which I believe I have been able to condense the articulation of a discourse.

It's a matter of showing you what relation this bears to the fact that analysts have a relation – and you would be wrong to think that I'm ignorant of this – to something that is called the human being. Yes indeed. Of course. But I don't use this label. I avoid this label so that you won't stick your necks out, so that you'll stay right where you ought to be, to the extent that you're capable of seeing what the difficulties are that arise for the analyst.

Let's speak no more of cognizance, because man's relation to a world of his own – obviously this is where we've been starting off from for a long while now – has never been anything but play-acting in the service of the discourse of the master. The only world of one's own is the world that the master strings along at his beck and call.

As for the famous *knowing thyself*, γνῶθι σεαυτόν, which is what supposedly maketh the man, let's take as our point of departure the following, which is straightforward and palpable. Indeed, if you so wish, cognizance has a locus. It has the locus of the body. The cognizance of oneself is hygiene. Let this be our starting point.

So, throughout the centuries, illnesses continued to exist. Everyone knows that illness cannot be remedied by hygiene. There is illness, and this is indeed something that grips the body. For centuries, illness was something of which doctors were supposed to have cognizance. During one of our recent talks I think I briefly underscored the failure of these two angles. All of this is plain to see in history. It's spread across it in all sorts of aberrations.

So, all the same, the question that I would like to make tangible for you today concerns the analyst who is now here and who seems to be taking up the baton. People speak about illness and at the same time people say that there is no such thing, that there is no mental illness, for example. They are quite right, in the sense that illness is a nosological entity, as used to be said. On no account is mental illness an entity. Rather, mentality has rifts. Let's put it like that, somewhat briskly.

Let's try to see, for instance, what is supposed in what I've written here, and which supposedly lays out where a particular chain is positioned. This chain is very certainly, and without the faintest ambiguity, *structure*.

$$\frac{S_1}{\cancel{S}} \longrightarrow \frac{S_2}{a}$$

Discourse of the master

You can see two signifiers in succession, and the subject is here only in so far as one signifier represents it for the other signifier. Then, something results from this for which over the years we have extensively developed enough reasons to justify notating it as the object *a*. Evidently, if it here takes this tetradic form, this is not a topology that is devoid of some kind of meaning.

This is the novelty that was introduced by Freud, and it's no small matter.

There was someone who did something very fine by crystallizing the discourse of the master on the basis of a historical perspective that he succeeded in grasping. That someone is Marx. This was a step forward. There is no cause to reduce this step to the first. Nor is there cause to mix the two together. One wonders on what grounds they would have to be in absolute accord. They are not in accord. They are perfectly compatible. They are nested. They are nested, and then there is certainly a step that takes its place quite comfortably, and that is the step of Freud.

All in all, what was the essential thing that Freud introduced? He introduced the dimension of over-determination. I afford an image of over-determination in my way of formalizing, in the most radical fashion, the essence of discourse, in so far as it occupies a pivotal position in relation to what I have just called a support.

After all, it was on the basis of discourse that Freud brought to light the fact that what was produced at the level of the support had to do with what was articulated by way of discourse. The support is the body.

We still have to pay attention when we say that it's the body. It's not necessarily *one* body. From the moment we take jouissance as the starting point, this means very precisely that the body is not on its own, that there is another one. It is not because of this that jouissance is sexual, since what I've just been explaining this year is that the least one can say is that this jouissance is not brought along. It's the jouissance of a bodily one-on-one. What is specific to jouissance is that, when there are two bodies, and even more so when there are more of them, naturally one cannot tell which of them is enjoying. It is for this reason that there might be several bodies involved in this affair, and even series of bodies.

One thing led to another and, goodness knows why, I found myself rereading a session of a Seminar I gave at the start of the last term of the academic year that I dedicated to the case of President Schreber. It is from 11 April 1956, right after the two first terms that are summarized in my *écrit* that goes by the title *D'une question préalable à tout traitement possible de la psychose*. I set out what is involved in structure. I'm calling it by its name, the name that it bears in my disquisition – *structure*. Structure is not always what the rabble believe,[1] but it's perfectly well expressed at this level.

It would have amused me to publish this Seminar, if the keybasher hadn't left a large number of lacunae because she hadn't heard me properly. If only she had accurately reproduced the sentence in Latin that I wrote on the blackboard. I no longer remember who the author was, and to find it again will certainly cost me some time, but no matter. I'll do it for the next issue of *Scilicet*. Everything that I said back then about the signifier – at a time when, in '56, it can't be said that it was in fashion – is still struck in a metal that I have no need to retouch.

What I said in this regard is precisely that what distinguishes the signifier is that it has no signification. I said it in a forthright way because back then I had to make myself heard by my audience. You do realize that, what is more, it was an audience of doctors. What the heck could they get out of it? They were just listening to a bit of Lacan. Well, a bit of Lacan . . . that is to say, this clown who was doing his marvellous trapeze act. Throughout that time, they already had an eye on how they would get back to their digestion, because one can't say that they are dreamers. That would be too fine. They don't dream. They digest. It's an occupation like any other.

What one has to try to see is that what Freud introduced – and people imagine that I misconstrue this because I speak about the signifier – is the return to this grounding that is in the body, and which means that, quite independently of the signifiers by which they are articulated, these four poles are determined by the emergence as such of jouissance, precisely as something that is ungraspable. This is what makes the other three rise up, and, in response, the first, which is truth.

Truth already implies discourse. This doesn't mean that it can be said. I've been knocking myself out saying that it cannot be said, or that it can only go midsay. However, for jouissance to exist, one has to be able to speak about it. In view of which, there is something else, which is called *the fact of saying*.

Well, all told, I spent the whole of last year explaining this for you. It took a while to articulate. You have to see in this my necessity, my way of moving forward. Precisely, I can never articulate it as a truth. You have to turn around it in keeping with your own destiny. More exactly, you have to see how it turns, how it swivels, as soon as it is touched, and even how, up to a certain point, it's unstable enough to lead to all sorts of errors.

Either way, if I came out with the title – which all the same shows some gall – *D'un discours qui ne serait pas du semblant*, on a discourse that would not be a discourse of semblance, then it was to allow you to sense, and you did sense it, that discourse as such is always a discourse of semblance, and that if there is something at some point that is authorized by jouissance, then this is precisely the fact of affecting a semblance. From this point of departure one can manage to conceive of something that we can only catch hold of here, namely surplus jouissance.

If there is someone who got to grips with this surplus jouissance in a way that was so self-assured, whose memory has to be hailed – *mémoire* as I write it, giving *mé* the same meaning as the *mé* in *méconnaisance* – who has been so well *mémorisé*,[2] so well memorialized that it's more a matter of his words having been made risible, then that someone is Plato.

Plato captured something that gives us to think that he's not only about Ideas and Forms, but also everything that can be got out of him by translating his statements with a certain grid that is, I admit, *vraisemblable*, plausible. Plato is nevertheless the one who put forward the function of the dyad as the chute down which everything has to pass, to leak. No *larger* without *smaller*. No *older* without *younger*. The fact that the dyad is the locus of our loss, the locus of this leak, the locus that forces Plato to forge this One of Idea, of Form, this One that immediately multiplies and becomes *un*-graspable, is because like the rest of us it is steeped in this supplement.

Indeed, I spoke about all this in the session of my Seminar of 11 April 1956. I spoke of the difference between the supplement and the complement. Well, I had already spelt this out very clearly in 1956. It seems that this might have served to crystallize something of the function that is to be fulfilled, the function of the analyst, and which seems to be so impossible, more so than others, that people think only of camouflaging it.

So, everything turns around this. After everything I've just set out concerning jouissance, truth, semblance, and surplus jouissance, there is this support, which is what happens at the level of the body and from which all meaning emerges, but in a non-constituted form. This is what forms the ground. *Ground* is the word that was used the other day by the person who was kind enough to come and speak to us about Peirce, to the extent that it was in Peirce's note that he had heard what I was saying.

I don't need to tell you that back when I wrote up Peirce's quadrants, it came to nothing. You can well imagine that remarks on the total ambiguity of the universal, whether it is affirmative or negative, and of the particular, too, . . . well, what effect could that have on those who dreamed only of finding again their same old tune?

The ground lies here. It is indeed a matter of the body with its radical meanings on which we have no purchase.

2

It is not with truth, semblance, jouissance, or surplus jouissance that one philosophizes. One is doing philosophy when there is something that fills in this support, which can be articulated only on the basis of discourse. What does it fill this support with? It has to be said that it is filled with what you are made of, and all the more so given that you are a bit philosophical. This happens sometimes, but in the end it's rare. You are above all *astudied,* as I once said.[3] You are in the place where the university discourse locates you. You are taken as *à-former.*[4] For some time now, a crisis has been afoot, but we will speak about this presently. It's secondary. The question is a different one, therefore.

You need to realize that what you depend on most fundamentally – because in the end the university did not appear just yesterday – is the discourse of the master. The discourse of the master was the first to arise, and this is the discourse that has endured and which stands little chance of being shaken. It could be compensated, balanced out, with something that would be, the day when this happens, the analytic discourse. At the level of the discourse of the master, one can say perfectly well what lies between the functions of the discourses such as they are articulated using this S_1, S_2, barred S, and a, and then, on the other hand, the body that represents you here and which, as an analyst, I address.

When someone comes to see me for the first time in my consulting room and I punctuate our entry into this business with a few preliminary consultations, what is important is the confrontation of bodies. It's precisely because it starts with this, with this encounter of bodies, that once one enters the analytic discourse, there will be no further question of this. It is still the case, however, that on the level at which discourse functions – which is not the analytic discourse – the question arises as to how this discourse has managed to capture bodies.

At the level of the discourse of the master, it's clear. As bodies, you are moulded by the discourse of the master. You can't hide this, regardless of your gambolling. This is what I shall call *sentiments*, and very precisely *bons sentiments*, fine sentiments. Between the body and discourse lies what analysts indulge in pretentiously calling *affects*. It's quite obvious that you are affected in analysis. But they claim that this is what constitutes an analysis. They have to hold on to something, to be sure they won't slip. What are fine sentiments formed by? We are very much compelled to come to this. At the level of the discourse of the master, it's quite clear. They are formed by jurisprudence. Given that I'm speaking here as a guest to the Law Faculty, it is as well not to forget this. It's as well not to misrecognize that fine sentiments are founded by jurisprudence, and nothing more.

Let's be clear. When something like this all of a sudden comes to move your heart because you don't know very well whether you might not be a little responsive to the way an analysis has taken a turn for the worse, if there were no deontology, if there were no jurisprudence, where would this heavy heart be? Where would this affect, as they say, be? One does have to try to speak the truth a bit once in a while.

A *bit* means that what I've just said is not exhaustive. I could also say something else that would be incompatible with what I've just said, and which would *also* be the truth. And this is indeed what happens simply on account, not of a quarter-turn, but of half a complete turn, of two quarter-turns, in the sliding of these functional elements of discourse.

In this tetrad there are vectors, the necessity of which can be established full well. These vectors are due neither to the tetrad, nor to truth, nor to semblance, nor to anything else of the kind. They stem from the fact that the tetrad is fourfold. On the sole condition that you require that there should be vectors going in both directions, namely that there should be either two incoming vectors and one outgoing, or one incoming and one outgoing, you will necessarily be led to the way they are laid out here. This is due to the number 4, and nothing else. Naturally, semblance, truth, jouissance, and surplus jouissance, cannot be added together. So, they cannot make four all by themselves. It is precisely in this that the real consists, in that the number 4 exists all on its own.

This is something that I also said on 11 April 1956, but I hadn't yet come out with all of this. Moreover, I hadn't even constructed all of this. Only, this is what proves to me that I'm on the right track because, back then, I said that the number 4 is a number that is essential when it comes to remembering. I find nothing surplus to requirement in this. I said it when it had to be said, at the time when it was a question of psychosis.

Don't trouble yourselves over the people who are walking out. They have to at this time. They have to go to the funeral of someone to whom I hereby pay my respects, someone from our School and who was very dear to me. I regret not being able to join them, in view of my commitments here.

What is there, in the analytic discourse, between the functions of discourse and this support, which is not the signification of discourse, and which does not depend on anything of what is said? Everything that is said is semblance. What's more, everything that is said is true. All that is said gives rise to jouissance. As I have written again today on the blackboard, *Qu'on dise, comme fait . . .* this fact of saying . . . *reste oublié derrière ce qui est dit.*

That which is said lies nowhere else than *in what is heard*. That's what speech is. The fact of saying is something else entirely. It's another plane. It's discourse. It's a matter of relationships, which hold each and every one of you together with people who are not necessarily the people here. What is called relationship, *religiō*, social binding, occurs as the level of a certain number of points of capture that are not produced by chance. These points of capture necessitate, save for a very occasional erring, a certain order in the signifying articulation. And for something to be *said* here takes something other than what you imagine under the name *reality*, because reality stems very precisely from the fact of saying.

The fact of saying has its effects, on the basis of which what is known as the fantasy is constituted. The fantasy is the relation between the object *a* – which is what is concentrated through the effect of discourse in order to cause desire – and this something that is condensed around it, as a split, and which is called the subject. It's a split because the object *a* always lies between each signifier and the signifier that follows it, and this is why the subject was always not *between*, but, on the contrary, *gaping*.

In Rome, where I have just been, I was able to put my finger on the fairly gripping effect, an effect in which I recognize myself full well, of the copper plates by a certain Fontana – who is apparently deceased – who after having shown great felicity as a constructor, a sculptor, and so on, dedicated his last years to making what in Italian is called *squarcio*. I don't speak Italian very well. I had this term explained to me. It's a gash. He made gashes in copper plates.

This produces a certain effect. It produces an effect for those who are a little sensitive. There's no need to have heard my disquisition on the *Spaltung* of the subject to be sensitive to this. The first person who comes along, especially if she is of the feminine sex, can experience a little wobbling.

Fontana was surely not one of those who completely misrecognize structure, and who think that it's overly ontological.

3

So, what is at issue in analysis?

If I am to be believed, it must be thought that it is indeed as I have said it is, namely that the analyst installs the object *a*, and does so *en corps* – with all the legitimate ambiguity of this term[5] – in the place of semblance. It is on account of this that something exists that is called the analytic discourse. What does this mean? At the point we've reached, that is, where we've started to see this discourse taking shape, we can see that, as discourse – not in what is said but in its fact of saying – it allows us to apprehend what is involved in semblance.

This is why it is striking, at the end of a cosmological tradition, as we were allowed to feel it last time, to see the question being posed as to how the universe came to be born. Doesn't this question strike you as a rather dated one? It dates from the depths of ages, but it's no less dated. What is striking is that this led Peirce to a purely logical articulation, and even a logician's articulation. This is the point at which the fruit detaches from the tree of a certain articulation that I shall call illusory, which down through the ages has culminated in this cosmology fused with a psychology, with a theology, and with all that ensued.

Here we put a finger on the fact that, as was set out for you last time, there is no discourse on the origin that does not deal with the origin of a discourse. There is no graspable origin besides the origin of a discourse. This is what is important for us when it's a matter of the emergence of another discourse, the analytic discourse. In relation to the discourse of the master – the terms and arrangement of which I will quickly draw up again – the analytic discourse entails the double inversion of the slanting vectors.

$$\uparrow \ \frac{S_1}{\$} \ \overset{\longrightarrow}{\times} \ \frac{S_2}{a} \ \downarrow$$

Discourse of the master

$$\uparrow \ \frac{a}{S_2} \ \overset{\longrightarrow}{\times} \ \frac{\$}{S_1} \ \downarrow$$

Discourse of the analyst

This holds all its importance. What Peirce dares to articulate for us, and here at the hinge of the cosmology of Antiquity, is the plenitude of what is at issue in bodily semblance. It is discourse in its relation, so he says, with the nothing. This means, with that around which any discourse necessarily turns.

Along this path, and by promoting set theory, I've been trying this year to suggest to those who hold the function of analyst that they should become versed, in order to train themselves, in this vein that exploits these statements that are formalized in logic. To train themselves in what? In the fact that there has to be a sifting apart of what earlier I called the filling in, the interval, the buffering, the gap, that lies between the body, jouissance, semblance, and discourse. This needs to be distinguished in order to realize that this is where the question is posed regarding something else, which is neither fine sentiment nor jurisprudence, and which bears a name, that of interpretation.

This was put up on the blackboard for you the other day in the form of what is called the semiotic triangle. It includes the *Representamen*, the *Interpretant*, and the Object. The relation is always ternary. The Representamen–Object pair is always to be reinterpreted, and this is what is at issue in analysis. The Interpretant is the analysand.

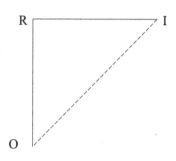

The semiotic triangle

This doesn't mean that the analyst shouldn't be there to help him, to give him a bit of a push in the direction of interpreting. It has to be said that this cannot be done at the level of just one analyst, for the simple reason that if what I say is true, then this would merely be the lode of logic, the extraction of articulations from what is said, and not from the fact of saying. To spell it right out, if the analyst in his function – I mean, *en corps* – does not know how to gather up sufficiently what he hears from the Interpretant, from the one whom he allows to speak in the capacity of analysand, well, this analytic discourse effectively remains where Freud said it would, without budging a line. But then, as soon as it becomes part of common discourse, which is nowadays the case, it enters the armature of fine sentiments.

According to Peirce's diagram, which was drawn up last time, what does it take for interpretation to progress, for it to be possible? What is at issue in this relation between interpretation and Object? What is this Object for Peirce? There is no end to the extension of each new interpretation, unless there should be a limit precisely in what the analytic discourse should bring about, provided it doesn't languish in its current stagnation.

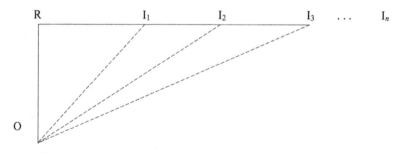

Endless interpretation

What needs to be replaced in Peirce's diagram so that it will match my articulation of the analytic discourse? Well, it's as easy as pie. For the effect of what is at issue in analytic treatment, there is no other Representamen but the object *a*. The analyst turns himself into the Representamen, in the place of semblance.

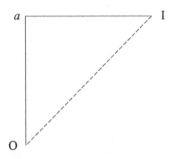

Where am I in the fact of saying?

The Object at issue is none other than what I've been examining here in my two formulas on the blackboard. It is none other than the fact of saying qua forgotten. This is the Object of the question that each of us poses – *Where am I in the fact of saying?*

If it is quite clear that neurosis has this staggered extension, this is very precisely because of this, which explains for us the wavering in what Freud put forward concerning desire, and especially desire in dreams. It's quite true that there are dreams of desire, but when Freud analyses one of his dreams, we can see which desire is at issue. It's the desire to posit the equation that desire equals zero.

At a time that was not much later than 11 April 1956, in 1957 precisely, I analysed the dream of Irma's injection.[6] This was transcribed as you can imagine it would be, by an academic, in a PhD thesis that is doing the rounds at present. The way that it was . . . I won't say *heard*, because he wasn't there – instead he worked from notes, and he thought he could add some of his own inventions to it. All the same, it's clear that if there is one thing that the sublime and divine dream of Irma's injection allows us to show, then it's what should have been exploited, given the time that's passed since I announced it, by anyone within the field of analysis. I left it to languish, because after all, as you're going to see, the thing isn't as consequential as all that. If, as I was reminding you recently, the essence of sleep is the suspension of the body's relation to jouissance, then it's quite obvious that desire, which is suspended from surplus jouissance, will not for all that be bracketed out.

One can clearly see what the dream works with, what it knits together. It uses elements from the day before, as Freud says it does. That is, it uses whatever is still lying utterly at the surface of memory, not in the depths. The only thing that connects the desire of the dream to the unconscious is the way in which it has to be worked through in order to solve the problem with a formula that includes $= 0$, in order to find the root whereby its functioning is annulled. If it is not annulled, as they say, you wake up. In view of which, the subject goes on dreaming in his life.

Freud underscores that if desire has some interest in the dream, then it's in so far as there are cases in which the fantasy cannot be resolved. That is to say, it is perceived that desire – allow me to express it like this since I'm nearing the end – has no reason for being. It's that something has occurred, which is the encounter from which neurosis stems, the Medusa's head, the *split* from earlier, seen directly, inasmuch as it has no solution. It is precisely for this that, in most people's dreams, it is indeed a matter of the question of desire, in so far as it refers far beyond, to the structure by virtue of which the *a* is the cause of the *Spaltung* of the subject.

So, what binds us to the one with whom we are setting off, stepping beyond the first apprehension of the body? Is the analyst there to give him grief for not being sufficiently sexuated, for not enjoying well enough, and goodness knows what else? What is it that binds us to the one who is setting off with us in the position that is called that of the patient?

The term *frère* is splashed across every wall. *Liberté, égalité, fraternité.* But I ask you, at the cultural point we've reached, with whom are we brothers? With whom are we brothers in any other discourse besides the analytic discourse? Is the boss the brother of the worker? Does it not strike you that this word *brother* is precisely the one to which the analytic discourse affords its presence, if only in that it brings it back to what are called family affairs? If you think this is simply to avoid class struggle then you're mistaken. It has to do with many other things besides the family racket. We are brothers with our patient in that, like him, we are sons of discourse.

To represent this effect that I designate as the object *a* – to accustom us to this *désêtre*, this deserted Being, by dint of being the support, the refuse, the abjection, onto which can be hooked what will, thanks to us, be begotten by the fact of saying, which will of course be an Interpretant – I invite the analyst to support himself, in such a way as to be worthy of transference, through this knowledge that can be questioned as such, on account of being in the place of truth. This knowledge can be questioned with respect to what has always been involved in the structure of knowledge, from *savoir-faire* through to the knowledge of science. From here, of course, we interpret. But who can do so if not the very one who engages himself in the fact of saying and who, brother that we are to him, will uplift us?

What is begotten by an analysis, what is begotten at the level of the subject, of the subject who speaks, of the analysand, is something that happens *with* – man thinks, said Aristotle, *with* his soul.[7] The analysand analyses *with* this piece of crap that is proposed to him in the figure of his analyst, the object *a*. It is *with* this something, this split thing, that must be begotten what is none other when all is said and done – to take up something that was put forward the other day with respect to Peirce – than the beam by which the scales of what is called *justice* can be set in balance. Our brother transfigured is what is begotten by the analytic conjuration, and this is what binds us to the one who is improperly called our *patient*.

It has to be said that this *parasexal* discourse can produce this kind of backlash. I would not like to leave you with just this saccharine treat. When it comes back at the level of a discourse, the notion of brother, however solidly it has been rubber-stamped by virtue of all sorts of jurisprudence throughout the ages, will produce its backlash at the level of the support.

In all of this, I haven't made the faintest mention of the Father. I consider that people have already said enough and explained enough about the Father to show you that it's around him who *unigates*, him who says no, that all that is universal can be grounded, must be grounded, and alone can be grounded. When we come back to the root of the body, if we reassert the value of the word *brother*, it will return full sail at the level of fine sentiments.

Since, nevertheless, it's not just about painting a rose-tinted future, you should know that what is on the rise, the ultimate consequences of which we have still not seen, and which is rooted in the body, in the fraternity of bodies, is racism.

You have not heard the last of this.

21 June 1972

APPENDICES

REPORT ON SEMINAR XIX

Jacques Lacan

First published in the *Annuaire de l'École pratique des Hautes Études, 1972–1973*, pp. 287–91; reprinted with minor editorial modifications in *Scilicet* 5 (1975): 5–10.

The title is a choice. Others *s' . . . oupirent*, suspire for worse. I abet not making as much my honour. At issue is the sense of a practice, psychoanalysis.

I will note that I doubled this seminar, with another bearing the entitling of the 'psychoanalyst's knowledge', seen through by the air of sarcasm of my inspiring by Saint-Anne where I was making a return.

In which respect does my Hautes-Études title justify that at Paris I–II, playing host, my having spoken of the One, this is what might have been asked of me, tacit as it was.

That such an idea should have occurred to no one follows from my granted position in advance within the field of psychoanalysis.

It raises those I have designated as suspiring for worse to the One.

As for the rest, I was fomenting no thought of the One, but on the basis of the fact of saying *y a dl'Un*, I was going to the full terms that are demonstrated by its use, to make psychoanalysis thereof.

This is already in the Parmenides, i.e. Plato's dialogue, by a curious vanguard. I recommended a reading of it to my audience, but did they do so? I mean: did they read it as I do? This is not irrelevant to the present report.

The date of the analytic discourse is indicative of applying, to a real like the arithmetic triangle, which is *mathematical* par excellence, that is, which is transmissible outside of meaning, the analysis whereby Frege generates the One from the empty set, born of its time – specifically, where it slides to the equivoque by the name of the number zero, to establish that zero and one makes two. Whereupon Cantor newly calls into question the entire series of integers and refers the denumerable to the first infinite, named $\aleph_0$, the first other One to transfer the cutting edge from the first: the same that, de facto, cuts it off from the twain.

This is precisely what Leibniz foresaw with his monad, but which, failing to extricate it from Being, he left in the Plotinian confusion that is favourable to the defence and illustration of the master.

This is where analysts take an imperious turn for the worse when they cannot accustom themselves to being promoted as abjection at the place defined by the One rightfully occupying it, with the aggravating factor that this is the place of semblance, specifically where *l'être* lays down the *lettre*, we might say.

How might they accustom themselves to it being on the analysand's side that the One is admissible, albeit put to work there (cf. below)?

What they can bear still less is the steadfastness of the One in modern science, not that the universe is maintained therein, but rather that the constancy of energy forms a pivot to the point that even quantum theory's refusals of univocity do not disprove this one and only constancy, indeed that probability promotes the One as the closest element to Nature, which is comical.

Turning oneself into a being of abjection presupposes the analyst as otherwise rooted in a practice that stakes everything on another real: the very same that is at stake for us in the fact of so saying.

And another thing is the remark that abjection in scientific discourse should hold the rank of truth, no less. This, manifest from the start in the hysteria of Socrates, and in the effects of science, coming back to light of day sooner than anyone can imagine.

But what can be found for the taking in analysts' me-at-the-least, when this is the blow I sustain?

Why, wherefore your daughter is mute, did Freud manage to account? This is the complicity we've just been saying, that of hysteria with science. As for the rest, the question is not as to the discovery of the unconscious, which has its material preformed in the symbolic, but as to the creation of an apparatus the real of which touches the real, namely what I have articulated as the analytic discourse.

This creation could only be produced given a certain tradition of Scripture, the hinging of which is to be sounded out with what it sets down of creation.

A segregation results from this, which I am not against, though a formation that is addressed to man one and all, such is my preference, even if, in keeping with my formulae not-all woman does it include.

This not that a woman should be less gifted when it comes to there sustaining herself, quite the contrary, and precisely because she does not suspire for worse of the One, being of the Other, to take up the terms of the Parmenides.

Bluntly to tell the truth that is inscribed by dint of Freud's statements on sexuality, there is no such thing as sexual relation.

This formula makes sense in summing them up. For if sexual jouissance is injected so deeply into the relationships of him that assumes being from speech – for this is what, speaking, being is – is it not so that he has no quantifiable relation to sex as specifying a partner, I would say to indicate what is required by science (and which it applies to the animal realm).

It is only too conceivable how the universitarian idea obfuscates this by classifying it under pansexualism.

Whereas, while the theory of cognizance was for a long time no more than man's relations with woman imagined in metaphor, it is precisely in taking an opposite stance that the analytic discourse is situated. (Freud throws out Jung.)

That analysis should have the task of voicing the critique of the inconsistency of the ancient sayings of love is what results from the very notion of the unconscious inasmuch as it is borne out as knowledge.

What the disposed experience of analysis brings us is that the faintest bias in the text of whatever the analysand's said offers us a purchase thereupon that is more direct than myth, which is aggregated only from the generic in language.

This is a return to the state of civil status, certainly, but why not take this humble path?

If there is solidarity – and no more to advance – between the non-relation of sexes and the fact that a being be speaking, then it's hither wise as valid as the erring habits of consciousness, locating what is presumed to be the crowning achievement of life, which is itself supposed to be a reproductive idea, when sex binds itself unto death as well.

Thenceforth it is in the knots of the symbolic that the interval that is located, by way of a non-relation, is to be mapped in its orography, which, in forming a world for man might equally be called *mur*, a wall, and to proceed from *l'(a)mur*.

Hence the watchword I have been giving to analysts, not to neglect this linguistic discipline in broaching the said knots.

Yet this is not so that they should dodge, following the fashion that affects a semblance of knowing in the university discourse, that which in this field outlined as linguistics, is real about it.

The signifier One is not one signifier among others, and it surmounts that whereby it is but be-twain these signifiers that the subject is supposable, by my so saying.

But this is where I recognize that this here One is but knowledge superior unto the subject, that is, unconscious insofar as it manifests itself as ex-sisting – the knowledge, I say, of a real of the One-all-alone, all-alone right where relation would be said.

Save but zero of meaning should be begotten from the signifier whereby the Other is inscribed in its being unto the subject barred, S(A̶), I write it.

This is why I have been calling the Ones of one of the lateral series of Pascal's triangle *nads*.[1] This One repeats, but is not totalized through this repetition: which is seized from the mere nothings of meaning, facts of non-sense, to be recognized in the dreams, the slips, and indeed the 'quips' of the subject so that he may venture that this unconscious is his own.

His own as knowledge, and the knowing of it as such affects without doubt.

But what? This is the question where one deceives oneself.

– Not 'my' subject (the one that I said just a moment past: that it constitutes in its semblance, I said its letter).

– Nor the soul, which is the imagining of imbeciles, at least they would have believe as much when one finds on reading them this soul *with* which man thinks, for Aristotle, the soul that is reconstructed by the likes of Uexküll, in the guise of an *Innenwelt* that is the trait-portrait of the *Umwelt*.

I say, ergo, that knowledge affects the body of the being that becomes Being only through spoken words, in parcelling out his jouissance, in thereby carving him up to the extent of producing the off-cuts from which I make the (*a*), to be read object *a*, or indeed abject, which is what will be said when I am dead, the time when finally I shall be tended to, or further fleshed out, th(*a*) first cause of his desire.

This body is not the nervous system, though this system does serve jouissance inasmuch as in the body it fits out the predation, or better still the jouissance of the *Umwelt* taken in the manner of prey – which of the *Umwelt* does not, therefore, figure the trait-per-trait, as they persist in dreaming it, a residue of a philosophical vigil, the translation of which into 'affect' marks the unanalysed.

---

[1] We should specify that the monad is, therefore, the One that knows itself all alone, aught of real of the voided relation; the *nad* is this empty relation insisting; there remains the inaccessible henad, the $\aleph_0$ of the sequence of integers, whereby two, which ushers it in, symbolizes in language the supposed subject of knowledge.

It is true therefore that work (dream-work, among other sorts) bypasses thinking, calculating, and even judging. It knows what it has to do. This is its definition: it supposes a 'subject', and this is *Der Arbeiter*.

What does think, calculate, and judge is jouissance, and jouissance being of the Other, requires that the *Une*, the One that makes a function of the subject, should simply be castrated, that is to say symbolized by the imaginary function that incarnates powerlessness, in other words by the phallus.

In psychoanalysis it is a matter of raising powerlessness (the same that makes the fantasy hear reason) to logical impossibility (the same that incarnates the real). That is to say, of completing the lot of signs in which the *fatum hominum* is played out. Here, it is enough to know how to count up to 4, the 4 where the three major numerical operations converge, 2 and 2, 2 times 2, 2 to the power of 2.

The One *pro tanto*, which I locate by way of non-relation, is not part of these 4, precisely in but forming the set of them. Let's not call it monad any more, but the One-fact-of-saying inasmuch as therefrom come to ex-sist those that in-sist in repetition, the founding of which requires three (I said so elsewhere), which goes very well towards setting the subject aside of these 4, by subtracting from him his unconscious.

This is what the year is leaving in suspense, in keeping with what is ordinary in thought which does not except itself for all that from jouissance.

Hence it becomes apparent that thought proceeds only along the path of ethics. This ethics still needs to fall in with the *pas* of psychoanalysis.

Does the One-Fact-of-Saying, in knowing itself One-all-alone, speak on its own? *Pas de dialogue*, I have said, none such dialogue, but this nonesuch of dialogue has its limit in interpretation – whereby is ensured, like for number, the real.

The result of this is that analysis upends the precept: *bien faire et laisser dire*, to the point that saying it well gives satis-fact-ion, since there is but more-thereof-to-say in response from the *pas-assez*, the nonesuch-ficient.

What the French lalingua so illustriates in the saying: *com-bien* for making a question of quantity.

Let's say that the interpretation of the sign renders meaning unto the effects of signification that the signifying battery of language substitutes for the relation it could never encipher.

But the sign in return produces jouissance through the cipher the signifiers permit: which forms the mathematician's d-es-ire, enciphering beyond jouis-sense.

The sign is obsession that cedes, makes an obcession (spelt with a c) to the jouissance that decides upon a practice.

I give my blessing to those who pass commentary in my regard, contending with the torment that sustains a worthy thought, namely: one that is not content to be beaten by tracks of the same name.

Make these lines the trace of hap-py chance, theirs without the knowledge thereof.

LIBRARY TO SEMINAR XIX

Jacques-Alain Miller

The bibliographical notes below follow those prepared by Jacques-Alain Miller for the 2011 Seuil edition of Book XIX (pp. 245–54), with the notable difference that references to French publications have been supplemented, wherever possible, with published English-language translations, while references to French translations have generally been replaced by original sources and/or renderings in English. – ARP

Antiquity

– For Lacan's references to Plato (first and foremost the *Parmenides*, but also the *Meno*, the *Cratylus*, the *Theaetetus*, and the *Symposium*), one may consult the bilingual Greek/French edition published by Belles Lettres; likewise for his references to Aristotle (the *Prior Analytics*, *Physics*, and *Metaphysics*). In English, the *Complete Works of Aristotle* were published as a two-volume set by Oxford University Press in translations revised by Jonathan Barnes, 1984 (corrected edition 1995).

– Euclid, quoted on page 126: Lacan owned a copy of the Dover reprint of *The Thirteen Books of the Elements*, translated by Sir Thomas L. Heath (Cambridge University Press, 1908).

– Archimedes, cited on page 123: concerning his application of the method of exhaustion, derived from Eudoxus of Cnidus, see his works 'On the Sphere and Cylinder', 'Measurement of a Circle', and 'Quadrature of the Parabola'. They were published in French translation by Belles Lettres in 1970 and 1971 as the first two volumes of his complete works; Heath's 1897 *The Works of Archimedes; Edited in Modern Notation with Introductory Chapters* pre-dates the identification and deciphering of the Archimedes palimpsest, and has thus been largely superseded by the scholarship of Reviel

Netz and Nigel Wilson (*The Archimedes Palimpsest, Vols I & II*, Cambridge University Press, 2011 and Netz's translation *The Works of Archimedes, Vols I & II*, Cambridge University Press, 2004); for an excellent overview see Heath's *A Manual of Greek Mathematics* (Oxford University Press, 1931).

– Boetius de Dacia, cited on page 75: see Roman Jakobson's article 'Glosses on the Medieval Insight into the Science of Language' in the seventh volume of his *Selected Writings* (Mouton, 1985, pp. 192–3); one may also consult the article by Sten Ebbesen, 'Theories of Language in the Hellenistic Age and in the Twelfth and Thirteenth Centuries' in *Language and Learning*, edited by D. Frede and B. Inwood (Cambridge University Press, 2008, pp. 299–319).

– Apuleius, cited on page 90: several translations of *The Golden Ass* are available, the most recent being by Sarah Ruden (Yale University Press, 2011); on his logic, one may consult *Apuleian Logic: The Nature, Sources, and Influence of Apuleius's Peri Hermeneias* by Mark W. Sullivan (North-Holland, 1967).

– Secondary sources: Karl Ludwig Michelet, cited on page 18, is a German philosopher (1801–93); his *Examen critique du livre d'Aristote intitulé Métaphysique*, written in French and published by J. Albert Mercklein in Paris in 1836, can now be consulted on Google Books. The article by Jacques Brunschwig, cited on page 90, appeared in *Cahiers pour l'analyse* 10 (1969): 3–25. On the Pythagoreans, cited on page 177, and the incommensurability of the diagonal of the square,[1] see, for example, the article by Jean-Toussaint Desanti, 'Une crise de développement exemplaire: la "découverte" des nombres irrationnels', in *Logique et connaissance scientifique* (Encyclopédie de la Pléiade, 1967, pp. 439–64). On modality in Aristotle, Lacan was later to read Jaakko Hintikka's contribution, *Time and Necessity: Studies in Aristotle's Theory of Modality* (Oxford University Press, 1973).

Logic and Mathematics

– Pascal: the 1654 *Traité sur le triangle arithmétique* was translated in abridged form by Anna Savitsky in D. E. Smith (ed.), *A Source Book in Mathematics* (McGraw-Hill, 1929, pp. 67–79). A full translation was made in 2009 by Richard J. Pulskamp, whose brief introduction points to some textual differences between the 1880 Hachette edition and the 1954 Pléiade edition. The latter is favoured as the source text of his translation, available online at: <www.cs.xu.edu/math/Sources/Pascal/Sources/arith_triangle.pdf>.

– Cauchy and Fourier are cited on page 123 in connection with the history of infinitesimal calculus; on this subject, see the classic book by Carl B. Boyer, *The History of the Calculus and Its Conceptual Development* (Hafner, 1949); and also Margaret E. Baron, *The Origins of Infinitesimal Calculus* (Pergamon, 1969).

– Boole and De Morgan are mentioned on page 154 for their role in the emergence of mathematical logic; Lacan was a reader of the 'Kneale and Kneale', *The Development of Logic* (Oxford University Press, 1962); see also Józef M. Bocheński, *A History of Formal Logic* (Notre Dame Press, 1961).

– Frege: his 1879 *Begriffsschrift* was first Englished by Peter T. Geach ('*Begriffsschrift*, a Formalized Language of Pure Thought Modelled upon the Language of Arithmetic', in *Translations from the Philosophical Writings of Gottlob Frege*, Blackwell, 1952, second edition, 1960, pp. 1–20), followed by the 1967 translation by Stefan Bauer-Mengelberg ('*Begriffsschrift*, a Formula Language, Modeled upon that of Arithmetic, for Pure Thought', in J. van Heijenoort (ed.), *From Frege to Gödel: A Source Book in Mathematical Logic, 1879–1931*, Harvard University Press, pp. 1–82), and then the 1972 translation by Terrell Ward Bynum (in *Conceptual Notation and Related Articles*, Clarendon, pp. 101–203), while the Preface and Part I were also translated by Michael Beaney (in *The Frege Reader*, Blackwell, 1997, pp. 47–78); Frege's 1884 *Grundlagen der Arithmetik* was translated by John Langshaw Austin as *The Foundations of Arithmetic* (Blackwell, 1950, revised second edition 1952), with selections and summaries included in *The Frege Reader* (op. cit., pp. 84–129); Frege's 1892 article 'Über Sinn und Bedeutung' was translated by Max Black as 'On Sense and Reference' (in *Translations from the Philosophical Writings of Gottlob Frege*, op. cit., pp. 56–78), later modified (mis-leadingly) to 'On Sense and Meaning' (B. McGuiness (ed.), *Collected Papers on Mathematics, Logic, and Philosophy*, Blackwell, 1984, pp. 157–77), which in Beaney's translation bears the more prudent title, 'On *Sinn* and *Bedeutung*' (*The Frege* Reader, op. cit., pp. 151–71).

– Dedekind, page 171: see, for example, his 1872 pamphlet *Stetigkeit und irrationale Zahlen* and the 1888 article 'Was sind und was sollen die Zahlen?', which were translated by Wooster Woodruff Beman as 'Continuity and Irrational Numbers' and 'The Nature and Meaning of Numbers', in *Essays on the Theory of Numbers* (Open Court/Kegan Paul, Trench, Trübner, 1901). Beman's translation was extensively revised by William Ewald in *From Kant to Hilbert: A Source Book in the Foundations of Mathematics, Vol. II* (Oxford University Press, 1996, pp. 765–79, 787–833). A French translation of the two essays, prefaced by Desanti and with an Introduction by Mohammed Allal Sinaceur, was published in 1979 as *Analytica* 12/13 (Navarin / Bibliothèque d'Ornicar).

– Peirce: Lacan was a reader of the *Collected Papers of Charles Sanders Peirce, Vols. I–VI*, edited by C. Hartshome and P. Weiss, 1931–35, and *Vols. VII–VIII*, edited by A. W. Burks, 1958 (Harvard University Press).

– Poincaré, page 74 and page 193: see 'L'expérience et la géometrie', the fifth chapter in the 1901 collection *La science et l'hypothèse*, recently translated as 'Space and Geometry' by Mélanie Frappier, Andrea Smith, and David J. Stump, in *Science and Hypothesis* (Bloomsbury Academic, 2017).

– Cantor: his complete works are available in German as *Gesammelte Abhandlungen mathematischen und philosophischen Inhalts*, edited by E. Zermelo (Springer, 1932). The two versions of 'Beiträge zur Begründung der transfiniten Mengenlehre' (1895, 1897) were translated by Philip E. B. Jourdain as *Contributions to the Founding of the Theory of Transfinite Numbers* (Open Court, 1915). Further key texts, and his correspondence with Dedekind, are included in Ewald's English-language translations in *From Kant to Hilbert, Vol. II* (op. cit., pp. 838–940). See also Joseph Warren Dauben's *Georg Cantor: His Mathematics and Philosophy of the Infinite* (Harvard University Press, 1979). For a study of Lacanian influence, see Nathalie Charraud's *Infini et inconscient, essai sur Georg Cantor* (Economica, 1994).

– Russell: Lacan was familiar at least with the following works: *The Principles of Mathematics* (Cambridge University Press, 1903); *Principia Mathematica* (with Alfred North Whitehead, Cambridge University Press, 1910, 1912, 1913); and *An Inquiry into Meaning and Truth* (Norton, 1940).

– Brouwer: Lacan alludes to Brouwer's theory of the 'creative subject' on page 152; see, for example, his text 'Consciousness, Philosophy and Mathematics', in *Proceedings of the 10th International Congress of Philosophy* (North-Holland, 1949, pp. 1243–9), and the study by Walter P. van Stigt, *Brouwer's Intuitionism* (North-Holland, 1990).

– Gödel, page 30 and page 156: Gödel's *Collected Works, Vols I–V* are published by Oxford University Press, 2001–12, under the editorship of S. Feferman; one may also consult the book by Raymond M. Smullyan, *Gödel's Incompleteness Theorems* (Oxford University Press, 1992); and, by the same author, the accessible *The Lady, or the Tiger? And Other Logic Puzzles* (Knopf, 1982), and *Forever Undecided: A Puzzle Guide to Gödel* (Knopf, 1987).

– Bourbaki, page 20: the first volumes of the (at present) twelve Books of the *Éléments de mathématique* treatise were published in French and English by Éditions Hermann. The 1970 volume on the *Théorie des ensembles* (Book I), comprising chapters previously published in 1939, 1954, 1956 and 1957, is slightly later than its English edition (*Theory of Sets*, Hermann, 1968). Likewise, the 1971 volume that comprises Chapters 1 to 4 of *Topologie générale* (Book III) was pre-dated by its English edition (*General Topology*, Hermann, 1966) and contains material first published between 1940 and 1942. Meanwhile, *Éléments d'histoire des mathématiques* groups together historical notes from the Books of the treatise; the first edition was published in 1960, followed by several further editions up to the 2007 Springer edition; the English-language translation by John Meldrum was first published by Springer in 1994 as *Elements of the History of Mathematics*.

– Thom: one may consult his 1972 book on *Structural Stability and Morphogenesis: An Outline of a General Theory of Models*, translated by David H. Fowler (Benjamin, 1975). A collection of papers dating from 1967 to 1981 was translated by W. M. Brookes and D. Rand as *Mathematical Models of Morphogenesis* (Ellis Horwood, 1983).

– The mention of *Naive Set Theory* on page 124 refers to the book by Paul Halmos (Springer, 1960).

– *Cantor a tort*, first mentioned on page 176, bears an author credit to Georges Antoniadès Metrios and a translation credit to Pierre Étienne Bessière (Sival-Presse, 1968). It is highly likely that both are pseudonyms.

The chapters one at a time

I The Small Difference

Lacan refers to his article in the *Écrits*, 'Propos directifs pour un Congrès sur la sexualité féminine'. On the Précieuses, Lacan had certainly read the classic study by René Bray, *La Préciosité et les Précieux: De Thibaut de Champagne à Jean Giraudoux* (Albin Michel, 1948); one can now read Myriam Dufour-Maître's *Les Précieuses: Naissance des femmes de lettres en France au XVIIe siècle* (Honoré Champion, 1999). Apollinaire's play *Les Mamelles de Tiresias* (1903), which is frequently cited by Lacan, was translated by Louis Simpson in 1961 as *The Breasts of Tiresias* (in M. B. Gale and J. F. Deeney (eds), *The Routledge Drama Anthology and Sourcebook: From Modernism to Contemporary Performance*, 2010, pp. 207–19), and by Maya Slater as *The Mammaries of Tiresias* (in *Three Pre-Surrealist Plays*, Oxford University Press, 1997, pp. 151–207). Regarding etymological dictionaries, Lacan owned the abridged two-volume set of Walther von Wartburg's *Französisches etymologisches Wörterbuch* (the full twenty-five volume work was only completed in 2002). The Damourette and Pichon, a constant touchstone for Lacan, is their treatise *Des mots à la pensée: Essai de grammaire de la langue française*, 1911–56, the eight volumes of which have been reprinted by Vrin.

II The Function Φx

If the question of the written was 'on the agenda', this was due in particular to Jacques Derrida (*L'écriture et la différence* had been published in 1967 and *De la grammatologie* in 1967). 'L'instance de la lettre dans l'inconscient' is in the *Écrits*. Anyone interested in logic in the Middle Ages will read with profit *The Cambridge History of Later Medieval Philosophy: From the Rediscovery of Aristotle to the Disintegration of Scholasticism, 1100–1600*, edited by N. Kretzmann, A. Kenny, and J. Pinborg (Cambridge University Press, 1988). I would also mention the works in French of Alain de Libera.

III From Anecdote to Logic

'The most recent steps in biology': Lacan is no doubt thinking of Crick and Watson's discovery of the structure of DNA and the results that led to Jacob, Lwoff, and Monod being awarded the Nobel Prize in 1965; he had read François Jacob's *La Logique du vivant, une histoire de l'hérédité* (Gallimard, 1970, translated by Betty E. Spillman as *Logic of Life: A History of Heredity*, Princeton University Press, 1973). August Weismann: we know that Freud refers to him in *Beyond the Pleasure Principle*; consult, for example, his *Essays upon Heredity and Kindred Biological Problems*, translated and edited by Sir Edward Bagnall Poulton, Selmar Schönland, and Sir Arthur Everett Shipley (Clarendon, 1891). The variations on 'I love her' are in Freud's text on President Schreber; there is a commentary by Lacan in his 'Discours de Rome' (in *Autres écrits*).

IV From Necessity to Inexistence

The pupil who 'came up with this, all on his own' is the psychoanalyst Octave Mannoni, cited for his 1963 article 'Je sais bien, mais quand même' (this phrase is translated by G. M. Goshgarian as 'I know well, but all the same' and by Wendy A. Hester as 'I know very well, but all the same'). 'La signification du phallus' is in the *Écrits*. Leopold Kronecker's anti-Cantorian comment is often quoted: 'Die ganzen Zahlen hat der liebe Gott gemacht, alles andere ist Menschenwerk'. The 'little book' on Arabic dactylonomy: I gave this book to Lacan, but have been unable to recall the title; one may consult Karl Menninger's classic book from 1934, translated by Paul Broneer from the revised 1958 edition as *Number Words and Number Symbols: A Cultural History of Numbers*, MIT Press, 1969, along with the references listed in my note on Al-Uqlidisi in *Ornicar?* 16, 1978. Leibniz's lucubration on identity can be found in *New Essays on Human Understanding*, IV, vii, 10.

V Topology of Speech (*A Talk at Sainte-Anne*)

The four discourses are set out in 'Radiophonie', in *Autres écrits*. 'Fonction et champ de la parole et du langage en psychanalyse' was reprinted in the *Écrits*. On archetypes, see Jung's 1912 book *Symbols of Transformation: An Analysis of the Prelude to a Case of Schizophrenia*, translated by R. F. C. Hull (Bollingen Foundation, 1956). Roman Jakobson: Lacan makes several mentions of the series of *conférences* that his friend was delivering concurrently at the Collège de France at the invitation of Lévi-Strauss. Van Gulik's *Sexual Life in Ancient China: A Preliminary Survey of Chinese Sex and Society from ca. 1500 BC till 1644 AD* was published in 1961 (E. J. Brill; revised edition, 2003). On André Gide, see Lacan's 'Jeunesse de Gide' in the *Écrits*. Jean Paul Richter's 1883 two-volume translation of Leonardo's *Notebooks* and Edward MacCurdy's more complete 1905 rendering have long stood as the reference editions in English. Lacan came up with 'lettre d'amur' in his third *entretien* at Sainte-Anne (see *Talking to Brick Walls*, Polity, 2017).[2] 'La métaphore du sujet' features in the appendices to the second edition of the *Écrits*. In 1958, Chaïm Perelman co-authored with Lucie Olbrechts-Tyteca *The New Rhetoric: A Treatise on Argumentation*, translated by John Wilkinson and Purcell Weaver, Notre-Dame, 1968.

VI I Ask You to Refuse Me My Offering

'Ne touchez pas à la hache' is the famed retort from General Armand de Montriveau in Balzac's *La Duchesse de Langeais*. The Antonella to whom Lacan appeals was then translating him into Italian; he calls her 'A' in his 'Préface à une thèse' (*Autres écrits*, p. 393). Wittgenstein's notorious aphorism is the last proposition in his *Tractatus Logico-Philosophicus*. Alexandre Kojève was Lacan's mentor and close friend, author of the famous *Introduction to the Reading of Hegel*, edited in 1947 by Raymond Queneau and translated by James H. Nichols Jr (Cornell University Press, 1969). On the potlatch, read the 1925 essay, *The Gift*, by Marcel Mauss (translated by Ian Cunnison, Cohen & West, 1954; then again by W. D. Halls, Norton, 1990; and more recently in an expanded edition by Jane I. Guyer, University of Chicago Press, 2016) and *The Accursed Share* by Georges Bataille (three volumes, 1946; translated by Robert Hurley in two volumes, Zone Books, 1988). Georges Théodule Guilbaud was a mathematician and a friend of Lacan's whom he frequently consulted; among his other achievements, Guilbaud introduced game theory into post-war France. Lacan develops the Borromean knot at great length from his twenty-second Seminar (*RSI*) onwards.

VII The Vanished Partner (*A Talk at Sainte-Anne*)

Simone de Beauvoir's *The Second Sex* was published in two volumes in 1949 (translated by Howard Madison Parshley, Vintage/Random House, 1953; and later by Constance Borde and Sheila Malovany-Chevalier, Cape, 2009). On Socrates, see in particular the eighth Seminar, on *Transference*.

VIII What is Involved in the Other

Hogarth: the S-shaped line is, according to him, the emblem of beauty; see his 1753 book *The Analysis of Beauty* and the note to Book XXIII of the Seminar (Polity, 2016, pp. 218–19). Lacan often asserted that he was the first to have pointed out the importance of Freud's *nachträglichkeit* (retroaction) and to have established its meaning (cf. in particular the case of the Wolf Man). Descartes: Lacan often commented on the *cogito*, and played at modifying it; see especially Seminars XII and XIV. 'La Chose freudienne' features in the *Écrits*, including Truth's prosopopeia. Lacan read the *Phänomenologie des Geistes* in German and in the French translation by his friend Jean Hyppolite (still in print by Aubier); there are several partial translations in English; for a full translation, see Sir James Black Baillie's *Phenomenology of Mind* (revised second edition, Allen & Unwin, 1931) and Arnold V. Miller's *Phenomenology of Spirit* (Oxford University Press, 1977). On the events that led to Lacan's 'excommunication' from the IPA (International Psycho-Analytic Association), see the bio-bibliographical information I supplied to *On the Names-of-the-Father* (Polity, 2013), the file in *Television/A Challenge to the Psychoanalytic Establishment* (Norton, 1990), and the opening lesson to Seminar XI, *The Four Fundamental Concepts of Psychoanalysis*. Lacan had been the target of an armed robbery in his consulting room; he was struck in the throat by one of his assailants, and this left him with a hoarse voice for several days afterwards; the identity of the aggressors was known; Lacan did not lodge a complaint.

IX In the Field of the Unian

John Stuart Mill came out with *A System of Logic, Ratiocinative and Inductive, Being a Connected View of the Principles of Evidence, and the Methods of Scientific Investigation* in 1843 (third revised edition, John W. Parker, 1851, reprinted in *The Collected Works of John Stuart Mill, Vols. VII–VIII*, University of Toronto Press, 1974). During this session, Lacan gets into a muddle over the number of subsets; I have given the formula that features in Claude Berge's 1968 book *Principles of Combinatorics* (edited by Richard Bellman as Vol. 72 of the Mathematics in Science and Engineering series, Academic Press, 1971).

X *Yad'lun*

Pliny the Elder: following the influential English rendering by Philemon Holland in 1601, the first full translation of the thirty-six Books of the *Natural History* was produced by John Bostock and Henry Thomas Riley in 1855. The Harris Rackham (*Vols I–V, IX*), William Henry Samuel Jones (*Vols. VI–VIII*), and D. E. Eichholz (*Vol. X*) translation was printed in the Loeb library (Harvard University Press, 1949–54); see also the selection by John F. Healy (Penguin, 1991).

XI An Issue of Ones (*A Talk at Sainte-Anne*)

'Brrom-brrom-wap-wap' comes from Lacan's first wife, Marie-Louise, née Blondin. By Berkeley, one may read *A Treatise concerning the Principles of Human Knowledge* (1710); and one may also consult Martial Gueroult's *Berkeley: Quatre études sur la perception et sur Dieu* (Aubier, 1956). Antonie van Leeuwenhoek and Jan Swammerdam, two Dutch scholars of the seventeenth century, were pioneers in the use of microscopy for biological observation; they are considered precursors of microbiology and cellular biology. On the biology of copulation, Lacan consulted in particular Charles Houillon's treatise on *Sexualité* (Hermann, 1967). Galileo's famous remark on infinity can be found in his 1638 book *Discorsi e dimostrazioni matematiche intorno a due nuove scienze* (translated by Henry Crew and Alfonso de Salvio as *Dialogues concerning Two New Sciences*, Macmillan, 1914; and later by Stillman Drake as *Two New Sciences*, University of Wisconsin, 1974).

XII Knowledge about Truth

Freud refers to Gustave Le Bon in his *Massenpsychologie und Ich-Analyse*. The *einziger Zug* features in Chapter VII on 'Identification'. Lacan refers to the mutilation of the hermai in his Seminar on *Transference* and in his *écrit*, 'Proposition du 9 octobre 1967 sur le psychanalyste de l'École' (*Autres écrits*). It may be presumed that the mention of Nietzsche refers to *Der Antichrist* (first translated, with some censorship, by Henry Louis Mencken as *The Antichrist*, Knopf, 1918, then by Walter A. Kaufmann in *The Portable Nietzsche*, Viking Press, 1954, and then by R. J. Hollingdale as *The Anti-Christ*, Penguin, 1968). Aristotle looks at tragedy in his *Poetics* (numerous editions available). It may be presumed that in referring to Surrealism, Lacan is thinking of André Breton's 1937 *Amour fou* (translated by Mary Ann Caws as *Mad Love*, Bison, 1988); for Stendhal, the reference is surely *De l'amour* (translated by Philip Sidney Woolf and Cecil N. Sidney Woolf as *On Love*, Mayflower, 1915, then by Gilbert and Suzanne Sale as *Love*, Penguin, 1975, and more recently by Sophie Lewis as *On Love*, Hesperus, 2009); for Baudelaire, Lacan must be thinking of the 1846 *Choix de maximes consolantes sur l'amour* (translated by Rainer J. Hanshe in *My Heart Laid Bare*, Contra Mundum, 2017, pp. 1–12); *L'Astrée*, the novel by Honoré d'Urfé (1607–27), was translated in 1657 by John Davies under the title *Astrea*, and Part I was translated, under the same title, by Steven Rendall in 1995 (Medieval and Renaissance Texts and Studies, SUNY). The reference to the miner rubbing down his wife can be found in 'Subversion du sujet et dialectique du désir', in the *Écrits*.[3] The 'instructive' remark by Gödel is in his 1944 article, 'Russell's Mathematical Logic', in *Collected Works, Vol. II*, op. cit., pp. 119–41.[4]

XIII The Founding of Sexual Difference

Russell's remark, which was often quoted by Lacan, is from the 1901 paper 'Recent Work on the Principles of Mathematics' (later published as 'Mathematics and the Metaphysicians', in *Mysticism and Logic*, Allen & Unwin, 1917): 'Mathematics may be defined as the subject in which we never know what we are talking about, nor whether what we are saying is true'; he wrote a three-volume autobiography (Allen & Unwin, 1951–69).

XIV Theory of the Four Formulae (*A Talk at Sainte-Anne*)

As I have indicated, the first three of the seven *entretiens* that Lacan initially delivered under the heading *Le savoir du psychanalyste* have been set apart in the book *Talking to Brick Walls* (Polity, 2017). The psychoanalyst mentioned for his use of set theory went by the name of Ignacio Matte Blanco; his book *The Unconscious as Infinite Sets: An Essay in Bi-logic* was published in London by Duckworth in 1975 (reprinted by Karnac, 1998). Lacan had earlier pointed out how, soon after his report on 'Fonction et champ . . .', the *International Journal* had published some considerations on language by his former analyst, Rudolph Loewenstein. The word *Verwerfung* features in the Schreber case; see the index of Freud's German terms in the *Écrits*. On imaginary numbers, an appellation that we owe to Descartes (Book III of *La Géométrie*, 1637), see Dominique Flament, *Histoire des nombres complexes: Entre algèbre et géométrie* (CNRS, 2003). Paul-Jean Toulet is a poet of whom Lacan was fond in his youth; his complete works were published by Éditions Robert Laffont in 1986; Lacan refers to *Contrerimes*, XXVI (*Œuvres complètes*, p. 12): *Comme les dieux gavant leur panse, / Les Prétendants aussi. / Télémaque en est tout ranci : / Il pense à la dépense.* The *Legenda aurea* by Jacobus da Varagine (*c.* 1260) was Englished by William Caxton in 1483 as *The Golden Legende*, later modernized by Frederick Startridge Ellis (Kelmscott, 1892); a more recent translation by William Granger Ryan was published in 1993 by Princeton University Press (two volumes). Lacan refers to his graph from 'Subversion du sujet . . .' in the *Écrits*.

XV The Desire to Sleep

The article 'L'Agonie du signe' is by Jean Paris, published in the eleventh issue of *Change* (themed *L'Atelier de l'écriture*, May 1972). The Seminar of 1954–1955 is Seminar I on Freud's technical writings, in which there is a commentary on the dream of Irma's injection.[5] The thesis that Lacan stigmatizes is Didier Anzieu's *L'Auto-Analyse de Freud*, which had been published in 1959 (translated by Peter Graham as *Freud's Self-Analysis*, International Universities Press, 1986). Henri Poincaré recounted to the French Société de Psychologie the circumstances of his invention of Fuchsian functions during a sleepless night ('L'Invention mathématique', 1908, translated by George Bruce Halsted as 'Mathematical Creation', in *The Foundations of Science*, The Science Press, 1913); the anecdote was taken up by the mathematician Jacques Hadamard in his *Essay on The Psychology of Invention in the Mathematical Field* (Princeton University Press, 1945). Lacan had been giving some lectures in Milan at the invitation of his Italian pupils.

XVI Bodies Captured by Discourse

The sentence on the blackboard (which had also been written up at the start of the previous session) appears in slightly modified form near the beginning of the article in which Lacan finalizes and extends the elaborations of . . . *or Worse*, namely 'L'étourdit', collected in *Autres écrits*; the four quantifying formulae are there designated as the formulae 'of sexuation'. Umberto Eco remained Lacan's friend; he went to listen to a lecture Lacan gave at the Italian Institute in Paris in the late 1970s: Eco evokes meeting Lacan in *Foucault's Pendulum* (translated by William Weaver, 1989).[6] The painting by Hieronymus Bosch is *The Conjurer*, in the municipal museum of Saint-Germain-en-Laye; it is attributed to his workshop.[7] On Marx, see in particular 'Radiophonie', in *Autres écrits*. The 1955–1956 Seminar, the third in the series, was published in 1981, shortly after Lacan's death, under the title *Les Psychoses*; the Latin sentence was from Cicero (see 'L'étourdit'). Peirce's quadrants are commented on and employed in Seminar IX, *L'identification*; they serve to demonstrate the universal and the particular in the affirmative and the negative. Lucio Fontana (1899–1968) founded 'Spatialism': this school sought to reveal the third dimension of pictorial space by making scratches, perforations, and incisions in the canvas; in Rome, Lacan had seen works from the series *Concetto spaziale, Attese*.[8]

NB: All characters in Chinese have been revised for this English edition.

JAM

Hieronymus Bosch and workshop, *The Conjurer*, *c.*1502, oil on wood,
53 cm × 65 cm, Musée Municipal, St.-Germain-en-Laye;
Photo: The Yorck Project / Wikimedia Commons/Public Domain

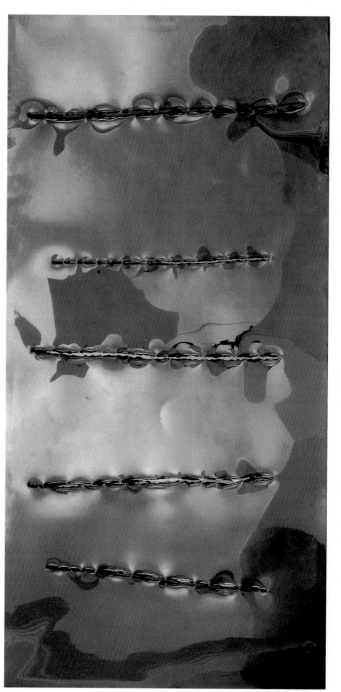

Lucio Fontana, *Concetto spaziale*, 1962, copper 38¼ × 77⅝ inches (97.2 × 196.5 cm)
Private Collection, courtesy of Sperone Westwater, New York

TRANSLATOR'S NOTES

Chapter I The Small Difference

1 Grammarians classify *pire* strictly as an adjective. The corresponding adverb is *pis*, and the comparative form *plus mal*. However, since *pis* has become increasingly outmoded, the erroneous adverbial use of *pire* has been on the rise. When in the following paragraph Lacan qualifies the adverb as *disjoint*, he may have in mind the 'disjunct adverb' (usually termed a *modalisateur* in French).

2 As Bertrand Russell notes in his 1908 article on 'Mathematical Logic as Based on the Theory of Types' (in J. van Heijenoort (ed.), *From Frege to Gödel: A Source Book in Mathematical Logic, 1879–1931*, Cambridge, MA: Harvard University Press, 1967, p. 157n), the term *variable apparente* had been coined five years previously by Giuseppe Peano in the fourth volume of *Formulaire de mathématiques*. The term has since been largely superseded by David Hilbert's term 'bound variable', though some have contested their equation (e.g., Montgomery Furth in his Introduction to Frege, G., *The Basic Laws of Arithmetic: Exposition of the System*, translated by M. Furth, University of California Press, 1964, pp. xxxii–xxxiii).

3 Here and throughout the present edition, the quantifying *tout* is rendered as 'all'. While this usage conforms to a long-standing tradition of Aristotelian term logic in English, it may be remarked that Robin Smith asserted (drawing on Peter T. Geach in *Logic Matters*, Oxford: Blackwell, 1972, p. 69) that translating ὑπάρχειν παντί as 'belongs to all' is an 'unnecessary barbarism', with the plural form, 'belongs to every', being more advisable ('Preface' to *Prior Analytics*, Indianapolis: Hackett, 1989, p. ix). This opinion is counter to that of W. and M. Kneale in their 1962 book *The Development of Logic* (Oxford University Press) who assert: 'in some modern versions of Aristotle's doctrine the difficulties of his account of opposition are unnecessarily aggravated by use of examples and formulae in the plural' (p. 61). Recent translators and commentators have tended to maintain the use of 'all', foremost among them Gisela Striker in her *Aristotle's Prior Analytics, Book I*, Oxford University Press, 2009; see also M. Malink's note on '*Every* and *all*' from his chapter on 'The Orthodox *dictum* Semantics' in *Aristotle's Modal Syllogistic*, Harvard University Press, 2013, pp. 55–6. Lacan

employs extensively the four French declensions: *tout* (masculine singular), *toute* (feminine singular), *tous* (masculine plural), and *toutes* (feminine plural), which in this edition have on most occasions been reproduced alongside the uninflected 'all'. It should be noted, however, that the distinction between *toute* and *toutes* is inaudible in spoken French, and thus in the absence of an article or other quantifying grammatical feature there is transcriptive uncertainty in some instances.

4 In § 11 on 'Die Allgemeinheit' from the *Begriffsschrift*, Frege writes of inserting *eine Höhlung* in the *Inhaltsstriche*, which Geach translates as a 'concavity in the content-stroke' (*Translations from the Philosophical Writings of Gottlob Frege*, second edition, Oxford: Blackwell, 1960, p. 16). Stefan Bauer-Mengelberg's 1967 translation (in van Heijenoort, J. (ed.), *From Frege to Gödel*, op. cit., p. 24) follows suit, as does Michael Beaney's 1997 translation (in *The Frege Reader*, Oxford: Blackwell, p. 69).

5 Originally coined by Molière in *Le Médecin malgré lui* (Act I, Scene 6), the phrase *il y a fagots et fagots* has passed into common idiomatic use in French to mean 'every alike is not the same'. The French *fagot* corresponds to its English-language cognate, signifying a bundle of twigs or small branches.

6 The French terms are *la canaillerie* and *la bêtise*, but the allusion is most probably to the distinction drawn in *Seminar VII* where Lacan reproduces the English vocabulary, referencing the tradition that reaches from Chaucer through to Elizabethan theatre. There, Lacan translates 'knave/knavery' as *canaille/canaillerie*, while 'fool' is rendered variously as *sot*, *innocent*, and *demeuré*.

7 The term was first coined at the end of the lesson of 19 May 1971. The Seuil edition transcribes as *hommoinzin* (*Le séminaire livre XVIII, D'un discours qui ne serait pas du semblant*, Paris: Seuil, 2006, p. 144). In 'L'étourdit' (*Autres écrits*, Seuil: Paris, 2001, p. 479) the spelling is *hommoinsun*. In the lesson of 9 June 1971, three possible forms are stipulated: *au moins un* ('at least one'); *hommoinzin*, punning on *homme* or *homo*; and *a(u moins un)*, highlighting the function of the object *a* (*Livre XVIII*, ibid., p. 153). Here in this opening lesson, Lacan pronounces the term in a way that suggests a terminal 'e' indicative of feminine declension (to accord with the feminine *erreur*).

8 *Seriner* is to repeat something incessantly, or to drum something into someone, as one might train a canary to sing. In their entry on *serin*, Bloch and von Wartburg trace the verb to 1812. Further to the avian signification, a *serin* in French is also a 'dimwit' or 'silly billy' (since 1821).

9 Damourette and Pichon list these forms of post-verbal negation, of which the latter two are rather antiquated, as examples of the negation that *forecloses*, in contrast to the 'discordential' negation represented by the pre-verbal *ne*. The special quality of these words is that they can be associated with *ne* to function as adverbs, producing a negative signification. (When the respective meanings of the latter three terms are rendered approximately in English as 'not a jot', 'not a drop', and 'not a speck', this special quality is lost, since the negation 'not' has been appended to the noun as it could be in any other negative construction.)

Cf. *Des mots à la pensée: Essai de grammaire de la langue française*, Vol. I (1911–1927), d'Artrey, chapter 7.

Chapter II The Function Φ*x*

1 *Hi-han* is the French onomatopoeia for a donkey's bray, equivalent to 'hee-haw' in English. An *appât* is 'bait' or a 'lure'. *Hi-han appât*, or *hihanappat* as Lacan will write it in the second paragraph of 'Joyce le Symptôme' (*Autres écrits*, op. cit., p. 565), is loosely homophonic with the informal *Y en a pas*, 'there is / are none'.
2 Lacan says, *au niveau du mythe d'Œdipe*, 'at the level of the Oedipus myth'. The present edition respects the alteration introduced in the Seuil edition.

Chapter III From Anecdote to Logic

1 Several French authors had used the title *Traité de logique* for their tracts on logic: Philibert Damiron in 1836 (third volume of his *Cours de philosophie*); Joseph Duval-Jouve in 1843; Edmond Goblot in 1918; Jules Tricot in 1928 (*Traité de logique formelle*); and Charles Serrus in 1945.
2 August Weismann used the Latinate *soma*, but not *germen* which was chiefly an intervention of French translators and commentators to refer to *Keimplasma*, 'germ-plasm' (occasionally 'germinative plasma' in English), the substance of *Keimzellen*, 'germ cells'.
3 Frege refers to the blackletter α that he uses to denote the bound variable in the *Höhlung* as a *deutschen Buchstaben*. Like much of the symbolic apparatus of the *Begriffsschrift*, the convention was not retained by the more influential authors who adopted and expanded its notational principles.
4 As in the previous chapter, Lacan's reference to *le mythe de l'Œdipe* is altered in the Seuil edition to *Totem et Tabou*.
5 The opening of this lesson was disturbed by a tirade from a member of the public.

Chapter IV From Necessity to Inexistence

1 Here, and seven paragraphs below, *nécessité de discours* might also be rendered as: 'necessitated by discourse'.
2 In modern usage, the French adjective *grotesque* extends wider than its English cognate to encompass the ludicrous, the ridiculous, and the preposterous.
3 The ambiguity is of course stronger in French (*un désir d'enfant*), since in English one would speak rather in terms of 'a desire for a child' and 'a child's desire'. Cf. the bilingual title of Wladimir Granoff's 1955 article in French, 'Desire for Children, Children's Desire: Un désir d'enfant', in *La psychanalyse* 2: 75–110, and Lacan's mention of the same in Book VIII of the Seminar (Paris: Seuil, revised edition 2001, p. 147).

4 Frege quotes Leibniz from the 1840 Johann Eduard Erdmann edition of Book IV of the *Nouveaux Essais sur l'Entendement Humain* (Ch. vii, § 10, p. 363), in *Godhofredi Guillelmi Leibnitii Opera philosophica*. Whereas Leibniz, in his definitions, spells out each number in roman letters, Frege uses arabic numerals (Frege, G., *The Foundations of Arithmetic*, translated by J. L. Austin, London: Blackwell & Mott, 1953 revised edition, § 6, p. 7).

5 On the Englishing of Frege's coinage *Gleichzahlig*, see Austin's footnote to § 68 of *The Foundations* (ibid., p. 79).

6 Austin translates 'Unter den Begriff "gleich 0 aber nicht gleich 0" fällt [. . .] kein Gegenstand' (§ 77), as 'under the concept "identical with 0 but not identical with 0" [. . .] no object falls' (ibid., p. 90).

7 Lacan has arranged the arithmetical triangle (see page 27) into an upper triangular matrix, as did Pascal himself. In this arrangement, the column 1, 3, 3, 1 corresponds to the subsets of the elements of a triad, i.e. 1 figure, 3 (monadic) vertices, 3 (dyadic) edges, and 1 (triadic) face. Having established the number of edges, it is then possible to read the horizontal row 1, 3, 6, 10, 15 . . . as the triangular numbers, i.e. the number of objects that can be arranged into a triangle, thus: a minimal triangle of 3 discrete objects is configured of a base of 2 and an apex of 1; then, a larger triangle of 6 is configured, with a base of 3 added to the previous 3; followed by a triangle of 10, with a base of 4 added to the previous 6; and so on. The next column, 1, 4, 6, 4, 1, corresponds to the subsets of a tetrad, i.e. 1 figure, 4 (monadic) vertices, 6 (dyadic) edges, 4 (triadic) faces, and 1 tetrad. Having established the number of faces, it is then possible to read the row 1, 4, 10, 20 . . . as the tetrahedral numbers, i.e. the number of objects that can be arranged into a tetrahedron, thus: a minimal tetrahedral of 4 discrete objects is configured of a base of 3 and an apex of 1; then, a larger tetrahedron of 10 is configured, with a base of 6 added to the previous 4; and so on. Note that the additional 'base' level of each new tetrahedral is derived from the triangular number that stands one position to the left in the row immediately above, just as the additional 'base' level of each new triangle is derived from the linear number that stands one space to the left in the row immediately above. The arithmetical triangle can be used to generate infinitely larger figurate numbers, beginning at the next level with the pentatope numbers.

8 At no point in the Seminar does Lacan enumerate the figurate numbers. However, the stenographer's typescript inserts the opening sequence of dyadic numbers, then the opening sequence of pentatope numbers, then the opening sequence of tetrahedral numbers, and finally the opening sequence of triadic numbers, in an apparent attempt to parse this and the previous paragraphs. The Seuil edition reproduces these sequences on pp. 59–60.

Chapter V Topology of Speech (*A Talk at Sainte-Anne*)

1 Isidore of Seville groups such terms in the category of 'medial (*medius*) nouns', and also writes of 'mongrel' (*nothus*) terms with corrupted (i.e.

inter-lingual) suffixes. See entry vii.13 in Book I of *The Etymologies of Isidore of Seville*, translated by S. A. Barney, W. J. Lewis, J. A. Beach, and O. Berghof, Cambridge University Press, 2006, p. 43.

2 The French reads: ... *parce que je ne pédale normalement*. The verb *pédaler* carries the same primary signification as the English 'to pedal'. The noun *pédale* is sometimes used, informally and vulgarly, to label a male homosexual, and Lacan appears to be playing on this meaning here. The sentence that follows could be understood as reasserting the primary sense of the verb.

3 The French verb *causer* also means 'to talk' or 'to converse'. Thus, *nous sommes causés par notre propre bla-bla-bla* could be rendered as 'we are spoken by our own blather'.

4 In his previous talk at Sainte-Anne, on 6 January, Lacan gave himself over to some extemporized punning on *(a)mur*, a condensation of *mur* ('wall'), *amour* ('love'), and the object *a* (see *Talking to Brick Walls*, Cambridge: Polity, 2017, p. 98). The opening comments from the present session, included in the appendix to *Talking to Brick Walls*, explore the theme of 'the love letter/the letter on the wall' in relation to the story of the writing on the wall at Belshazzar's feast (ibid., pp. 108–9).

Chapter VI I Ask You to Refuse Me My Offering

1 Lacan offers no commentary on these characters. Reading right to left, they transliterate to Pinyin as: *qǐng* (please/invite/ask) *jù shōu* (refuse/reject) *wǒ* (I/me/my) *zèng* (offer/give) / *gài* (ancient form: because/probably/indeed) *fēi* (fusion of negative particle and copula: not be) *yě* (emphasis: thus/indeed not). The text is therefore a partial equivalent to *je te demande de me refuser ce que je t'offre, parce que c'est pas ça*; partial in that any analogues of *te* and *ce que* have been omitted. Although any source remains unidentified, the *zōngpái* script and the Old Chinese signification of 蓋 suggest a citation from an ancient text. The characters are missing from the Seuil edition (cf. Jacques-Alain Miller's response to a query on this matter in *Lacan Quotidien* 6 (25 August 2011): 6–7).

2 The French word *conférence* would in similar contexts translate fairly straightforwardly into English as 'lecture', but Lacan's ensuing comments seem to comprehend the more formal and antiquated use that links directly to the etymological root of conferring, conversing, consulting, and deliberating (from the Latin *conferre*). This signification coincides largely with the English 'conference'.

3 The *Dictionnaire universel d'histoire et de géographie* includes, as one would expect, an entry on Anicius Manlius Severinus Boëthius.

4 The French *ache* as in 'h' is homophonic with *hache* as in 'axe', thus the full sentence is homophonic with: 'Don't touch the axe'. For the bibliographic reference, see p. 227.

5 According to the rules of accordance for the *passé composé* in French, the past participle respects the gendered attribute of the *complément d'objet direct*, the pronoun that is directly attached to the verb. Thus, in this case, assuming the addressee denoted by *t'* to be female, the close of

the declaration should read: . . . *combien je t'ai aimée*. The full sentence could be rendered as: 'you shall never know how much I loved you'.

6 Lacan uses a lower-case d for *destinateur* and a capital D for *destinataire*. Jakobson's vocabulary is sometimes rendered in English, including by Jakobson himself, using Addresser and Addressee.

7 Lacan expressly conflates the D of Demand with the D for *destinataire* in the triangle diagram. It should also be borne in mind that the French *demande*, especially when preceded, as here, by the indefinite article, also translates as 'request'. Thus, the form rendered here as 'I ask you . . .' is, in French, *je te demande . . .*

8 Up to this point, Lacan's audience would in all likelihood have understood *Je te demande de me refuser ce que je t'offre* as 'I ask you to reject what I'm offering you', i.e. with the relative pronoun *ce que* standing in for a noun, and *offre* functioning in the present indicative tense. Here, Lacan reiterates that he entertains a different meaning, with *ce que* being essentially reducible to the conjunction *que*, and *offre* functioning as what he calls a *substantif verbal*. In the present translation, an analogous ambiguity is rendered by means of the alternation between 'offering' as a noun and 'offering' as a gerund. This has led to the suppression of Lacan's remark, in this same sentence, that the verbal substantive is 'purported to be a lesser substantive, but is nevertheless quite something'. This remark comes in echo of the earlier comment concerning the dubious classificatory distinction between 'concrete substantives' and others.

9 *Je te bouffe* could also mean something like 'I'm biting your head off' or 'I'm eating you alive'.

10 Again, *ce que tu désires que je te demande* might initially suggest 'what you want me to ask you'.

Chapter VII The Vanished Partner (*A Talk at Sainte-Anne*)

1 First coined in the early twentieth century, the term *partouze* (also spelt *partouse*) refers to group sex, in a similar colloquial register to 'gang bang' or 'orgy'. While the term resembles *partout*, 'everywhere', it is derived from *partie*, as in a *partie de cartes* (a game or a round of cards) and the argotic suffix *-ouse*, which is used to form nouns.

2 The aitch added to *Autre* introduces an aspect of haughtiness or elevation. With a French pronunciation, *Hun* is identical to *Un* ('One') prefixed by a voiced aitch. Lacan had previously used *Hun* in the written text 'Lituraterre' of the year before, in his coinage *Hun-en-peluce*. Cf. 'Lituraterre' in *Hurly-Burly* 9: 34.

3 Lacan is turning *sa femme*, 'his wife', into a verb. The *s* followed by the apostrophe indicates a reflexive form, reminiscent of *s'affamer*, 'to starve oneself', or perhaps even *s'affirmer*, 'to affirm oneself'.

4 Lacan says, *les aventures mythiques d'Œdipe*, 'the mythical adventures of Oedipus'. The Seuil edition alters to *les aventures mythiques du Père primitif*, which is respected in the present edition. See Chapter II, endnote 2, and Chapter III, endnote 4.

5 *Type désespéré* could also be a 'hopeless guy'.

6 In the Baxter–Sagart system, the Old Chinese pronunciation is notated /*tˤa/; in the Zhengzhang system, /*taː/.

7 Lacan says *nous continuons à nous entretenir*, which is at once an allusion to the *entretien* format of his presentations at Sainte-Anne and a jocular acknowledgement of their aspect of 'getting in shape' as far as formal logic is concerned.

Chapter VIII What is Involved in the Other

1 This remark features at the start of what is most commonly classified as the fifth argument or 'hypothesis', not the seventh. Lacan is drawing on the Auguste Diès translation ('. . . si le non-Un n'est pas?' in the 1923 Budé edition of Plato's *Œuvres complètes*, Vol. VIII). For εἰ μὴ ἕν μὴ ἔστιν (160b6), F. M. Cornford takes issue with the Diès rendering, and tries 'if a not-one (no thing) does not exist' (*Plato and Parmenides*, Routledge & Kegan Paul, 1939, p. 219); but is in turn challenged by R. E. Allen (*Plato's Parmenides*, Yale University Press, 1997, revised edition, pp. 329–30), who offers, 'if not unity is not' (p. 55). R. S. Brumbaugh gives 'if it is not the case that the one is not' (*Plato on the One*, Yale University Press, 1961, p. 165); while S. Scolnicov gives: 'if the not-one is not' (*Plato's Parmenides*, University of California Press, 2001, p. 148). See also the formalization by S. C. Rickless in *Plato's Forms in Transition*, Cambridge University Press, 2006, pp. 212–13, *D5AI*; and the comparison of the Diès and Cornford renderings by D. O'Brien in '*Einai* copulatif et existentiel dans le *Parménide* de Platon', in *Revue des Études Grecques*, Vol. 118, 2005, §X, pp. 236–7.

2 The Seuil edition inserts *parmi les réalistes* to resolve an anacoluthon in the typescript. Lacan says only: *C'est en ça que je me classe . . .*

3 The French *face* and *fasse* are homophones. *Fasse* is the present subjunctive of *faire* in the third-person singular.

4 The pun is stronger in French: *l'ontologie est une honte*. For a more intricate extension of the same pun, see p. 426 of 'Radiophonie' in *Autres écrits*, op. cit.

5 There is likely a paranomasia here exploiting the signification of *un savon* as 'a telling-off' or 'a reprimand'.

6 Again, the Seuil edition, which is here respected, resolves an apparent anacoluthon. Lacan says: *Ce qui veut dire qu'on ne peut pas écrire que ce qui y fait obstacle, à savoir la fonction phallique, ne soit pas vrai.* ['This means that you cannot write that what forms an obstacle here, namely the phallic function, is untrue.']

7 Lacan plays on the proximity between *Autre* and *entre* to transform *entreposer* ('to store' or 'to stock') into *Autreposer*. In this coinage, one can also hear *Autre-poser*, 'to Alter-posit', or 'to posit Otherwise'.

Chapter IX In the Field of the Unian

1 The written form *Yad'lun* is an attempt to capture the concentrated pronunciation of *Y a de l'Un*, itself an informal contraction of *Il y a*

de l'Un. Thus, not only does the content of the expression indicate the prominence of the One, but its very form presents as a unitary element. Compare the orthography here with that on p. 215 of the written report in the appendix.

2 Lacan is again drawing on the Diès translation, which here gives *s'il est Un* (op. cit. p. 72). For εἰ ἕν ἔστιν (137c4), Cornford prefers 'if there is a One' (op. cit., p. 116). O'Brien concludes that a systematic comparison of all the occurrences formulated in the second part of the *Parmenides* confirms Cornford's translation of the verb in an existential sense, and disqualifies the Diès reading as a copulative verb (op. cit., p. 245). See also the discussion by C. C. Meinwald in *Plato's Parmenides*, Oxford University Press, 1991, pp. 40–5. Brumbaugh gives 'if one is' (op. cit., p. 55); Scolnicov gives 'if the one is' (op. cit. pp. 78, 80); as does Rickless (op. cit., pp. 106–11, 114 (*DIAI*)). Allen, meanwhile, gives 'if Unity is' (op. cit., p. 17). A further likely source for Lacan's discussion is F. Regnault's 1968 article from the *Cahiers pour l'analyse*, recently translated by K. Peden and P. Hallward as 'Dialectic of Epistemologies', in *Concept and Form, Vol. I, Selections from the Cahiers pour l'analyse*, Verso, 2012, pp. 119–50.

3 Whereas in English it has become customary to distinguish orthographically between Aristoteles (of The Four Hundred and of The Thirty Tyrants) and Aristotle (of Stageira), French uses the single proper name Aristote for both instances of Ἀριστοτέλης. Some commentators in English have, however, preferred 'Aristotle' for the youth in the *Parmenides*, notably Meinwald (op. cit.) and Rickless (op. cit.).

4 For ἀδολεσχίας (135d4), Cornford gives 'idle talk' (op. cit., p. 103), as do Allen (op. cit., pp. 15, 207) and Scolnicov (op. cit., p. 74). Cf. Brumbaugh, op. cit., p. 22.

5 *L'essence-maître* and *l'essence-esclave* are Diès's renderings of ὅ ἔστι δεσπότης and ὅ ἔστι δοῦλος (133d6–133e1). Cornford gives 'the essential Master' and 'the essential Slave' (op. cit., p. 96); Allen gives 'what it is to be a master' and 'what it is to be a slave'; Scolnicov gives 'that which is master' and 'that which is slave' (op. cit., p. 70); Rickless gives 'what a master is' and 'what a slave is' (op. cit., p. 87).

6 Probably an allusion to Deuteronomy 15:12–18, though perhaps also to Genesis 37:27–8, and/or to Exodus 21:2–11, 20–1. Compare, however, Leviticus 25:39–55.

7 The Seuil edition introduces a modification here by inserting the general formula for computing the number of 2-element subsets in an *n*-element set (*n*-choose-2) in place of Lacan's formula that places $n(n-1)$ as the numerator and 2 as the denominator. Lacan's slip, saying 'seven times eight is forty-two', has also been emended (see the note on p. 229).

8 The stenographer's typescript, which is the source text for the Seuil edition, gives *que l'Un ne sache être comme être*, but no such *ne* is audible on the audio recording. Cf. *Parmenides*, 160c7–d1: πρῶτον μὲν ἄρα γνωστόν τι λέγει, ἔπειτα ἕτερον τῶν ἄλλων, ὅταν εἴπῃ ἕν, εἴτε τὸ εἶναι αὐτῷ προσθεὶς εἴτε τὸ μὴ εἶναι· οὐδὲν γὰρ ἧττον γιγνώσκεται, τί τὸ λεγόμενον μὴ εἶναι, καὶ ὅτι διάφορον τῶν ἄλλων.

9 Cf. *Parmenides*, 160b5, *passim*.

10 For τὸ ἐξαίφνης (156d3), Cornford gives 'the instant' (op. cit., p. 200), as do Brumbaugh (op. cit., p. 148), Allen (op. cit., p. 49), Scolnicov (op. cit., p. 137), and Rickless (op. cit., p. 193).

Chapter X Yad'lun

1 This mention of the ahistorical character of the *Parmenides* may indicate that, despite the reservations expressed in the previous lesson, Lacan nevertheless held the youth Ἀριστοτέλης to be the same as Aristotle the philosopher. Alternatively, this may be an allusion to the long-held notion (from Athenaeus of Naucratis down to Eduard Zeller) that the meeting between Parmenides and Socrates must be a 'poetic fiction'. Compare, however, T. L. Heath, *Aristarchus of Samos, the Ancient Copernicus*, Cambridge University Press, 1913, pp. 62–3, footnote 4.

2 The translation *si l'un est un* was first given for εἰ ἓν ἔσται τὸ ἕν (137d3) by Victor Cousin (*Œuvres de Platon*, Vol. XII, Paris: Rey, 1846, p. 28). Diès gives 'si l'Un doit être un' (op. cit., p. 23), which is endorsed by Regnault ('Dialectique d'épistémologies', *Cahiers pour l'analyse* 9: 53). Cornford gives 'if the One is to be one' (op. cit., p. 116); Scolnicov gives 'if the one is to be one' (op. cit., p. 80); and Allen gives 'if unity is to be one' (op. cit., p. 17). Cf. Rickless (op. cit., p. 108).

3 For οὐδαμοῦ ἂν εἴη (138a2) and ἐστίν που τὸ ἕν (138b5), Cornford gives 'it cannot be anywhere' and 'the One is not anywhere' (op. cit., p. 119). Brumbaugh gives 'the one [...] will be nowhere' and 'the one is not anywhere' (op. cit., pp. 62, 64); Allen gives 'it would be nowhere' and 'unity is nowhere' (op. cit., p. 18); Scolnicov gives 'it would be nowhere' and 'the one is not anywhere' (op. cit., p. 82). See also Rickless (op. cit., pp. 117–18, *DIA6*).

4 For ἂν περιέχοιτο ὑπ' ἐκείνου ἐν ᾧ ἐνείη (138a4), Cornford gives 'it would be encompassed all round by that in which it was contained' (op. cit., p. 119). Brumbaugh gives 'it would be encircled by that in which it was' (op. cit., p. 62); Allen gives 'it would be contained in a circle by what it was in' (op. cit., p. 18, and footnote 65 on p. 231, which takes issue with Cornford); and Scolnicov gives 'it would somehow be encompassed round by that in which it would be' (op. cit., p. 82).

5 For ἄπειρον ἄρα τὸ ἕν (137d7), Cornford gives 'it is without limits' (op. cit., p. 118). Brumbaugh gives 'the one is unlimited' (op. cit., p. 59); Allen gives 'unity is unlimited' (op. cit., p. 17); and Scolnicov gives 'the one is unlimited' (op. cit., p. 81) and 'the one is undelimited' (pp. 81–2). See also Rickless (op. cit., pp. 115–16, *DIA4*).

6 W. B. Ewald translates 'das Uneigentlich-unendliches' (*Grundlagen einer allgemeinen Mannichfaltigkeitslehre*, Leipzig: Teubner, 1883, p. 166) as 'the improper infinite' ('Foundations of a General Theory of Manifolds', in *From Kant to Hilbert: A Source Book in the Foundations of Mathematics, Vol. II*, Oxford: Clarendon Press, 1996, p. 882). G. Chaitkin prefers 'non-genuine-Infinite' ('On the Theory of the Transfinite; Correspondence of Georg Cantor and Cardinal J. B. Franzelin (1885–1886)', in *Fidelio* 3(3): 101, 103).

7 In 'Beiträge zur Begründung der transfiniten Mengenlehre', Cantor uses the terms '"Teil" oder "Teilmenge"' (1895 version of 'Beiträge zur Begründung der transfiniten Mengenlehre', § 1, in *Gesammelte Abhandlungen*, Berlin: Springer, 1932, p. 282), which P. E. B. Jourdain renders as '"part" or "partial aggregate"' (*Contributions to the Founding of the Theory of Transfinite Numbers*, London: Open Court, 1915, p. 86). As Lacan notes in the following chapter, the former vocabulary of 'aggregates' and 'parts' has since been superseded by that of 'sets' and 'subsets'. His pertinacious use of 'part' may be intended to evoke the Greek μέρος, used in Euclid's *Elements* (VII, g′–d′), and in the *Parmenides* (153d7–8); a coincidence noted by Diès and, previously, by Sir Thomas Heath (*A History of Greek Mathematics, Vol. I*, Oxford: Clarendon, 1921, p. 294).

Chapter XI An Issue of Ones (*A Talk at Sainte-Anne*)

1 The allusion is to the verb phrase *faire avec les moyens du bord*, which may be rendered as 'to make do with what is to hand' or '. . . with what is lying around'. When voicing his nonce word *bord-homme*, Lacan does not make a liaison 'd' at the end of *bord* ('rim' or 'frontier'), thus producing a phone that resembles the first two syllables of *borroméen*.

2 The neologism is not Lacan's own. The spelling in the Seuil edition, *hénologie*, matches the orthography that has come to dominate since Leo S. J. Sweeney first set down 'henology' in 1961 ('Basic Principles in Plotinus' Philosophy', in *Gregorianum* 42:510). However, Étienne Gilson had previously coined *énologie* in 1948 (*L'être et l'essence*, Paris: Vrin, p. 42).

3 Lacan's *s'éventailler* is a neologism in French. An *éventail* is a 'fan'. The closest verb form is *tailler* ('to trim', 'to prune', 'to chisel', etc.).

4 An *Auvergnate* is an inhabitant of the Auvergne. Cf. Alfred Delvau's jocular *Dictionnaire érotique moderne* (Brussels, 1864): 'AUVERGNATE. Qui appartient au troisième sexe – puisqu'elle n'est pas homme et ne veut pas être femme.'

5 Conveniently, the English verb 'to found' carries both the sense of 'to establish' and 'to melt'. See also Chapter XIII, endnote 1.

6 For 'Unter einer "Menge" verstehen wir jede Zusammenfassung M von bestimmten wohlunterschiedenen Objekten m unsrer Anschauung oder unseres Denkens [. . .] zu einem Ganzen' ('Beiträge zur Begründung der transfiniten Mengenlehre', op. cit., §1, p. 282), P. E. B. Jourdain gives: 'By an "aggregate" we are to understand any collection into a whole M of definite and separate objects m of our intuition or our thought' (*Contributions to the Founding of the Theory of Transfinite Numbers*, op. cit., p. 85).

7 That is, the pentahedroid, or 5-cell (C_5), this being the object that corresponds to the pentatope numbers in the arithmetical triangle (see Ch. IV, endnote 7, above). On the audio recording (the apparent source for the stenographer's typescript), there is a hiatus just before this sentence, which may account for the sudden skip from the columns for cardinals 3 and 4 to the column for cardinal 5.

8 Lacan uses *distinct* and *défini* for Cantor's *bestimmten wohlunter-schiedenen* (see endnote 6 to this chapter).

Chapter XII Knowledge about Truth

1 Lacan says: *Voilà comment de toujours on aurait appelé ça. L'est-ce? point d'interrogation.* Even in stipulating the question mark, the juxta-position of *Ça* and *Es* – the French translation and the German source of the term that James Strachey translated as the *Id* – is particularly striking.
2 This is a probable reference to the Mouvement de libération des femmes, which held its first public meeting in 1970. It grew out of the Mouvement démocratique féminin. It is unlikely that Lacan's term *modèles-modèles* is an allusion to fashion models (more commonly *mannequins* in French).
3 Though the term 'creative subject' abounds in the mathematical litera-ture, 'creating subject' is a more loyal translation of L. E. J. Brouwer's *scheppende subject*.
4 Lacan likely intends *bc* instead of *ba*, since the four partitions of the three-element set {a,b,c} are: {ab/c}, {a/bc}, {ac/b}, {abc}. These could be arranged as follows:

Chapter XIII The Founding of Sexual Difference

1 See Chapter XI, endnote 5.
2 *La bourgeoise* carries the same indecorous and disparaging tonality as 'her indoors' or 'the missus', but with the further connotation of 'she who rules the roost'.
3 'Il court, il court, le furet' ['He runs, he runs, the ferret'] is the title of a children's song (transcribed in 1870 by Jean-Baptiste Weckerlin), sung during 'Pass the parcel' and other party games. The title refrain, or the tune of the refrain, is often used independently of the song to insinuate that someone is being made to hunt for something, or is being given the runaround. Cf. Lacan's allusion to the *jeu du furet*, the 'hunt-the-ring' parlour game, in *Talking to Brick Walls*, op. cit., p. 99.
4 Similar use of such reflexive forms as *se penser*, *se dire* and, below, *s'articuler* is often translated into English as a passive construction ('to be thought', 'to be said', etc.) on the grounds that the grammatical subject does not hold grammatical agency. Here, however, there is a firm attribution of grammatical agency to the *Ça* and to the One.
5 As above, the signifier \dø\ might equally be transcribed: *d'eux*.

6 According to some transcripts, this sentence had been written up on the blackboard at the start of the lesson.

Chapter XIV Theory of the Four Formulae (*A Talk at Sainte-Anne*)

1 Lacan is punning on the expression *séparer le bon grain de l'ivrai*, 'to sort the wheat from the chaff'.
2 The French pronunciation of *saints* is homophonic with *seins*, 'breasts'.
3 Concerning the English terms that correspond to *canaillerie* and *bêtise*, see Chapter I, endnote 6.
4 Another pun, this time on the two senses of *fini*: both 'finished' and 'finite'.
5 On the audio recording, this sentence is interrupted midway by the first of several barrages of bangers being let off outside the chapel. This is the disturbance to which Lacan alludes at the end of the talk (p. 184) and at the start of the following chapter (p. 189).
6 *C'est un repère* perhaps contains a pun on *père*, 'father'.
7 Lacan says *l'homme* with a definite article, but *femme* with no article. What is here rendered as 'man' might also be understood as 'mankind'.
8 This may be an allusion to the *Parmenides* (139c 8). Although Diès translates αὐτῷ as 'par lui-même', Alexandre Kojève coins 'l'Un-tout-seul' specifically in reference to this passage (*Essai d'une historie raisonnée de la philosophie païenne*, Vol. I, Paris: Gallimard, 1968, p. 212). See also Lacan's footnote to his 'Report', on page 218 below.
9 Here and in the following paragraph, Lacan's reference to *l'Œdipe* is altered in the Seuil edition to *Totem et Tabou*, as it was in Chapters II, III, and VII.
10 The term *femme virile* is used in French when the term 'mannish woman' might be used in English.
11 Here Lacan is punning on the homophonic coincidence in French between the stem *vir-* and conjugations of the verb *virer*, 'to veer'. There is no shared etymology. *Parer à virer* is a command used in a nautical context: 'prepare to go about!'
12 As above, *mythe d'Œdipe* is altered in the Seuil edition to *mythe de Totem et Tabou*.
13 This diagram is a considerably modified version of the one recorded in the stenographer's original typescript, reproduced with slight alteration on page 207 of the Seuil edition. The typescript carries a warning that the accuracy of the diagram as there recorded is uncertain.

Chapter XV The Desire to Sleep

1 For *immixtion des sujets* (*Le séminaire de Jacques Lacan, livre II*, Paris: Seuil, pp. 192, 228; *Écrits*, Paris: Seuil, 1966, p. 16), S. Tomaselli gives 'inmixing (*sic*) of subjects' (*The Seminar of Jacques Lacan, Book II*, Cambridge University Press, 1988, pp. 160, 194) as does B. Fink (*Écrits* in English, New York: Norton, 2006, p. 10). See, too, R. Grigg's

footnote on page 193 of *The Seminar of Jacques Lacan, Book III*, Norton/Routledge, 1993.

2 The exclamation from the man in the audience is *Une pollution!* The indefinite article indicates that he is denoting a *pollution nocturne*, a 'nocturnal emission', in jocular response to the preceding discussion on sleep. In the present translation, the signifier 'pollution' is favoured due to Lacan's ensuing response.

Chapter XVI Bodies Captured by Discourse

1 Lacan here employs one of his favourite locutions, *Ce n'est pas* [. . .] *ce qu'un vain peuple pense*, which derives from Voltaire's *Œdipe*, Act IV Scene 1: 'Nos prêtres ne sont pas ce qu'un vain peuple pense'. The line was rendered by Thomas Francklin in 1761 as 'These priests are not what the vile rabble think them'.

2 *Mémorisé* is pronounced syllable by syllable in a way that suggests *mes mots risée*, 'my words, a laughingstock'.

3 Cf. R. Grigg's note on *astudé* on page 9 of his translation of *Book XVII* (Norton, 2007). The rendering 'astudied' appears on page 105 of the same. The prefixed '*a*' may function both as a privative and, crucially, as object *a*, the student holding the position of the *a* in Lacan's formalization of the university discourse. The verbal pun is on *étudié*, which means 'studied' in the sense of 'well thought out' or 'carefully considered', and *enseigné*, 'taught'. There is a further overtone of *astreinte*, 'obligation' or 'constraint', as Lacan observes in his intervention of 19 April 1970 (*Lettres de l'École Freudienne* 8: 211).

4 Respecting the orthography adopted in the Seuil edition, *à-former* could be rendered as 'for training'. Note, however, that the homophonic *a-formés* is also plausible: 'a-formed' or 'a-shaped'.

5 *En corps* ('in body') is homophonic with *encore*, 'again', 'still' or 'more'.

6 For the correct date, see the previous chapter (p. 192) and the 'Library to Seminar XIX' (p. 231).

7 For βέλτιον γὰρ ἴσως μὴ λέγειν τὴν ψυχὴν ἐλεεῖν ἢ μανθάνειν ἢ διανοεῖσθαι, ἀλλὰ τὸν ἄνθρωπον τῇ ψυχῇ (*De anima*, I, 4, 408b 13–15), R. D. Hicks gives 'Doubtless it would be better not to say that the soul pities or learns or thinks, but that the man does so with the soul (*De anima*, Cambridge University Press, 1907, p. 33); more paraphrastically, Walter Stanley Hett gives 'Probably it is better not to say that the soul pities, or learns, or thinks, but to say rather that the soul is the instrument whereby man does these things' ('On The Soul' in *Aristotle in Twenty-Three Volumes, Vol. VIII*, Loeb, 1953, p. 47); D.W. Hamlyn gives, 'For it is surely better not to say that the soul pities, learns, or thinks, but that the man does these with his soul' (*Aristotle's De Anima*, Book I, Oxford: Clarendon, 1968); Ronald Polansky gives, somewhat equivocally, 'It is better perhaps not to say the soul pities or learns or thinks, but the human being due to the soul' (*Aristotle's De Anima: A Critical Commentary*, Cambridge University Press, 2007, p. 113); while more recently Christopher Shields has given the limpid rendering, 'For

it is perhaps better not to say that the soul pities or thinks, but that the human being does these things with the soul' (*De anima*, Oxford: Clarendon Press, 2016, p. 14). In his Commentary, Shields (p. 144), unpacks the two possible readings of τῇ ψυχῇ as i. 'with the soul' or ii. 'in virtue of his having a soul' / 'by means of having a soul', further noting that Jonathan Barnes prefers the latter (cf. 1972, 'Aristotle's Concept of Mind' in *Proceedings of the Aristotelian Society*, 72:101–114) which he rejects in favour of the former (referring the reader to his 1988 article, 'Soul as Subject in Aristotle's *De anima*' in *Classical Quarterly* 38: 140–9). Lacan first uses the paraphrastic formula 'l'homme pense avec son âme' in the opening lesson of *Seminar III*.

Appendices: Library to Seminar XIX (Jacques-Alain Miller)

1 Reading *l'incommensurabilité de la diagonale du carré* for *l'incommunicabilité de la diagonale du carré* (p. 246 of the Seuil edition).
2 Lacan punned on *l'(a)mur* and *a-murs-ement* at the end of the *entretien* of 6 January 1972 (*Talking to Brick Walls*, op. cit., p. 98). 'Lettre d'amur' is from the opening section of this same *entretien* (3 February 1972), which is included as an appendix to *Talking to Brick Walls* (ibid., pp. 108–9). See above, Chapter V, endnote 4.
3 Miller inverts the husband and wife: in Lacan's example, 'sa femme le frictionne' (*Écrits*, p. 827).
4 While Gödel's 1944 paper contains some discussion of the theory of integers and transfinite orders (cf. pp. 134–6), the remark that more closely matches Lacan's comment is the third note defining technical terms in the 1947 paper 'What is Cantor's Continuum Problem?' (*Collected Works, Vol. II*, op. cit., pp. 186–7; revised in the 1964 reprint, pp. 264–5).
5 The Seminar of 1954–5, which includes the commentary on the dream of Irma's injection, is *Séminaire II* (sessions of 9 and 16 March), translated by Sylvana Tomaselli as *The Ego in Freud's Theory and in the Technique of Psychoanalysis* (Cambridge University Press, 1988).
6 Eco's character 'Dr Wagner' seems to be loosely based on Lacan.
7 Lacan mistakenly attributes the painting to Brueghel. This is emended in the Seuil edition (p. 223), which includes a reproduction of the 1502 panel (reversed right to left).
8 Judging by Lacan's description, he had also seen works from the *Concetto spaziale, New York* series (1962), which are executed on copper plates. The Seuil edition includes a reproduction of a 1968 canvas from the *Concetto spaziale, Attese* series.

Index